Praise for
When You Wonder, You're Learning

"In this book, Gregg Behr and Ryan Rydzewski have accomplished an amazing feat: they have sequenced the human creative genome. They reveal how the DNA strands of curiosity, communication, and collaboration were interwoven in the miracle of *Mister Rogers' Neighborhood*. And how parents and educators can transmit this DNA from themselves to children who will become loving parents, confident professionals, and caring citizens. At this point in our nation's—indeed, the world's—history, there is nothing more important."

—Dr. Milton Chen, executive director emeritus,
George Lucas Educational Foundation

"Recent films, biographies, and tributes have attempted to capture the kindness and genius of Fred Rogers. *When You Wonder, You're Learning* is a beautiful complement to all that has been written, as it looks beyond the man to peel back the curtain and reveal the science used by Fred, and others who have followed, to inspire the development of caring and empathetic children into whose hands our future rests. I cannot imagine a more important time for a book such as this."

—Paula Kerger, president and CEO, PBS

"*When You Wonder, You're Learning* is a compelling, beautifully written call for seeing, supporting, and loving the individual complexities of every human being, whether they're kids or adults, our own children or a neighbor's. Living up to the kindness and humanity that Fred Rogers embodied will never be easy, but with this essential book—full of fascinating science and moving scenes from *Mister Rogers' Neighborhood*—Behr and Rydzewski have given us the tools."

—Dr. Todd Rose, former director of the Mind, Brain, and Education program at Harvard University and bestselling author of *The End of Average: How We Succeed in a World That Values Sameness*

"Building on the legacy of an incomparable humanist, Pittsburgh's Mister Rogers, *When You Wonder, You're Learning* will inform you, inspire you, change how you engage with children, and flat out make you a better person. It's a brilliant, stirring exposition on the vital role of humanism in educating our children, and it strikes at issues near and dear to any teacher, parent, or policymaker. I loved every word of it."

—Ted Dintersmith, education philanthropist and author of *What School Could Be: Insights and Inspiration from Teachers Across America*

"I'm so grateful to Gregg Behr and Ryan Rydzewski. *When You Wonder, You're Learning* brings me back to the days of sitting with Fred in his office, bowled over by the depth of his philosophy, and inspired by his urgent and radical message of love. Here are two authors who *get it*, who have the courage to try to *explain it*, who demonstrate their mastery of Fred's message in the craftsmanship of the work itself. Beautifully constructed, full of deeply researched and well-earned wisdom, *When You Wonder, You're Learning* is a dazzling accomplishment that offers a much-needed wake-up call about the enduring strength of the human spirit."

—Jeanne Marie Laskas, *New York Times* bestselling author of *Concussion* and *To Obama: With Love, Joy, Anger, and Hope*

"The enduring legacy of Fred Rogers is based on a couple of things. One, of course, is his role as the greatest American exemplar of the deep, fundamental human values by which most people aspire to live. But the other reason is the extraordinary importance of Rogers as a teacher and his approach to learning. He understood that through their curiosity and sense of wonder, children offer the purest expression of the joy of learning. And so he focused not on facts and numbers, but on the natural, joyful instinct of children to inquire and to learn. *When You Wonder, You're Learning* is a timely and powerful exploration of Rogers' approach and will quickly become an important instrument for advancing learning and Fred's legacy. Its authors, Gregg Behr and Ryan Rydzewski, have brought Fred Rogers the educator to life. We are indebted to them for adding this book to the body of Fred's teachings."

—Maxwell King, senior fellow at the Fred Rogers Center and *New York Times* bestselling author of *The Good Neighbor: The Life and Work of Fred Rogers*

"*When You Wonder, You're Learning* is a timely gem for anyone who supports the development of children of all ages. It is at once practical yet aspirational, affirming yet instructive. Chock-full of research and anecdotes, it reminds us that the uniquely human traits of curiosity, creativity, kindness, and generosity are not only essential but attainable for fulfilling work and life. The exquisite weaving in of the stories of *Mister Rogers' Neighborhood* will conjure a powerful memory of Mister Rogers' calm affirmation, 'I like you just the way you are.' I am in love with this book and can't wait to give it to parents and teachers in my life!"

—Karen Cator, former CEO, Digital Promise

"Just when parents and educators need him most, *When You Wonder, You're Learning* revives Fred Rogers. It reminds us that children thrive on love, curiosity, and a can-do attitude. Through artful prose that weaves together humanity, love, science, and history, Behr and Rydzewski navigate us beyond the loneliness, fear, and digitalization of our current world, inviting us back to the hopeful simplicity of the Neighborhood. A must-read for anyone who cares about children."

—Dr. Kathy Hirsh-Pasek, professor at Temple University and coauthor of *Becoming Brilliant: What Science Tells Us about Raising Successful Children*

"Want to be a better parent or teacher? *When You Wonder, You're Learning* reveals in accessible and delightful ways how we—as grownups who care so very much about our kids' tomorrows—might help them develop habits of mind and social awareness to handle what's ahead. This book is spot-on; it's a blueprint for our times."

—Rebecca Winthrop, senior fellow and codirector of the Center for Universal Education at the Brookings Institution

"Gregg Behr and Ryan Rydzewski deftly blend the timeless parables from the Neighborhood of Make-Believe and personal philosophies of Fred Rogers with contemporary examples of scientists and educators who are prioritizing the foundational social and emotional skills that are essential for learning, proving there's always been a method to the kindness."

—Paul Siefken, president and CEO, Fred Rogers Productions

"The unrelenting goodness of Mr. Rogers' iconic television show is still felt today. Behr and Rydzewski reveal the humble wisdom of Mister Rogers in *When You Wonder, You're Learning.* Through a blend of social science research, child development theory, and the life of Rogers himself, they illuminate the values of the Neighborhood. What better way to honor Rogers' legacy than to give readers a road map for how to nurture and sustain genuine wonder in today's children?"

—Kyle Schwartz, teacher and author of *I Wish My Teacher Knew* and *I Wish for Change*

"Mister Rogers is the essential role model for all teachers and parents. He taught us to admire, inspire, and raise confident kids. Behr and Rydzewski's engrossing book is a long overdue explanation of the scientific nuts and bolts behind the Neighborhood approach."

—Jordan Shapiro, author of *Father Figure* and *The New Childhood*

When You
Wonder,
You're
Learning

When You Wonder, You're Learning

MISTER ROGERS'
Enduring Lessons for Raising Creative, Curious, Caring Kids

Gregg Behr and Ryan Rydzewski

hachette
BOOKS

New York

Hachette Go, an imprint of Hachette Books
Hachette Book Group
1290 Avenue of the Americas
New York, NY 10104
HachetteGo.com
Facebook.com/HachetteGo
Instagram.com/HachetteGo

First Edition: April 2021

Hachette Books is a division of Hachette Book Group, Inc.
The Hachette Go and Hachette Books name and logos are trademarks of Hachette Book Group, Inc.

The publisher is not responsible for websites (or their content) that are not owned by the publisher.

Print book interior design by Amy Quinn.

Library of Congress Cataloging-in-Publication Data

Names: Behr, Gregg, author. | Rydzewski, Ryan, author.
Title: When you wonder, you're learning : Mister Rogers' enduring lessons
   for raising creative, curious, caring kids / Gregg Behr and Ryan
   Rydzewski.
Description: First edition. | New York : Hachette Go, 2021. | Includes
   bibliographical references.
Identifiers: LCCN 2020049994 | ISBN 9780306874734 (hardcover) | ISBN
   9780306874727 (ebook)
Subjects: LCSH: Rogers, Fred. | Mister Rogers' neighborhood (Television
   program) | Child rearing. | Child psychology--Popular works.
Classification: LCC HQ769 .B414 2021 | DDC 649/.1--dc23
LC record available at https://lccn.loc.gov/2020049994

ISBNs: 978-0-306-87473-4 (hardcover); 978-0-306-87472-7 (ebook)

Printed in the United States of America

LSC-C

Printing 1, 2021

For our parents, who smiled us into smiling, talked us into talking, and loved us into loving

Contents

Contents

Foreword

Even by Pittsburgh's frigid November standards, it was cold out there.

But I didn't mind very much, despite my inner Floridian. I was due that day to visit the neighborhood hospital. And though hospital visits aren't typically cause for cheer, least of all for little old ladies like me, I knew this one would be different. I knew this one would be special.

I put on a cardigan—one of his—and zipped it against the chill.

The hospital's atrium was already full. The room fell quiet as I pushed through the door, and someone sat down at the lobby's piano and played a familiar chord. Then, all at once, the doctors and nurses started to sing.

> *It's a beautiful day in the neighborhood,*
> *A beautiful day for a neighbor . . .*

What music! The old lyrics filled the lobby, sounding almost new. I stopped, as I always do, to sing along.

Afterward, in the hospital nursery, I met the reason for my visit: Six newborn babies, all dressed in tiny red sweaters and little blue booties made to match my late husband's shoes. Six little Freds, brand new to the world, with so much to wonder and learn. I loved them from the moment we met.

Maybe you saw the pictures. It was a big to-do, staged to celebrate World Kindness Day and the sixty-fifth anniversary of WQED, the television station where Fred had made *Mister Rogers' Neighborhood*. The pictures made their way to the internet, and social media did what social media does. By the end of the day, the whole *country* loved those babies, and I think I know why.

Pittsburgh, you see, wasn't the only place that was cold that day. Half the nation had frozen solid. The front page of the *New York Times* said that in McAllen, Texas, temperatures fell from ninety-two degrees to just thirty-one, all in a couple of hours! The other words on the page— *eviction*, *hate crime*, *brutality*, and *Sandy Hook*, among them—said all there was to say about the temperature of everything else.

It was November 13, 2019: World Kindness Day in a world where kindness is hard to find. Where more and more people feel hardened and messed up, whether by politics or poverty or the ever-growing gulfs between our neighbors and ourselves. As Fred's wife of fifty-one years, I'm often asked what he'd think about this—this coldness that's crept across our country. And I always say the same thing: Fred Rogers would think, first and foremost, about the children.

I think those tiny babies made us stop and do the same. I think they showed us that despite the cold, kindness and warmth can endure. Swaddled in their sweaters, they showed us that even though Fred had gone to heaven some time ago, he'd left us the *Neighborhood*'s blueprints. And we could rebuild it wherever we'd like—even in a hospital nursery on a frigid November day.

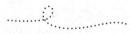

In 1920, a Frenchman named Antoine de Saint-Exupéry enrolled at the Beaux-Arts school in Paris, hoping to become an architect. He dropped out before he finished his studies, but he'd learned enough about blueprints to pen the most memorable line in *The Little Prince*, a novella he published many years later. *"L'essentiel est invisible pour les yeux,"* Saint-Exupéry wrote. "What is essential is invisible to the eye."

Fred loved *The Little Prince*, and he loved that quote best of all. He loved it so much that he hung it in his office. Reading it now, Saint-Exupéry's quote puts me in mind of a house: We call an old house beautiful when its wood is polished and fine, when it's furnished with well-made things, when there's art on the walls and the garden's in bloom. But what's *essential* about the house is almost always hidden from view. We don't see the minds that dreamed it or the labor that built it. We don't see the nuts and bolts that brace it or the love that lives in its rooms. And if we ever want to rebuild it—or add a modern wing—then we have to grasp its design. We have to get into the crawl spaces and pull up the carpets and have a look at what's beneath.

We have to go back to its blueprints.

You might say the same of the *Neighborhood*. So much of what made the program essential was invisible to the camera, built so carefully into Fred's scripts and songs that you'd never know it was there. When Fred put on a sweater at the start of each episode, we only knew that it made us feel safe. We never saw the hours he spent with scientists and teachers and experts in child development, engineering that very feeling. When he took us to visit a factory, we only knew that we'd gone somewhere fun. We never saw it as part of a plan to nourish curiosity, encourage creativity, and show us that right down to our favorite crayons, the things we love about life come from our fellow neighbors. Grasping these intentions—and the designs that helped Fred fulfill them—is key to rebuilding the *Neighborhood*.

Lots of people are doing that now, each in their own way. People tell me that Fred is as popular today as he was when he was alive! And doesn't that makes sense? Who better to turn to when kindness seems lacking than the kindest person we've known? Who better to beat back the cold than the man in a cardigan sweater?

As his wife, of course, I find it marvelous. I sometimes say that I'm the luckiest widow in Pittsburgh. Every day, I can be close to him. I can put on his old sweaters or sing his old songs or meet adorable little babies in a nursery. I'm grateful. And when I consider the lives that my husband has touched, I'm grateful even more.

But sometimes I worry.

I worry that as the world grows meaner, kindness like Fred's can look less and less attainable. I worry we'll forget that Fred was just as human as we are. We'll forget that he sometimes had doubts, that he sometimes felt defeated, that he sometimes felt angry. We'll forget that he wasn't a saint.

Don't get me wrong: Fred was the same in real life as he was on television. The Fred you saw on the *Neighborhood* was the Fred you saw on the street and the Fred I saw at home. That's just who he was—Fred always gave his authentic self.

I mean only that there was nothing magic about him. There were no miracles in the *Neighborhood*. Everything you saw and everything you felt stemmed from his deliberate efforts and designs. He made kindness look easy, but even for Fred, kindness was anything but. "Try your best to make goodness attractive," he liked to say. "That's one of the toughest assignments you'll ever be given."

If we can say anything about my husband, it's that he accepted that assignment every hour of his life. No one worked harder at being Fred Rogers than Fred Rogers himself. I trust that this won't diminish his aura—in my opinion, the extent of his efforts only makes him *more* remarkable. But we ought to resist holding him up beyond the reach of us mortals. Because the truth of Fred's ministry was that every last one of us can be as caring, kind, and influential in children's lives as he was. Every last one of us can do a version of what Fred did.

That's why this book is so important, and why I'm so delighted that Gregg and Ryan wrote it. *When You Wonder, You're Learning* explores what's essential about the *Neighborhood*, making it visible to parents, teachers, and anyone else who cares about children. It breaks down the tools for learning that Fred taught and the reasons they're still significant. It contains, in a very real sense, the blueprints my husband left us, and it introduces the people building *Neighborhoods* of their own: places where kindness and warmth endure, despite the cold that creeps outside. Places where children are cared for and safe, even when the wind kicks up and the temperature starts to fall.

Back at the hospital that frigid November day, I asked the parents of those six beautiful babies if they were nervous to go home. Invariably, their answer was yes. Who could blame them? Beyond that nursery was parenthood: a state of astonishment, joy, and the nagging feeling that you're royally screwing it up. Even friendly advice can be nerve-racking. Fred himself felt that too many tips led to anxiety and overthinking.

So instead I offered the simplest, truest thing I know: *Being there for each other and supporting each other is what it's all about.*

This is a book about the many ways we can do that.

* * *

Once, in the 1970s, Fred asked me to appear on his program, just as I'd had a handful of times before. On cue, I knocked on his television door and crossed his make-believe threshold. I said I was happy to be back in the *Neighborhood* again, and I was.

I still am.

"It gives me a good feeling," Fred told his television neighbors, "to know that I can be with her."

Well, Fred, it gives *me* a good feeling to know that you're with us now—in these old sweaters of yours, in those six newborn babies, and in the six chapters of this beautiful book.

Joanne Rogers
Pittsburgh, Pennsylvania
August 2020

Trouble in the Neighborhood

On February 19, 1968, if you had tuned to the National Educational Television network—a sort of proto-PBS—you would've noticed a curious introduction to a program you'd never seen.

After panning over a miniature model town, the camera settles in someone's living room. A tall, gawky young man strolls through the front door, singing a catchy, nonsensical tune about wanting to be your neighbor. He swaps his coat for a more-comfortable sweater, changes his shoes, and leans toward the camera to speak to the nation for the very first time.

His opening lines aren't exactly gripping. In fact, one of the first things he tells you is that it took him a long time to learn to tie his shoes. "But I kept practicing, and practicing, and practicing, and finally, I learned quickly," he says. There's some banter about a porch swing and the purpose of a ladder, and then he sings a song about liking you—yes, *you*—just the way you are.

You wouldn't have known it then, but you'd just witnessed the TV debut of one of the most legendary teachers of all time. Nothing you'd seen on-screen was haphazard or random. On the contrary, he'd engineered all of it—from his sweater to his porch swing to his songs—for a particular purpose. And over the course of more than nine hundred of these "television visits," as the host would come to call them, that purpose would gradually grow clear.

Though today we tend to remember his gentle warmth and kindness, Fred Rogers was more than a nice guy in a cardigan. In fact, what made *Mister Rogers' Neighborhood* so effective in the first place had less to do with Fred-Rogers-the-television-host than it did with his ingenious application of the learning sciences. An accomplished scholar in his own right, Rogers worked with the leading minds of his day—including world-famous pediatricians, psychologists, and child-development experts, some of whom you'll meet in the following pages—to ensure that everything children saw in the *Neighborhood* enriched their lives and nurtured their growth as human beings.

Like all great teachers, Rogers used what he knew to captivate and even enchant his students. He blended the *Neighborhood*'s science so seamlessly with its art that it's all but invisible now: What looks like an inexpensive costume is instead a perfect conduit for curiosity. A strange-sounding song lyric sends a message of self-acceptance. Rogers based every story, every song, every script on what had been proven to benefit children. If anything, he was almost *too* good at hiding the science behind the show; today, his legacy as a scholar has largely been forgotten.

It's doubtful, though, that Rogers would have cared. "What if you were offered an hour of television live every day?" he once asked. "Can you imagine what it's like to try to fill that up with something of value? I wanted to give the best I could."

By all accounts, that's exactly what he did. From its 1968 debut until its final episode in 2001, the *Neighborhood* helped whole generations navigate rapid, sometimes unsettling change. It made millions of kids feel valued and loved, and in turn helped millions of kids value and love their neighbors. Studies of children who regularly watched the program found that compared to their peers, *Neighborhood* viewers grew more patient, more playful, more cooperative, and more social. And of course, many of those children went on to raise children of their own. Fred Rogers' impact on the last half century is incalculable.

But following his death in 2003, the *Neighborhood* gradually disappeared from American airwaves, becoming a pleasant (if fading) memory in the minds of the children who watched it. With its cardigan-clad host, its distinctive Pittsburgh accents, and its dated special effects, the program can seem—at least at first glance—hopelessly detached from the rest of modern media. It's slow, it's quiet, it's *not exciting* by design. And aside from some minor tweaks, it looked the same at its end as it had at its beginning. It's tempting to think the *Neighborhood* fell behind the times.

But perhaps we've gotten it wrong. Perhaps we've let the times drift away from the *Neighborhood*. Clearly, there's still a cultural craving for what the program offered: its animated spinoff, *Daniel Tiger's Neighborhood*, is streamed more than forty million times per month. An acclaimed documentary, a bestselling biography, and a biopic starring Tom Hanks have all created a Mister Rogers renaissance, one that highlights his unrelenting *goodness* in a world that seems to lack it. Amid the nostalgia and the good feelings and our reverence for Fred-Rogers-the-man, all that's missing now is an exploration of what he did, how he did it, and why it worked.

"Ourselves, Five Hundred or a Thousand Years Ago"

In a tiny town in western Europe, the kids have taken over. They've swarmed the river and the fields. They've climbed every tree and stormed every building. In the streets, chaos: Kids waddle on stilts, blow bubbles, and bang drums. They don homemade hats and strange wooden masks. They leapfrog through the alleys, swinging sticks at piñatas and shaking their rattles with glee. And best of all, there's not an adult to be found—a childhood fantasy more than four and a half centuries old.

Artist Pieter Bruegel the Elder's 1560 oil painting, *Children's Games*, is perhaps the Western world's most detailed window into what childhood looked like hundreds of years ago. Bruegel's encyclopedic work depicts more than seventy toys and games, nearly all of which children would recognize today. Though time-traveling tweens might recoil at the lack of Renaissance-era iPhones, they'd likely find solace in a game of King by Your Leaue (hide-and-seek) or Sunne and Moone (tug-of-war).

They'd also find that their sixteenth-century peers weren't nearly as alien as they might have expected. Historians of childhood have spent whole careers reconstructing the youths of past generations, digging for details in schoolmasters' reports, church records, diaries, parenting manuals, and more. What they've found is that kids in other times and places were basically "ourselves, five hundred or a thousand years ago," writes the British scholar Nicholas Orme.

While children's individual experiences have varied in every conceivable way, certain aspects of childhood are timeless and classic. Kids have always needed special care and special people to provide it—parents and relatives, yes, but also (depending on the era) wet nurses, wizards, and witches. They've always crawled away behind their parents' backs, driven by the need to look, explore, and wonder. They've always reached for the sweetest food on the table, fought with and hugged their siblings and friends, and surprised and tested their teachers. And they've always grown up too fast and made lives of their own too soon.

"So it was in the Middle Ages," writes Orme, "and for long before that."

And so it was in Pittsburgh in 2007. At the time, Gregg had just taken a new job as executive director of the Grable Foundation, a family philanthropy dedicated to improving children's lives. Ryan was a college student preparing to become a teacher. As we started down our respective paths, we talked with as many parents and educators as we could, asking each of them different versions of the same basic question: What do children need?

It seemed straightforward enough. In a very basic sense, all kids need the same things—food, shelter, safety, love. Given our vocations, we expected slightly more specific requests: extra help with fractions; funding

4

for classroom computers; a new floor for the school gym. What we heard instead would change the course of our lives.

We heard it from rookie teachers and classroom veterans. We heard it from progressive, reform-minded principals and old-school librarians. We heard it from counselors, museum curators, parents, and grandparents: *We're just not connecting with kids the way we used to.* The details differed, but nearly everyone we spoke to felt a disconnect, as if something seismic had shaken childhood's foundation.

At first, we chalked it up to that time-honored frustration: *Kids these days.* Such a feeling is nothing new; generational hand-wringing might be our oldest tradition. (A child-rearing tract from the Puritan era describes kids as "vile and abject persons, liars, thieves, evil beasts, [and] good for nothing.") Anyone who works with or cares for children has a difficult, demanding job.

But the more we listened, the more we realized adults' concerns went far beyond frustration. Their unease was philosophical, almost *existential* in nature. The people we spoke to had been among the first to detect a turning point: the moment the world's rate of change exceeded our ability to keep up.

For the first time, a generation of kids had spent their entire lives online. Their relationships with peers, parents, and even themselves had been forged in ways the world had never seen. They'd been raised with the ability to communicate instantly with anyone—anywhere, anytime. The answer to almost anything they'd want to ask could be found in a matter of seconds. They could create and consume art with tools that, until recently, had been confined to science fiction. If Pieter Bruegel the Elder had been around to re-create his famous painting, the modern version might largely consist of tiny glowing screens.

Hence the disconnect between kids and adults: Kids were growing up in a world vastly different from our own. As adults, we'd yet to reconcile what's timeless and classic about childhood with the rapid ways the world had changed. But plenty of people were working on it—whether they knew it or not.

Project Oxygen

In 2008, Google asked a team of statisticians to help solve a problem. Since the company's founding, its culture had been created and driven by software engineers: a breed famous for preferring computers to people, for wanting to be left alone, and for their zealous aversion to conventional office life. Not surprisingly, such a culture bred a distaste for hierarchy: When *everyone* is the smartest person in the room, who needs a boss?

It's a dilemma the company had struggled with since its inception. In fact, for a brief period in 2002, Google eliminated engineering managers altogether, though the experiment fizzled when employees brought every issue—from the major to the trivial—to the company's cofounder, Larry Page. The company conceded that it needed managers, if only to keep things organized. Still, Google took "a pretty simple approach to management," reported the *New York Times*: "Leave people alone. Let the engineers do their stuff. If they become stuck, they'll ask their bosses, whose deep technical expertise propelled them into management in the first place."

To validate that approach, the company asked its statisticians to determine—once and for all—which characteristics made for good bosses. Dubbed Project Oxygen, the multiyear initiative shocked the company. The statisticians collected and coded more than ten thousand data points from performance reviews, employee surveys, exit interviews, and more. Their analysis found that "technical expertise—the ability, say, to write computer code in your sleep—ranked dead last" among the things that mattered most. The other, more important skills included a boss's ability to communicate clearly and to take a collaborative approach to problem-solving. More than anything else, Googlers craved accessible managers who cared about employees and their well-being.

It was an early lesson in what would matter as the digital age developed: One of the world's most powerful technology companies discovered the importance of human qualities above all else. To be sure, technical expertise was still imperative. But what Project Oxygen suggested—and what parents, educators, and researchers have since confirmed—is that today's kids need more than the ability to read, write, and do arithmetic. Tomorrow's thriving adults will be the people you can go to with problems; who can listen, ask questions, and help think through complex issues; who know how teams work and who can nurture other people's strengths. They'll be endlessly curious and radically empathetic. They'll be, in other words, the type of people that Project Oxygen identified—people with qualities that can't be replaced by machines.

We should pause here to say that by no means are we equating "working at Google" with "living a successful life." The purpose of learning is far nobler than preparing future workers. It's about kids discovering their potential and their purpose, becoming more fully themselves. It's about raising creative, curious, caring neighbors and citizens—people who can build stronger, more inclusive communities and a more just and loving world. Still, Google remains a useful example, if only because the company's core function—organizing and navigating the world's data—will become ever more essential as technology advances.

Adults once memorized the Pythagorean theorem, the atomic number of carbon, and the function of the Fourth Amendment. Today, those facts fit comfortably in children's pockets. So, too, does the full range of humanity's history, art, opinions, and lies. To thrive in such a world, kids will have to be able to make sense of it all, discerning what's true, what's useful, and what's relevant to their lives.

It's the same lesson we'd eventually learn in Pittsburgh. At about the time that Google was briefing its statisticians, a group of parents and educators here were conducting a sort of Project Oxygen of their own. Gregg had invited them out to breakfast to think through some difficult questions: In a time of rapid, remarkable change, what and how should children learn? What's relevant? What's engaging? What *matters*?

The breakfasts started small: a few teachers and parents getting together for pancakes and coffee. Eventually, they started bringing their friends, and then their friends brought friends of their own. Soon, the breakfasts became standing meetings, growing in size and scope. Scientists, gamers, artists, and others started showing up, trading stories and discussing their fields. They talked about what interested them, what led them to their work, what moved them. They talked about their own joys and struggles with learning, the strengths that had gotten them through life, and the things they wished they'd known earlier. Most of all, they talked about their childhoods.

A certain theme emerged. When these adults—people who were thriving in the world by almost any measure—considered the substance of their formative years, none mentioned the hours spent drilling for exams. None had found their life's purpose in a state standard. The content they'd acquired had surely played a role, but their true moments of learning and definition had little to do with memorized facts or mandatory seat time.

Instead, they'd been inspired by an incredible teacher. They'd fallen in love with a novel or the way paint spreads on a canvas. Or they'd been asked a question that upended their world, sparking a lifelong search for answers. Nearly everyone who joined us could trace their success to specific skills and mindsets: curiosity, creativity, communication, and more. Emerging learning science suggested they were onto something, and over time, it became the group's mission to provide these tools using the new ways of learning available to modern kids.

That mission would take the group through countless classrooms, the labs of leading learning scientists, and even the White House. The network we formed, Remake Learning, would grow to include thousands of parents, educators, libraries, universities, museums, and others working to make learning more engaging, more relevant, and more equitable. Its family-friendly festival, Remake Learning Days, would take root across our city, our region, and eventually, our country.

But in the beginning, our question was where to start. Fortunately, there was someone watching over us—a neighbor who'd spent a lifetime showing us the way.

Remaking the Neighborhood

With its stilts and costumes and songs, *Mister Rogers' Neighborhood* sometimes resembled *Children's Games*. Rogers himself was once asked why his educational television program didn't focus on facts—on letters and numbers, fractions and spelling. "I would rather give [children] the tools for learning," he responded. "If we give them the tools, they'll want to learn the facts. More importantly, they'll use the facts to build and not destroy."

This is a book about how Rogers managed to do so—and how his modern-day equivalents are working to do the same. Using the latest technology of his time, Rogers honored what was timeless and classic about being a kid, while also providing the same tools for learning that scientists now consider critical. The skills and mindsets he taught have been shown to boost everything from academic learning to children's well-being. They've been shown to be up to *ten times* more predictive of long-term success than test scores, and they can benefit kids of every background and age. They cost next to nothing to develop, and they hinge on the very things that make life worthwhile: self-acceptance; close, loving relationships; and a deep regard for one's neighbor.

What ultimately matters, Rogers once wrote, "isn't how a person's inner life finally puts together the alphabet and numbers of his outer life. What really matters is whether he uses the alphabet for the declaration of a war or the description of a sunrise—his numbers for the final count at Buchenwald or the specifics of a brand-new bridge."

The *Neighborhood* may be off the air, but its lessons are as relevant as ever. To thrive in the age of the algorithm, kids today—and their parents, too—will have to excel at what Rogers taught best: being human.

ONE

When You Wonder, You're Learning

Curiosity

Even by the standards of this particular Neighborhood—where a tiger lives in a clock, polka dots litter the streets, and a trolley travels from another dimension—it's an admittedly curious scene.

King Friday XIII, the long-suffering sire of Make-Believe, is furious. He's just been pranked by two purple pandas: creatures who speak in robotic tones and flaunt their simple superpower. (The pandas can appear and disappear with a snap of their fingers.) Identical except for their height, the pandas use their power to trick the tortured ruler, causing Friday to confuse the taller panda for the shorter one, if only for a moment.

Of course, in most puppets, a harmless stunt like this one would fail to inspire outrage.

But King Friday XIII is not most puppets.

"I don't like being *fooled* like that," he declares, projecting as much anger as his puppet master can muster. King Friday isn't a villain, exactly—he's a reactionary and sometimes inept, but he tends to give wickedness a wide berth. He's a musician, a poet, and a former pole-vaulter—a true renaissance king—and he's even been known to show kindness. Once, upon meeting a starving magician, he established the King Friday Queen Sara Saturday Royal Foundation for the Performing Arts, or KFQSSRFFTPA for short.

But like any autocrat, King Friday has his flaws. He's vain, he's insecure, and most of all, he doesn't like to be *fooled*.

And this time, he won't get fooled again. "I shall make a rule," he declares.

By now, Make-Believe's subjects know the drill: King Friday forbids whatever foils his moods and whims. Over the years, he's outlawed harmonicas, bare hands, bad feelings, play, and puppets who don't look like him, all with varying degrees of success. Friday's decrees are almost always short-lived—usually, he changes his mind or simply forgets as he tends to other kingly concerns.

In this scene, though, he makes a rule so egregious—so contrary to the nature of Make-Believe—that to follow it would threaten the Neighborhood itself. Not only would it stilt Make-Believe's progress and dim its denizens' futures, it would drain the joy out of life and make learning impossible, condemning the Neighborhood to stagnation, decay, and the slow-moving horrors of indifference.

But in a moment of humiliation and shortsightedness, King Friday XIII issues his edict anyway.

"Cancel. All. Curiosity."

⋯⋯⋯⋯⋯

This scene—scripted by and starring Fred Rogers in a late-stage, turn-of-the-millennium episode of *Mister Rogers' Neighborhood*—is more than just make-believe. Kicking off a five-part series about curiosity, the image of a king trying to suppress his people's questions has roots in real life: Throughout history, countless rulers have sought to cancel curiosity themselves. As any tyrant knows, the less inquisitive a society is, the less free it becomes.

In 1937, the Nazis staged the infamous *Degenerate Art* exhibition, where more than seven hundred works of modern art were defaced and ridiculed. Actors posing as critics wandered through the crowds, loudly proclaiming that modern art—a style that invites interpretation by provoking questions—was not art at all, but rather a product of mental illness and Jewish perversion. As a result, many of the exhibition's attendees left less willing to question how the Nazis treated their neighbors.

It's a tactic that's been used for centuries. During China's Cultural Revolution, militants destroyed libraries to eradicate opposing ideas. In the United States, schools were first burned and bombed, then segregated and budget-starved to prevent Black children from learning. In the antebellum South, enslaved people caught with books were beaten or killed. Campaigns to cancel curiosity stretch all the way back to antiquity: Consider the cautionary tale of ancient Greeks succumbing to the Sirens. Or Adam and Eve in the Garden of Eden, dooming mankind by tasting the forbidden fruit. Or Lot and his family fleeing the biblical city of Sodom, forbidden by God to look back. (When Lot's wife gives into her curiosity and sneaks a final glance, she's transformed into a pillar of salt.)

"To ask questions of the universe, and then learn to live with those questions, is the way [one] achieves his own identity," said the writer James Baldwin. "But no society is really anxious to have that kind of person around. What societies really, ideally, want is a citizenry which will simply obey the rules of society."

Perhaps it's no wonder, then, that some of our oldest stories and sayings suggest ambivalence—or even outright hostility—toward the inquisitive. Curiosity leads to exploration. Exploration leads to questions, and questions threaten the status quo.

Curiosity is power.

And when that power is cultivated, it can change lives, topple dictators, and even reshape the planet. Hundreds of thousands of years ago, for example, one of humanity's predecessors had a question. *Homo erectus* wouldn't have called it that; the invention of words was still a long way off. But somewhere on an African savanna, or in a cave on the Sinai Peninsula, a mystery appeared: *What might happen*, our ancestor wondered, *if I picked up those rocks over there and bashed them together?*

Thus began one of the most important experiments of all time. According to one theory, the discovery of fire gave way to cooking and better nutrition, which led to the doubling of hominid neurons. Equipped with unprecedented brainpower, humans grew more and more sophisticated, learning to talk to one another, to build societies and cities, and to spread out across the globe. They developed ideas—that the Earth is six thousand years old, or that cavities are caused by tiny worms in our teeth—and replaced those ideas with better ones through science. They invented music, medicine, and *Mister Rogers' Neighborhood*. They even left the planet, launching a Martian rover that—perhaps out of gratitude—they called *Curiosity*.

Best of all, our predecessors passed this power to us. Nearly every human being is born curious. Babies as young as nine weeks old tend to focus on what's new and unfamiliar rather than what's constant or routine. Before they learn to speak, they learn to point: "A baby's way of saying 'tell me' is to point to an object while looking at her mother," writes Ian Leslie, author of *Curious: The Desire to Know and Why Your Future Depends On It*. As toddlers, kids become dogged investigators, asking *why* at every opportunity. Curiosity is so ubiquitous—so fundamental to who we are as a species—that psychologists put it on par with the drive to eat, sleep, and reproduce. Not only is it "the linchpin of intellectual achievement," as one scientist puts it, evidence suggests that curiosity will only grow more essential in coming decades.

But there's a catch. While almost all of us are born curious, far fewer actually stay that way. Curiosity can fade shockingly fast; disparities emerge even among babies, growing wider over time. It doesn't take a tyrant to cancel curiosity—even the most well-meaning adult can dim a child's desire to know. If curiosity isn't nurtured, it tends to be "transitory, to die out, or to wane in intensity," wrote the philosopher John Dewey in 1910. "In a few people, intellectual curiosity is so insatiable that nothing will discourage it, but in most, its edge is easily dulled and blunted."

That's a problem, especially today. It's been estimated that today's young people could change jobs as many as *fifteen times* over the course of their lifetimes and that many of their jobs will require work that hasn't been invented. The future will require today's young people to forge careers that cross sectors and industries, requiring constant learning. Those without the ability or desire to keep up could find themselves automated out of a job or otherwise left behind. Meanwhile, the curious will be rewarded.

It's happening already. Consider the priorities of any number of leaders and intellectuals: Apple CEO Tim Cook seeks employees with "obsessive curiosity." Addressing a crowd of college graduates, Oprah Winfrey said this: "I wish you curiosity." Bill Gates and Warren Buffett, when asked about their success, both credited their desire to learn more about the world. And Ta-Nehisi Coates, the National Book Award–winning writer, has described himself as "irrepressible in terms of my curiosities."

The list goes on, but curiosity's value extends far beyond wealth or professional success. Curious people can question their circumstances and fight for something better. They can appreciate the world's marvels and the importance of conservation. Above all, curious people are learners: people who can look closely at an orange blossom or a mural or a fellow human being and wonder.

What Curiosity Can Do

"Did you know?" Fred Rogers used to sing. "Did you know when you wonder, you're learning?"

Throughout the *Neighborhood*'s thirty-one-season run, Rogers served as curiosity's most famous televangelist, nurturing children's inquisitiveness in ways that—when viewed from today's world of pinging phones and breaking news—can seem almost quaint. Pick any episode at random and you might find Rogers exploring a pinwheel, or carefully drawing a rainbow, or narrating a documentary about citrus farms. He makes a point, again and again, of telling viewers how many questions he has and how much he wants to know about the world. He's so genuinely interested in *everything* that viewers can't help but be interested, too. And when he looks at the camera and asks if you've ever wondered how people make crayons or if you've yearned to visit an eraser factory, you surprise yourself by how quickly you think, *Yes!*

Thinkers, teachers, and scientists have long been interested in the power of wonder. From Jean Piaget to B. F. Skinner, psychologists have probed curiosity's origins; today, behavioral scientists and neuroscientists are shedding new light on its functions. But even before the advent of modern learning science, Rogers seemed to sense that curiosity drives learning—a thesis that brain scans and studies are now confirming in droves. Consider these lines from "Did You Know?" a song Rogers debuted in 1979:

> *Did you know? Did you know?*
> *Did you know that it's all right to wonder?*
> *There are all kinds of wonderful things!*
> *You can ask a lot of questions about the world*
> *And your place in it.*
> *You can ask about people's feelings;*
> *You can learn the sky's the limit.*
> *Did you know? Did you know?*
> *Did you know when you wonder, you're learning?*
> *Did you know when you marvel, you're learning*
> *About all kinds of wonderful,*
> *All kinds of marvelous,*
> *Marvelously wonderful things?*

Like so much of Rogers' work, "Did You Know?" was inspired by his childhood. "Fred McFeely, his maternal grandfather, was wonderfully supportive of Fred's sense of curiosity, his sense of learning, and his sense of exploration," says Maxwell King, author of *The Good Neighbor: The Life and Work of Fred Rogers*. "Fred McFeely understood that the most natural thing in the world for a child is to be exploring and learning and wondering about how the world works and how one fits in."

When Rogers was young, for example, he was curious about where kittens came from. While questions about reproduction sometimes strike fear in the hearts of parents, Fred McFeely had an idea: He'd let little Freddy watch a cat give birth. The experience satisfied Rogers' curiosity in a developmentally appropriate way, with a trusted adult—his grandfather—serving as a guide. "I'll always remember that as a wonderful time," Rogers later said. "[My grandfather] helped me to understand it so well, and he told me, 'You know, Freddy, it's all right to wonder about things and ask about things.'"

Watching a cat give birth might seem like a strange thing to remember several decades after the fact. It might seem odder, still, that Rogers would show his viewers another cat doing exactly the same thing. But the reality is that this is stuff kids wonder about, and according to learning scientists, Rogers was right: When kids wonder, they *are* learning—or at least they're far more likely to.

"Inciting children's curiosity is the best way to ensure that they will absorb and retain information," writes psychologist Susan Engel, one of the world's leading experts on curiosity's development. In 2009, a team of Caltech researchers demonstrated this by posing a series of trivia questions to a group of volunteers. They asked participants to guess the answers to the questions and rate their level of curiosity about each—that is, to tell the researchers how much they *wanted* to know the answers. Later, the volunteers were shown each question again, followed by the correct response. The research team watched their brains light up via functional magnetic resonance imaging—in effect, watching the volunteers' brains process information in real time.

They found that when volunteers were curious, their brains indicated "the type of feeling you have before the curtain goes up on a play you have wanted to see for a long time," writes author Mario Livio. "The researchers also found that when the correct answer was revealed to the subjects, the regions of the brain that were significantly energized were those typically associated with learning, memory, and language comprehension and production."

In other words, the more curiosity that participants reported feeling—the more they wondered—the more powerfully their brains were primed for learning.

On one hand, this might not surprise you. Anyone who has ever struggled to stay awake during a boring presentation knows how difficult it can be to learn information that doesn't pique your interest. On the other hand, the Caltech study allowed scientists to measure just how much difference curiosity can make: Ten days later, when asked to recall what they'd learned, participants more easily answered the questions they'd been curious about. This helps explain why Rogers never forgot watching the birth of those kittens.

A later study from the University of California at Davis found an even more surprising benefit. When participants were highly curious about the information in front of them, they also more easily learned *other* information, even when it was unrelated. As one researcher put it, "Curiosity may put the brain in a state that allows it to learn and return any kind of information, like a vortex that sucks in what you are motivated to learn, and also everything around it."

When you wonder, you're learning, indeed.

Such findings should be great news for parents, teachers, and anyone else concerned with children's learning. Since kids are naturally curious, harnessing their desire to ask and answer questions should be a no-brainer. Now that we know just how powerful curiosity can be, we'd expect learning environments to be like little laboratories—places where it's all right to wonder; where kids explore the *whats* and *hows* and *whys* of the problems that intrigue them; and where their brains light up day in and day out, making schools and libraries and museums the most joyful places on the planet.

And in a few lucky places, that's exactly what's happening. At the Carnegie Science Center in Pittsburgh, Jason Brown stands beneath a towering, room-size replica of the human brain, full of twinkling lights that map the constellations of neurons that carry our thoughts and feelings. All around him, the center's three-foot visitors dart from exhibit to exhibit, their parents struggling to keep up. One presses a button that says, "Why Do I Fart?" letting out a long recording of human flatulence. Shrieks of discovery and delight ring throughout the building.

"Sometimes we forget that learning is supposed to be fun," says Brown. It's something the center's director knows from experience: As a kid, he had no particular love for science. "I remember doing formulas for reactions of acids and bases in school, and never once did I think, 'Wow, this is amazing,'" he says. It wasn't until he mixed ammonia and Drano at home—a mixture that exploded in his driveway—that he developed an interest. "I think I just needed to see some destruction," he says, laughing. "After that, I was hooked."

Brown's curiosity had simply needed to be captured, priming his brain for learning. Today, the center he leads offers kids and families a similar (and safer) chance to feel what he felt in his childhood driveway. Everything here is designed to do such priming: There's a theater for live liquid-nitrogen demonstrations; a million-volt Tesla coil for making lightning; display boxes full of fake animal poop; and the Air Hockeybot, a computerized arm that calculates a puck's location and speed one hundred times per second, making it virtually unbeatable to human opponents. ("In my five years of working here," laments Brown, "I've won only once.")

Walking through the center, it's impossible not to gape at such things in astonishment. And that's exactly the point—when children are captivated, they start asking questions, and the more questions they ask, the more they're likely to learn. For adults, the key is to keep encouraging such wonder. "As a society, I think we've gotten too used to just giving kids the answers," says Brown. "Sometimes, the best answer isn't an answer at all. Instead of telling them, 'X happens because Y,' it's often better to ask, 'Why do *you* think X happens? Have you ever seen anything like that before? What happens if you press that button? What else does this make you wonder about?'"

Of course, families don't have to visit a science center to find something that stokes curiosity. Tesla coils are cool, but so are bugs and flowers and cardboard tubes. Given ample opportunities and encouragement, kids will ask questions about just about anything, as psychologist Michelle Chouinard and her colleagues demonstrated by analyzing some 230 hours of recorded conversation between four children and their respective caregivers. The children had been recorded at regular intervals from the time they were fourteen months old until they were just over five years old. Chouinard's team wanted to find out how asking questions can aid a child's development: What kinds of questions do children ask? What do they want to know about? And what do they do with the answers they get?

The kids asked a *lot* of questions—more than one hundred per hour on average. They spanned several topics and ranged from simple information gathering ("What is this?") to more abstract explorations ("Why would someone do that?"). Chouinard concluded that curiosity is "a central part of what it means to be a child."

Adults, however, don't always treat it as such. When Susan Engel went searching for curiosity in elementary school classrooms, she found the opposite of what Chouinard and her team had encountered. "For the most part, kindergartners asked very few questions and spent little time investigating the environment. In any given two-hour stretch, we'd see anywhere from two to five questions or explorations," Engel recounts. "In 5th grade classrooms, the situation was even more striking. A typical two-hour stretch of time often didn't yield even one student question. That means

11-year-olds often go for hours at a time in school without indicating anything they want to know about."

Though Chouinard and Engel studied different populations in different places, their diverging results suggest that hypothetically, the same child who asks two questions per minute at home might hear fewer than two questions per *hour* in class. Engel notes that even in the livelier classrooms she observed, genuine wonder was usually absent. In most cases, kids followed clear-cut directions toward a predetermined objective.

Of course, there are plenty of good reasons to limit children's inquiry. Curiosity is a powerful driver of learning, but it's not without drawbacks. For one, the sort of total curiosity that most of us are born with—the kind that makes us grasp our toys, stick them in our mouths, and hurl them across rooms—is essential to our early explorations of the world. But as we age, this kind of curiosity can become a liability. Imagine trying to work when any sort of novelty—a new car outside the window, a new colleague down the hall—sparks an all-consuming fascination. No one would get anything done. Nor would anyone learn much, because every new thing would drag our focus from the last. If you've ever looked up from your Twitter feed only to find that several hours have passed, you have a sense of what this feels like.

Likewise, curiosity's age-old association with danger—think Lot's wife or the old saying about curiosity killing the cat—isn't entirely without merit. There's a reason childproofing is a billion-dollar industry: Kids have a knack for putting themselves in peril when they want to know something, whether it's what's behind that electrical outlet or how deep that swimming pool might be. Curiosity is why we have toilet locks and childproof pill bottles. It's why professional childproofers can charge thousands of dollars to assess private homes and sell safety solutions to nervous parents. And it's why Gregg's daughter, wondering what her house would look like from a second-story balcony, once scaled a safety gate and climbed over a railing before she'd even learned to walk. Fortunately, despite her expert ascent, her parents managed to pull her back to safety.

But it's doubtful that these reasons alone account for the yawning curiosity gaps that Engel found in classrooms. In many learning environments, there's a disconnect between what kids *naturally* do (ask questions that interest them) and what they *actually* do (work within the confines of an adult's plan). There's a disconnect, too, between what kids want to know (how kittens are born) and what we, as adults, want them to learn (how fractions reduce). Engel recalls one particularly ironic back-and-forth: "In one classroom I observed, a 9th grader raised her hand to ask if there were any places in the world where no one made art. The teacher stopped her midsentence with, 'Zoe, no questions now, please; it's time for learning.'"

The truth is that we can wind up chastening children's curiosity when we're actually trying to channel it. How many of us have come home exhausted after a long day, only to shortchange, redirect, or otherwise ignore a child's inquiries? In the moment, it's sometimes easier to say *I don't know* or *Ask your mother* or even *Where's your iPad?* But over time, our cues can signal that we neither value nor encourage children's questions.

Curiosity is so fragile, in fact, that we can cancel it without even speaking. As mentioned earlier, when babies want to know about something, they point to it. But they'll only *continue* to do so if their pointing results in answers. Moreover, those answers have to be good answers: In one study, researchers found that when incompetent or inattentive adults give bad information, babies become less likely to point. "It's sobering to think that even at such an early age, infants are capable of telling whether or not you're an idiot," writes Leslie.

Other cues can be even subtler. Research has shown that kids are much more likely to explore unfamiliar objects if adults make encouraging faces or otherwise show their own interest in the object. In other words, children can "catch" our curiosity if we model it. If we want to raise curious kids, it helps to be curious ourselves, both visibly and verbally.

"It's what *you* bring to the children every day—your listening, your caring, your enthusiasm, and your responding to their ideas, thoughts, and feelings—that encourages and inspires children to ask questions and to be imaginative," Rogers wrote to adults. "By responding thoughtfully to children's questions . . . you're encouraging their curiosity. Even when you don't know the answer, you're letting them know it's good to wonder and ask."

Curiosity Can Be Taught (and Caught)

In the 1950s, if you wanted to understand what makes children tick, Pittsburgh was the place to be. For a few years, the superstars of child development all worked in the same place: the Arsenal Family & Children's Center, cofounded in 1953 by the rock star pediatrician Dr. Benjamin Spock. Having recently published *The Common Sense Book of Baby and Child Care,* Spock was the era's most celebrated authority on childhood; even today, his book remains a bestseller. As a professor at the University of Pittsburgh, he launched Arsenal as a training site for students studying child development. His colleague at the center, the German American psychologist Erik Erikson, had just published a landmark book of his own, which introduced the world to the concept of an "identity crisis," among other things.

The presence of Spock and Erikson alone would have been enough to cement the center's legacy. To study child development at Arsenal would have been akin to studying music with Beethoven and Bach. But a third colleague—one who's lesser known to the world but every bit as influential—is the reason the lessons learned at Arsenal would eventually impact millions of children beyond the center's tiny brick building in Pittsburgh.

"Margaret McFarland knew more than anyone in this world about families with young children," Erikson used to say. A child psychologist, educator, and professor in the Department of Psychiatry at the University of Pittsburgh's School of Medicine, Dr. Margaret McFarland taught kindergartners in Melbourne and college students in Massachusetts before returning to her hometown to help cofound Arsenal. It was there that one day, a young man from the nearby theological seminary came knocking at her door.

The budding minister named Fred Rogers had decided that he wanted to work with children through television. His teachers at the seminary, however, weren't entirely sure what to do with such a request—"Nothing like that had ever been fashioned from Presbyterian fabric," notes Maxwell King. Eventually, a professor suggested that Rogers contact McFarland to study child development under her guidance.

The suggestion led to a lifelong friendship and professional collaboration that would eventually shape whole generations of kids. Rogers studied with McFarland for years at Arsenal; later, he'd meet with her each week to discuss scripts and songs for the *Neighborhood*. As Rogers' mentor, McFarland left an indelible mark on the program: "To know and love Fred Rogers," one journalist wrote, "is to know and love Margaret McFarland."

Rogers often said that one of the most profound lessons he learned from McFarland was the Quaker idea that attitudes are caught, not taught. He recalled how McFarland had once invited a famous sculptor to Arsenal: "Dr. McFarland said to him, 'I don't want you to teach sculpting. All I want you to do is to love clay in front of the children.' And that's what he did. He came once a week for a whole term, sat with the four- and five-year-olds as they played, and he 'loved' his clay in front of them."

The directive worked. The adults who'd worked at Arsenal for years said that neither before nor since had the children there used clay so imaginatively, Rogers recalled. By simply delighting in his work, the sculptor had made children wonder about clay and what they might do with it themselves. They'd caught his curiosity.

Nearly every episode of the *Neighborhood* followed this lead in one way or another. Rogers introduced kids to diverse TV neighbors who were passionate about any number of crafts and occupations: There was Yo-Yo Ma loving the cello; Wynton Marsalis loving the trumpet; Bill Nye loving science; Julia Child loving recipes; LeVar Burton loving books.

"The best teacher in the world is the one who loves what he or she does, and just loves it in front of you," he said, echoing McFarland. "And that's what I like to do with the *Neighborhood*. I love to have guests and presenters in a whole smorgasbord of ways for the children to choose . . . some child might choose painting, some child might choose playing the cello, but there are so many ways of saying who we are and how we feel."

In the very first nationally broadcast episode, Rogers visits Mrs. Russellite, an eccentric neighbor who collects lampshades. Rather than judging her choice of hobby, Rogers indulges it—he shows genuine interest in her collection and even puts a lampshade on his head. Throughout the rest of the series, Rogers unrelentingly exposes viewers to adults who wonder and who assure children that their questions have value. For parents, the program reinforces McFarland's message to the sculptor: Love learning in front of your kids. Let them catch your curiosity. Listen to their questions, learn their interests, and let *them* lead the journey toward knowledge.

Trusting kids to be curious is a crucial first step in that journey—a step we've collectively learned to skip in a culture that prizes efficiency over exploration and mastery over inquiry. Consider, for example, a simple button—the kind one might find on a cardigan sweater. Imagine sitting at a desk with nothing before you except that button. What's your first reaction?

"A lot of adults will immediately say, 'Okay, now what? What am I supposed to *do* with this button? They'll assume they're supposed to make something or have some sort of next step," says Melissa Butler, a nationally acclaimed educator, consultant, and writer. "And despite all the research that's out there about children's curiosity and how many questions kids ask, we often assume that children are the same way—we assume they'll find the button boring."

As founder of the reimagining project, LLC, and director of the Children's Innovation Project, Butler believes differently. Because buttons are so basic, she says, kids can bring their full selves to them. Children who haven't been granted access to a particular experience or certain prior knowledge aren't prevented from engaging with such a simple object. In fact, "kids don't have to know anything other than *who they are* in order to engage fully in something like a button," she says. And eventually, given enough time and encouragement, kids will start to notice things about the button—and they'll want to find out more.

"Oh, you found a bump? You found a tiny scratch? I wonder what else you can find," says Butler. "Setting limits on materials and focusing on one small thing allows children to really slow down. They notice what's there, what's not there, what might have been there before, and what might be dreamed there. Too often, we don't allow questions to emerge from what children are interested in. If we would just do that and listen, then their curiosity evolves."

Butler has focused on a slow, simple approach to teaching and learning for more than two decades—an approach Rogers himself emphasized on his program.* "The more space we can give children to *not* know, to *not* make a finished project, and to *not* be 'done,' the more space we allow for curiosity that's internalized and intrinsically motivated," she says. "Because that's what learning is: it's constant wondering. It's keeping yourself in a perpetual state of not knowing."

Susan Engel and her graduate student Madelyn Labella demonstrated this in a particularly striking experiment. They brought eight- and nine-year-olds into a lab to do a science project called "Bouncing Raisins," which required kids to drop raisins into a concoction of ingredients. With one group of children, Labella stopped partway through the project and said, "You know what? I wonder what would happen if we dropped [a Skittle] in the liquid instead of a raisin." With the other group, Labella and the children completed the project without straying from its instructions. Labella then left both groups alone in their respective rooms, telling them they could do whatever they wanted while she was gone. Sure enough, the

---

* You can see "beautiful things when you look carefully," Rogers would tell his viewers.

kids who'd seen Labella deviate from the task continued to experiment in her absence, dropping more objects into the liquid to see what might happen. The children who'd completed the project as instructed tended to do nothing at all.

Not only did this experiment reinforce the importance of modeling and allowing curiosity, it suggested a powerful way to pique children's interest. Scientists have found that something irresistible happens when we mix the familiar (raisins and Skittles) with the unknown (what happens when they're dropped into liquid). Ian Leslie notes that when people are presented with different landscape images, they tend to prefer those that include water, perhaps the most familiar substance on Earth. "But what's really interesting is that the most consistent and universal predictor of preference in these studies is *mystery*: scenes that hint at something we cannot see," he writes. "The reassuring presence of something we know is good for us gives us pleasure. But so does the promise of what lies beyond, the information we don't yet know."

In other words, we feel most curious when we're aware of a gap between what we're familiar with and what we want to know. It's hard to feel curious about something we know absolutely nothing about. Take, for example, the term *clinical lycanthropy*—if it doesn't ring any bells for you, then it probably doesn't sound all that intriguing. But what if you learn that clinical lycanthropy is a psychiatric disorder, and an exceedingly rare one at that? Then you might be inclined to pursue a few extra details—you become aware of what you don't know. Then, discovering that it refers to people who believe they've been turned into cows or wolves, the term becomes more intriguing still. The more you know, the more you *want* to know. Under the right conditions, you're driven to learn all you can until you perceive yourself as an expert, at which point curiosity begins to wane.*

---

* This explains the popularity of books, news reports, and TED Talks that purport to explain why everything you know about a given subject is wrong.

This framework for curiosity, known as the information-gap theory, was developed by George Loewenstein, the great-grandson of famed psychologist Sigmund Freud and a professor at Carnegie Mellon University, just next door to where Rogers filmed his program. Loewenstein's theory suggests that children need to have some basic knowledge about a subject before they can develop a sustained interest in it.

That's why Rogers spent so much time exploring whatever happened to be in his TV living room, says Roberta Schomburg, a longtime consultant for Fred Rogers Productions who now directs the Fred Rogers Center at Saint Vincent College in Latrobe, Pennsylvania. "What always intrigues me is the way that he found something deep in the little, familiar things that surround us every day," she says. "He liked to look carefully and discover something new in whatever was already part of the environment, like his fish tank. He didn't expect children to be curious about something they knew nothing about. Instead, he trusted them to notice something new about things that were already there."

Rogers knew that for kids to learn effectively, the information at hand has to connect to what they're familiar with and what they want to know more about. It has to strike that tantalizing balance between familiarity and mystery—the very balance on which the *Neighborhood* was built.

Curiosity's Components

"Once upon a time," writes journalist Tom Junod, "Fred Rogers took off his jacket and put on a sweater his mother had made him, a cardigan with a zipper. Then he took off his shoes and put on a pair of navy-blue canvas boating sneakers. He did the same thing the next day, and then the next . . . until he had done the same things, those things, 865 times, at the beginning of 865 television programs, over a span of 31 years."

Indeed, the basic format of the *Neighborhood* changed so little through the decades that the program's famous first frames spark a sort of Pavlovian response among the program's viewers. When Rogers visited Koko, a twenty-eighty-year-old who'd grown up watching the *Neighborhood*, the first thing she did was take off his shoes for him—a gesture that might have been unremarkable, if not for the fact that Koko was a 280-pound gorilla.

Even Koko understood Rogers' routine. Though viewers don't know the specifics of what's to come in any particular episode, they know the general outline: Rogers will show them around his house or his neighborhood for a while before the trolley takes them to Make-Believe. Afterward, the trolley brings viewers back to the "real" world, where Rogers unpacks what they've seen. Then he sings his departure song and anticipates the next episode: "I'll be back when the day is new / And I'll have more ideas for you!"

Given the immense innovations that arose in both television programming and the world at large during the *Neighborhood*'s multi-decade run, Rogers' adherence to the same basic format might seem old-fashioned or out of touch. After all, those same decades saw the debuts of both the Atari and the PlayStation 2; of cordless phones and the internet. But Rogers knew that without familiarity—and by extension, the trust that familiarity fosters—children's curiosity can wither. It sounds counterintuitive, but children's sense of adventurousness is paradoxically tied to their sense of safety. Kids need *both* to feel confident enough to explore the world around them.

Learning science has shown this again and again. In the 1970s, researchers Mary Ainsworth and Silvia Bell at Johns Hopkins University recruited fifty-six one-year-olds and their mothers for a series of experiments.* First, they placed a mother and her child in a room with some toys, which the one-year-old would then explore. They then asked the mother to leave the room, recording how the child reacted to the separation. Then, when the mother returned, they observed how the child reacted and what the child did next. The researchers found that kids with

---

* We should note here that all the participants were white and middle class, so the results here are not nationally representative.

a "secure attachment" to their mothers—that is, kids who felt confident in their enduring relationship—greeted their mothers warmly before turning back to the toys. Others, however, clung to their mothers and refused to resume exploring, suggesting that their fear of abandonment overrode their curiosity. Leslie sums this up in a decidedly Rogers-like way: "The more we love home, the more likely we are to strike out," he writes. "Curiosity is underwritten by love."

A few years later, scientists showed this another way, this time by placing rats on a raised platform with several extended walkways. One of the walkways had no sides—imagine a pedestrian bridge with no railings. When left to roam the platform, the rats mostly explored the enclosed walkways, perceiving them as safer. But when researchers injected them with anti-anxiety drugs, the rats explored the open walkway, too. The implication is that fear can dampen our desire to explore the unknown.

When that fear accumulates over time—whether due to trauma, an unsafe environment, or the absence of caring adults—it can damage children's drive to explore the wider world. Curiosity is power, yes, but it's also a privilege—one extended to kids whose basic survival needs have already been met. If kids are hungry or hurting or scared, they're less likely to have the luxury of wondering. This is one of many factors that put kids from poverty at a disadvantage: They're often forced to devote precious cognitive resources to things their more affluent peers take for granted. Some kids are more likely to wonder where their next meal is coming from rather than what a meteor is made of.

To the extent that he could, Rogers designed the *Neighborhood* as a safe haven in which every child could feel secure. In 1969, during his now-famous testimony before the Senate Subcommittee on Communications, Rogers explained his mission: "I give an expression of care every day to each child."

The routines he established on his show were an expression of that care. Hedda Bluestone Sharapan joined the *Neighborhood* as an assistant director on the first day of production in 1966, later serving as an associate producer and director of early childhood initiatives at Fred Rogers Productions. Today, she's a senior fellow at the Fred Rogers Center and a child development consultant for *Daniel Tiger's Neighborhood*. Rogers, Sharapan explains, wanted to emphasize clear expectations.

"We're not going to surprise you," she says of the *Neighborhood*'s philosophy. "We're going to tell you where you're going, and we're going to give you an introduction to it, and we're going to take you there. When we come back, we're going to talk about where we've been. You had a sense that the world was trustworthy and predictable. You could relax and be ready to learn."

Rogers went beyond establishing safety—he also emphasized *warmth*, right down to his gentle tone and soft sweaters. And rightly so: Learning scientists have linked an educator's disposition to the degree of engagement that learners convey. In 2018, for example, a group of researchers studied the effects of greeting middle-school students at the classroom door. This seemingly minor gesture yielded stunning benefits. Student engagement increased by 20 percent, while disruptions decreased by nearly 10 percent. A simple show of warmth effectively added an extra hour of learning to the school day.

Such warmth permeates every aspect of the *Neighborhood*. "Fred called each program a 'television visit,'" says Sharapan. "When you walk into a room as a visitor, what makes you feel safe? The environment has a lot to do with it—how things are set up, whether they convey comfort, and how people are welcoming you with their voice and body language."

Consider Rogers' unflinching eye gaze. He stares directly into the camera for lengths of time that might seem discomfiting to today's adults.* To

---

* It's uncomfortable in part because the media we consume have sped up considerably. According to Ben Berger, a political science professor at Swarthmore College, the length of an average shot in American movies fell from nearly 30 seconds in 1953 to just 2.5 seconds in 2007, with television tracking along a similar line. By contrast, Rogers allowed no more than two cuts per minute on the *Neighborhood*, making for substantially slower TV. "Who among us," laments Berger, "having seen *The Electric Company* as a child, could go back to watching *Mister Rogers*?"

children, however, his gaze mimics that of a supportive parent. His trolley, too, serves as a device, ferrying viewers from the living room to the Neighborhood of Make-Believe and back, helping young children learn to cope with comings and goings—which, as we've seen, helps them relax and feel comfortable enough to be curious.

Once familiarity—and with it, a sense of safety and warmth—has been established, Rogers adds curiosity's other ingredient: mystery.

This is where the fun begins. The *Neighborhood* made viewers feel safe, to be sure. But safety was a prerequisite, not the main event. What drew kids to the *Neighborhood* was something else entirely: the knowledge that such a program could, as children's author E. B. White once put it, "arouse our dreams, satisfy our hunger for beauty, take us on journeys, enable us to participate in events, present great drama and music, [and] explore the sea and the sky and the woods and the hills."

The *Neighborhood* delivered. The bulk of the program's seasons are organized around "theme weeks" that cover a lot of ground: There's a week for divorce, love, mad feelings, secrets, and curiosity, just to name a few. Over the course of a single week in February 2000 ("Mister Rogers Talks About Curiosity"), Rogers visits a vegetable garden, takes a ride in a bucket lift, puts on an astronaut costume, and builds a musical instrument. Each episode taps two proven catalysts for creating mystery: what Engel calls "the invisible and the exotic." The purple pandas that appear throughout the week are perfect examples—they're visitors from a far-away planet who can literally disappear. No wonder Rogers deploys them as curiosity's agents.

The *Neighborhood* also piqued curiosity through art. Though it's tempting to dismiss stories and songs and drawings as diversions or add-ons—things kids do after the "real" work of learning—Rogers took the opposite tack. In the *Neighborhood*, the arts aren't extracurricular; they're curiosity's very foundation. "The artistry of the program," McFarland once wrote, "stimulates the children's interest in the world around them and fosters their learning."

Here again, learning science has proven Rogers right. Arts experiences have been shown to feed curiosity by teaching kids to be careful, thorough observers of the world. Kids who study the arts may become stronger critical thinkers with better life outcomes: According to one nationally representative study, each year of arts study correlates with a 20 percent reduction in the likelihood an adolescent will be suspended from school. Young people who've studied the arts are almost 30 percent more likely to hold a four-year college degree by early adulthood and 26 percent *less* likely to get arrested. And while it's unclear whether the arts boost academic outcomes—at least as measured by test scores—evidence suggests that in the long run, exposing kids to the arts can significantly improve their lives.

The arts capture children's interest in ways that bare-bones information simply can't. Consider a time-honored tradition found in classrooms across the world: the textbook. Textbooks have been helping kids memorize definitions, rules, and facts for more than a thousand years, and for good reason. As vessels for vast amounts of specialized information, textbooks are unbeatable, especially in classrooms where resources are scant or teachers are untrained.

But in the era of mass production, successful textbooks have to appeal to the broadest possible market. That means publishers have almost universally dropped art and style in favor of more straightforward presentations of material, creating the blandness with which we're all too familiar. However, a number of studies have found that kids actually learn better when they encounter the opposite: stylized, even complicated texts that deploy seductive details and jump down rabbit holes to make their points. This makes intuitive sense in light of popular nonfiction titles. When adults want to learn about complicated, esoteric topics, they tend to seek out texts that satisfy their curiosity in an entertaining way. Most of us wouldn't rush to Amazon for the latest textbooks on advanced forestry, yet Peter Wohlleben's *The Hidden Life of Trees*—which reveals the science behind arboreal communication—topped nonfiction lists for weeks.

With art comes nuance, idiosyncrasy, and some degree of difficulty. This, too, is beneficial, learning scientists say. A number of studies suggest that the harder we work to acquire information, the more thoroughly we'll ultimately understand it. Presenting that information through art—as Rogers did—is one way to induce difficulty without diminishing curiosity or enjoyment. Researchers have found that even something as simple as printing material in hard-to-read fonts can help students retain knowledge. Inducing difficulty also leads learners to make mistakes—which, when paired with corrective feedback, has been shown to deepen learning as well.

But the arts do more than nurture curiosity about content. They also provoke questions about other people. The arts, after all, are a form of storytelling, and humans are naturally drawn to stories—especially those that concern other humans. Studies have shown that kids as young as four years old prefer stories about people or people-like characters to stories about animals or inanimate objects. They also crave stories about groups of people rather than individuals, perhaps because they're curious about the many ways people can interact with each other.

No wonder, then, that the Neighborhood of Make-Believe thrilled so many children. Populated by humans and human-like puppets with distinct personalities, Make-Believe offered several protagonists with which kids could identify: the stubborn ruler, King Friday XIII; the curious Prince Tuesday; the anxious Henrietta Pussycat; the mischievous Lady Elaine; and the timid Daniel Striped Tiger; among many others.

When children identify with fictional characters, they share in those characters' feelings, vicariously experiencing joys and struggles from a safe vantage point. "Precisely because [fiction] is make-believe and has no immediate real-world consequences," writes psychologist Peter Gray, children "can experience the challenges and difficulties more clearly, think about them more rationally, and develop more insight about them than we might from real-world experience."

It's through this process that kids learn to empathize with people who are different from themselves. We'll talk more about empathy later on, but for now, it's enough to know that stories help kids try to imagine themselves in one another's shoes. And the ability to do that is *at least* as important as what a child knows.

That's the premise of the *Saturday Light Brigade*, a nationally broadcast public radio program that airs documentaries, interviews, and live performances created by kids. Chanessa Schuler runs the program's *Crossing Fences* series, in which Black boys interview Black men in their communities to create short, professionally produced oral histories. While Schuler helps them workshop their potential interview questions, kids are free to pursue the lines of inquiry that interest them most. "Some of them want to ask questions, like 'If you were a superhero, which one would you be?'" she says, laughing. "But when they're asking about things they truly want to know about, they elicit some really amazing answers."

The men the kids interview for *Crossing Fences* are community leaders, and the opportunity to sit with them and ask honest questions helps kids relate to them on a more human level, says Schuler. "Say you interviewed your high school teacher," she says. "Now you're back in the classroom, and things have changed. You know your teacher as a *person*. So how is your interaction going to be different from here on out? You're going to see him in a whole new light. You can relate to him." And when kids relate to adults, they're far more likely to learn from them.

Though the *Saturday Light Brigade* teaches the art and craft of radio production, "We're not a media-training shop," says Larry Berger, the program's founder and president. "We're not trying to create journalists, necessarily. We're just trying to create complete people."

The key, he says, is giving kids permission to be curious—and providing the tools and a platform for expressing that curiosity. As kids get older, it can be hard for them to admit what they don't know; if they're even a little scared of being perceived as ignorant, they'll refrain from asking questions. "But if we train them—if we give them reporter's notebooks and explain that we want them to do a story so that *other people* can understand it—suddenly, we've given them permission to ask anything in the world," says Berger. "It's a kind of liberation."

Experts say there's deep value in creating spaces like this, where kids can ask honest, respectful questions of one another. The Reverend Paula Lawrence-Wehmiller, an educator who helped advise the *Neighborhood*, argues that much of the world's prejudice, for example, results from stifled curiosity—or, as she puts it, "our inability to expose our ignorance about each other." We don't like to be *fooled*, and so we sometimes hide our not-knowing by resorting to assumptions and stereotypes and biases. We might even try to cancel curiosity ourselves.

But the *Neighborhood* teaches the opposite. "It is in the context of a truthful relationship with children," writes Rev. Lawrence-Wehmiller, "that Fred Rogers encourages children to ask questions to be in the habit of unburdening themselves of hurtful ignorance. He creates a sanctuary for children, a place where they feel safe to be themselves, to express their wonderings and fears, or even to be allowed to be shy about them."

This is epitomized in what is today among the *Neighborhood*'s most famous scenes. On February 18, 1981, Rogers introduced viewers to Jeffrey Erlanger, a young boy from Madison who'd been diagnosed with a spinal tumor when he was just seven months old. Erlanger's resulting surgeries had left him without the use of his arms and legs, and when he appeared on the *Neighborhood* at age ten, he arrived at the front of Rogers' television house in an electric wheelchair.

As the scene unfolds, Rogers spends several minutes asking Erlanger the same questions that any child might want to ask: Would you show me how you make your wheelchair go? Did it take you a long time to learn how to use it? Can you tell my friends what it is that made you *need* this wheelchair? What do you do when you feel blue?

Erlanger answers each question earnestly and Rogers praises him for speaking so freely about his challenges. Then, in an unforgettable duet,

Erlanger joins in as Rogers sings "It's You I Like," a song that begins with this poignant verse:

> *It's you I like,*
> *It's not the things you wear,*
> *It's not the way you do your hair—*
> *But it's you I like.*
> *The way you are right now,*
> *The way down deep inside you—*
> *Not the things that hide you,*
> *Not your fancy chair—*
> *That's just beside you.*
> *It's you I like.*

This was Rogers turning curiosity into empathy before viewers' very eyes. By asking honest questions in a safe, supportive space—a sanctuary—Rogers showed children and adults alike how curiosity can help us understand and celebrate each other's differences. The scene also taught Erlanger something about himself. He became a community activist in Wisconsin and, until his death in 2007, committed himself to improving the lives of others.

At its best, the *Neighborhood* taught viewers that curiosity can resolve the uncertainties and mysteries that hold us back as human beings.

And that, readers, brings us back to where we began.

⋯⋯⋯⋰⋱⋯⋯⋯

It's dark now in the Neighborhood of Make-Believe, but King Friday XIII hasn't fallen asleep. Neither has Queen Sara, nor X the Owl, nor Henrietta Pussycat. Though curiosity has officially been canceled, the puppets here have been kept awake by a question: Will they ever see their beloved Prince Tuesday again?

He's been missing now for who knows how long, having fled his father's ban on knowledge-seeking. He's thought to be on AOP—Altogether Other Planet—but the team dispatched to find him has yet to send word. And really, could anyone blame the young prince for leaving? Who would want to stay in a place like this—a place without questions, without wonder, without learning? Certainly not someone as curious and caring as Prince Tuesday.

From his castle balcony, the king looks up at the night sky, purpled by the overhead lights of WQED's Studio A. Perhaps he'd been wrong to cancel his subjects' curiosity. Curiosity, after all, is part of who they are as puppets. It's how their creator made them. And besides, there are worse things in life than being *fooled*—worse things like missing your son.

Suddenly, there's a flash in the sky, and the rescue team returns from AOP. With them is Prince Tuesday, safe and unharmed. For a moment, the king's anger comes surging back: "Do you see what can happen with curiosity?" he thunders at this son.

But the young prince is ecstatic. He's seen wonderful, distant planets—things he never would have seen had he not set out on his own. And while it's true that he'd gotten a little lost, he says, he'd never meant to worry anybody. He'd just wanted to know what's out there.

King Friday, vain and impulsive though he is, stares at his son in the starlight. He has a choice now: He can double down on canceling curiosity, or he can tell Prince Tuesday that it's all right to wonder—that there are, indeed, all kinds of wonderful, marvelous, marvelously wonderful things for children like him to learn.

And though many things are mysteries in this particular Neighborhood, in this case, the right decision is clear. In the wondrous world of Make-Believe, King Friday decides, curiosity will carry the day.

WHAT MIGHT YOU DO?

- When kids are in a state of wonder, they're more likely to retain what they see, hear, and experience. Pay attention to what elicits children's curiosity—when their interest is piqued, their brains are primed for learning. When kids ask why the wind blows or why leaves change color in the fall, it's sometimes helpful to ask open-ended questions in return, especially if you're not entirely sure of the answer yourself. The process of discovery can be just as important as finding the factually correct answer. Adults and children can launch lines of inquiry together simply by wondering aloud—asking *why* and *what if*. *"What if we put grapes in our pancakes rather than blueberries?"* Or, *"Why do we need to put more air into the soccer ball?"* Or, *"What's inside of this toy?"*

- "Once, I saw a teacher who had in her classroom something called an 'Ask It Basket,'" says Hedda Sharapan. "When the children would ask a question, she would write it down and say, 'That's a great one to put into the Ask It Basket.' Whether or not you could answer it as the adult—either in that moment or later on—that simple action told children that their questions matter."

- Kids can "catch" curiosity, so it's important for them to see adults indulging interests of their own. What makes *you* curious? What do you love to do, and why? If you're not sure, this is a great excuse to reexamine old hobbies—to pull out those abandoned paintbrushes or dust off that old guitar. It's also helpful to verbalize your questions and thoughts: *"I wonder what would happen if I mix these colors together."* Or, *"How does this knob change an instrument's sound?"*

- It can be difficult for kids (and adults) to let go of the expectation that everything they encounter is part of a project that needs to be finished or done in a certain way. Be patient and encourage kids to examine things on their own terms. It can take time and even a bit of practice to let their curiosity flourish. *Let them rebuild that LEGO creation without the instructions—or ask them to add something unexpected.*

TWO

Mud Pies and Block Buildings

Creativity

The piano plays a familiar tune, the famous front door swings open, and there's Mister Rogers, smiling, clad in blue pants and a blue dress shirt and soon, a blue cardigan sweater. He sits down on a blue cushion and ties his blue canvas shoes. Behind him, the blue wall of his TV living room meets his blue TV window. It's a beautiful TV day, and Rogers wants to tell you something.

"I just never knew there were so many different kinds of spoons!"

Yes, spoons. He holds up a handful and debuts them one by one, giving the cameras a close-up of each. Look: Here's a teaspoon. Here's one that *looks* like a teaspoon, but actually, it's for grapefruits. Here's a sugar spoon, a serving spoon, a spoon for ladling gravy, and a spoon that's very old. So many different spoons, with different functions and stories. Do you ever use spoons to dig? And did you know that sometimes, moms and dads have very fancy spoons? And do you ever wonder where spoons come from?

Before you can answer—indeed, before you can question the point of all of this—Rogers makes his way to Picture Picture, the picture-frame-turned-television that hangs on his wall, and starts a documentary. It's a film about—you guessed it—how people make spoons.

"Look how *slowly* he works," says Rogers. Set to a gentle, jazzy soundtrack, the film shows an artist drawing pictures and making models and bringing new spoons into being. "Both men *and* women design spoons," Rogers reminds us. We watch machines churn out prototypes, workers make revisions and refinements, and inspectors in pursuit of perfection. "Spoons," says Rogers. "Spoons! So many spoons! That's very interesting, isn't it?"

It sure is. The documentary ends, but Rogers is just getting started. He's got a friend, you see, with a special spoon talent—one you're really going to like. She's coming by a little later, so we'll have to wait awhile first. And while we wait, we'll let our minds wander, and we'll start to daydream. We'll start to make-believe.

"Let's think of something that would have spoons in the story," says Rogers. "Spoons, and the king, and Lady Aberlin, and—well, let's just make it up together."

.......⋮..............

Spoons, the king, and Lady Aberlin. *Let's make it up together.* It sounds like the start of an improv skit: Fuse these nouns by constructing a story. Use your imagination.

Be creative.

For most of Rogers' audience, such a directive would pose no trouble—any friend of a five-year-old knows how quickly kids can spin a story. In fact, among young children, creativity is almost universal. In 1968, Dr. George Land tested the creative potential of more than a thousand five-year-olds using a test he'd developed for NASA. A full 98 percent scored so high that they qualified as creative geniuses.

The implication is that human beings are born creative. Though genes and heredity have been found to play a part, nearly all of us are gifted with at least some ability to imagine new solutions to problems—whether we're generating lists of novel ideas (an ability called *divergent* thinking) or drawing from diverse, interdisciplinary fields (*convergent* thinking). "Every child is born with a unique endowment, which gives him an opportunity to make something entirely different from everybody else in the world," Rogers once said. "You see it when you watch children at their own play: There are no two mud pies the same. Block buildings have infinite variety."

The advantages of such an endowment can't be overstated. Researchers have found that the more creative an animal species is, the more likely it is to survive when introduced to new situations, new environments, and new threats. In the Tōhoku region of northern Japan, for example, a species of crow drops walnuts near slow-moving cars. The cars run over the walnuts, cracking them open, and the crows swoop in to eat. Their creativity has turned the region's abundant walnut groves into a steady source of food.

No wonder we revere it so much. Barack Obama once called creativity the country's "single greatest asset." Nearly every celebrity we adore is a creative professional, and in 2019, LinkedIn—the world's largest job network—declared creativity the most in-demand skill on the planet.

So why is it that so many adults don't *feel* particularly creative? Why is it that unless we're novelists or actors or painters, we tend to regard creativity as a mystery—something reserved for the Toni Morrisons and Bob Dylans and Gabriel García Márquezes of the world? What happened to all those tiny geniuses from George Land's study?

Fortunately, Land stuck around to find out. Five years after his first experiment, he retested his original subjects, who were now ten years old. This time, the percentage of kids who scored in the "highly creative" range fell from 98 percent to 30 percent. When they turned fifteen, Land tested them again, and the share of geniuses fell even further—to 12 percent. By the time Land tested the cohort as adults, just 2 percent had retained their creativity. By Land's measure, the trait ubiquitous among five-year-olds had, in American adults, become less common than red hair.

"What we have concluded," wrote Land and his colleagues, "is that non-creative behavior is learned."

They weren't the first to suggest this. In 1906, the psychologist Théodule-Armand Ribot held forth on creativity's demise as only a Frenchman can: "The majority of people gradually get lost in the prose of everyday life, bury the dreams of their youth, consider love an illusion, and so forth," he wrote. "This, however, is only regression, not annihilation, because the creative imagination does not disappear completely in anyone. It merely becomes incidental."

Creativity, in other words, doesn't simply vanish. It's just that somewhere along the way, we learn to stop indulging it.

This has been well documented. Mention the "fourth-grade slump" to researchers and educators, and they'll solemnly nod. There are lots of exceptions, of course, but on average, creativity wanes as kids approach middle school. They stop drawing. They stop making up stories. They set down their instruments and let them gather dust. By adulthood, their music has largely fallen quiet.

This is partly due to natural changes in the brain. Young kids are creative not because they have better imaginations than their parents—on the contrary, they have fewer experiences from which they can draw—but because they don't self-censor. Ask a five-year-old to tell you a tale involving spoons and a fictional puppet-king, and she won't worry about whether it's good enough or funny enough or even coherent. She'll just do it.

But as kids enter adolescence, a part of the brain called the *prefrontal cortex* starts to rewire itself. This is where judgment and inhibitions live, and it's where creativity can take a nosedive. "The child begins to have a critical attitude toward his own drawing," explained Lev Vygotsky, the legendary Soviet psychologist, in 1930. Over time, "he comes to the conclusion that he cannot draw, and for this reason, he stops. We also see this curtailment of childish fantasy in the fact that the child loses interest in the naïve games of earlier childhood and in fairy tales and fantastic stories."

This has its advantages. A childlike lack of restraint would surely wreak havoc on our personal and professional lives, both of which require a certain level of tact. When your boss asks for a progress report, it's probably best to leave out spoons and puppets and make-believe. (Unless your boss is Mister Rogers.) We develop self-consciousness because our social standing, and arguably our survival, requires a baseline understanding of how others perceive us.

But the flip side is that we take our censors too seriously. Because we're so often worried about what other people think, we go out of our way to avoid the humiliation and failure that creative endeavors risk. There's a reason some comedy clubs offer discounts on front-row seats: It's the only way they can induce people to sit there and thus risk having to become a part of the show. The more self-conscious we become, the more our creative confidence dwindles.

Rogers knew this well. "What happens if children hear that their mud pies are no good and their block buildings have no importance? That their paintings and dances and made-up games and songs are of very little value?" he once asked. "Children, like laboratory rats, can learn quickly not to experiment with wrong answers."

Unfortunately, they may be learning this earlier and earlier, scientists say. In the late 1950s, a scholar named E. Paul Torrance developed a series of tasks designed to measure creativity. Though far from perfect, the so-called Torrance test became a standard way to gauge divergent thinking— that is, the ability to produce novel, useful solutions to problems. (One task, for example, asks kids how they'd improve a toy truck.)

In 1958, Torrance tested four hundred kids. Scholars tracked the cohort for the next fifty years, "recording every patent earned, every business founded, every research paper published, and every grant awarded," according to a 2010 story in *Newsweek*. "What's shocking is how incredibly well Torrance's creativity index predicted those kids' creative accomplishments as adults. Those who came up with more good ideas on Torrance's tasks grew up to be entrepreneurs, inventors, college presidents, authors, doctors, diplomats, and software developers." Subsequent cohorts scored better and better on the Torrance test, suggesting that overall, kids were growing more creative over time.

Until suddenly, they weren't.

When Kyung Hee Kim, a researcher at the College of William and Mary, analyzed the Torrance scores of more than 270,000 American children, she found that creative thinking has steadily declined since 1990, particularly among young children—the same group once found to be almost universally creative. The trend was so striking that Kim gave it a name: the creativity crisis.

Though her research stops short of pinpointing a cause, Kim has her suspicions: a tendency to jam-pack children's schedules with homework and structured activities; an overreliance on standardized testing; cuts to electives and arts classes; and the several hours per day that kids of all ages spend in front of their screens. Whatever the culprit, the problem remains the same: The fewer improvements kids make to toy trucks today, the fewer breakthroughs we can count on tomorrow.

And oh, do we need breakthroughs. Consider the problems today's kids face—climate change, systemic racism, widening inequality, hunger, water shortages, disinformation campaigns, health care costs, and global instability, just to name a few. Each of these problems is multifaceted beyond the grasp of any one person or field. Solving them will require collaboration, communication, and all the other tools that Rogers taught. Above all, it will require creativity—the ability to generate new ideas and synthesize existing ones.

In their book, *Becoming Brilliant: What Science Tells Us About Raising Successful Children*, psychologists Roberta Michnick Golinkoff and Kathy

Hirsh-Pasek put it bluntly. "How many different uses can you think of for a paper cup?" they ask. "Imagine your car is stuck on the ice. Can you think to put a board under the back wheels to give it traction? And these are just the day-to-day problems we face. How will society meet the challenges of climate change and poverty without creativity?"

That's not all. Yes, creative kids become successful adults, and yes, there are countless economic and moral reasons to care about creativity. But even more importantly, creative pursuits scratch an existential itch, helping us voice the joys and hopes and disappointments that define our time on Earth. Novelist Kurt Vonnegut, a sort of philosophical twin to Rogers, said it best. Creativity and the arts, he wrote,

> are not a way to make a living. They are a very human way of making life more bearable. Practicing an art, no matter how well or badly, is a way to make your soul grow, for heaven's sake. Sing in the shower. Dance to the radio. Tell stories. Write a poem to a friend, even a lousy poem. Do it as well as you possibly can. You will get an enormous reward. You will have created something.

While creative thinking may be in decline, it doesn't have to be. Like curiosity, children's creativity can be nurtured and sustained. It can be kept front and center in their lives. It just takes some help from creative adults, and there are still plenty of places where kids are able to find them.

Amid the bookstacks and computer tables in Pittsburgh's Carnegie Library, an oblate, hive-like structure about the size of a school bus rises from the floor. At first glance, this room within a room looks like a collection of things confiscated—a librarian's nightmare of electric guitars, amplifiers, microphones, TVs, and a whirring 3D printer that's constructing, at this moment, a set of monster claws to be worn as part of a costume. Stepping into the structure—a monument to noise, electronics, and imagination—feels like leaving the library around it altogether.

This is The Labs, a dedicated space for teenage creativity. The goal, says teen librarian Simon Rafferty, is to show kids that the library isn't what they think—"that it's actually a fun, cool place to be."*

Judging by the dozens of kids who stream through the doors each afternoon after school, *fun* and *cool* might be understating things. In and around The Labs are top-of-the-line game consoles, a drum set, DSLR cameras, computers equipped with Photoshop and iMovie, and even a fully enclosed, self-contained recording studio—all for use by any kid, at any time, at zero cost. Regardless of a teen's interests or grades or family income—and in this part of Pittsburgh, family incomes are modest at most—The Labs exists to meet his or her creative needs.

When teens come to The Labs, there's no set schedule, no homework, no pressure. Some kids come just for the recording studio, and that's fine. Others want to dabble in a little bit of everything—playing the instruments, using the sewing machines, and trying their hand at photography. "Because we're different from, say, a school, where kids are a captive audience, kids have to *want* to come to our space and *want* to use our equipment and *want* to be creative," says Rafferty. "And so we have to give them lots of choice and lots of freedom, because that's what gets kids—especially older kids—in the door. Our job is to give them the space and equipment they need to pursue their interests, whatever those happen to be."

Kristin Morgan is the lead librarian for digital learning. Her office, just upstairs from The Labs, looks a bit like a Hollywood warehouse: long shelves filled with robot parts, circuit boards, audiovisual equipment, and Otamatones—small, tadpole-shaped synthesizers from Japan. One could conceivably build a set, film a movie, record its soundtrack, and print promotional posters using just what's in this room. In fact, half of Morgan's job is ensuring that teens of every background can access the tools they need to turn their ideas into reality. The other half is making sure that such access is meaningful—and that, says Morgan, starts with building relationships.

---

* "Teen librarian" is Rafferty's title—he's not a teenage employee of the library.

By getting to know the kids who come to The Labs each day, the library's staff learns their interests and ideas, as well as the best ways to develop them. "Adults need to build trust by working with kids day in and day out," says Morgan. "When adults do that, they can become a supportive critic—someone who can gently push kids forward. We want them to exceed anyone's expectations and achieve amazing things, right? Well, that requires someone who's willing and able to guide kids and to be an advocate for them and their work."

To that end, she and Rafferty—along with a host of teaching artists—take both low- and high-touch approaches toward working with teens. Kids are welcome to experiment with most of the library's equipment on their own. If they want to learn a specific skill, The Labs also offers drop-in workshops: informal, loosely structured classes through which kids can earn a "badge"—a credential certifying their proficiency in, say, audio recording or beat making. (Badges give kids even more equipment privileges.) And for kids who want to level up even further, The Labs offers weeklong "summer intensives" focused on everything from street art to filmmaking to photography.

None of this, says Morgan, would work without relationships. "It's one thing to open your doors and say to kids, 'Hey, we have all these tools that can help you be creative,'" she says. "It's another to get to know them on a level that lets you say, 'We're hosting this class next week or next month, and here's why I think you'd be a good fit for it and why I want you to be a part of it.' Kids really crave that—when you honor their efforts, you validate their creativity. And you show them that they belong."

Rafferty remembers a sixth-grader who came to The Labs and discovered graphic design for the first time. "He started playing around with the library's equipment, and he got *really* into it," he says. "He learned every tool, every method, every application he could. When he got to high school, he even arranged his classes so he could dig deeper into it. And then it became a career for him."

By providing equipment, mentorship, and a path toward further learning, "[The Labs] helped that kid discover himself in a small way," Rafferty says.

He pauses for a moment and reconsiders. "Maybe in a big way."

Creativity Starts with a Spoon

Creativity is one part *doing*: dabbling, seeking help, and deepening one's understanding of an art or a science. But what about those ideas we get when we're not even trying—when we're walking the dog, maybe, or zoned out on the highway? Isn't there something to be said for the muses—for inspiration?

Yes and no. Think of it this way: Unless you're a physicist on par with Albert Einstein, a grand theory of quantum mechanics isn't suddenly going to strike you. Likewise, unless you're a trained composer, that tune you've found yourself humming will likely fall short of Beethoven's Fifth. And while it's true that outsiders can sometimes disrupt a field—that biologists solve physics problems and cellists write great books—there's almost always some overlap. Biologists and physicists are both trained to do science; musicians and authors are both trained to tell stories.

Creativity is almost wholly dependent on knowledge and experience—there's simply no getting around it. Hence the platitudes you've heard all your life: *Genius is 1 percent inspiration and 99 percent perspiration. Chance favors the prepared mind.* And so on.

That's why, when Rogers kicks off a five-part series on creativity and make-believe, he does it with something simple—something every child can access.

"What is it that you like to eat your food with?" he asks, lifting an imaginary spoon to his mouth. Rather than leading with something whimsical, something fantastic, or something that breaks all the rules, Rogers starts with—of all things—a kitchen utensil.

Right away, he sets the stage for a universal truth: To be creative, it helps to grasp the basics. No one paints a masterpiece without first studying color. No one—not even Mozart—writes a concerto without first know-ing some chords. And no one makes a beautiful spoon without knowing what a spoon *is* and how it might be used.

The grunt work of building a knowledge base on which creative ideas can stand is almost always hidden from view and thus almost always for-gotten. When we watch a movie, we only see the final cut. We're spared the dozen takes of a single scene, the cinematographer learning to hold a camera, the screenwriter spending weeks on just the right punch line. The best creative works belie the labor that goes into them, making it easy to think they simply arrived in the world fully formed and without effort.

Rogers stops this myth in its tracks. "Fred wanted children to know that things happen in a process," says Hedda Sharapan. "It takes this step and that step and that step. He wanted children to understand that a lot of things have to happen to create something. And he wanted to applaud the workers—to show his young viewers that the people who make things are important people in our world."

Within the first few minutes of make-believe week, for example, he takes us behind the scenes of a spoon factory, where he lays bare the cre-ative process in its slow, painstaking entirety: A spoon maker first draws a picture of his intended product. Then he makes a model, slowly chipping away at a chunk of metal until it starts to resemble the idea in his head. Then he churns out prototypes, which are cleaned and polished and tin-kered with until they're made exactly right. The segment's final shot—a slow pan over dozens of shiny spoons—reveals a product born of deliber-ate effort rather than divine inspiration.

Anyone, Rogers explains, can make a beautiful spoon. Anyone can be creative. It just takes some work.

It's a message he revisits again and again, using everything from spoons to paintings to clocks to make his point. When there's an opera in the *Neighborhood*, it never happens in a void—kids always see the plan-ning and preparation and rehearsals required to stage it. Likewise, "at the end of a sequence about a factory or farm," writes William Guy, a

Pittsburgh-based author, "Rogers points out that there is nothing magical about what it produces. The product, he notes, resulted from an idea that arose in a human mind, an idea that human beings carried out— something his viewers might do in the future."

In other words, Rogers shows kids that creative dreams are attainable. He shows them that their mud pies and block buildings really *do* have value, not just for their own sake but for the gourmet meals and soaring skyscrapers they suggest. And he shows them the hidden perspiration it takes to bring one's ideas into the world.

When Wasting Time Can Be Worth It

As soon as the spoon segment ends, Rogers gets a phone call. His friend was scheduled to stop by, he says, but she's gotten held up—so now, we'll have to wait. We'll have to sit here for a while with nothing much to do.

We'll have to get a little bored.

It's a prospect that strikes terror in us all. Boredom is a beast we'll do most anything to slay, and over the years, we've gotten pretty good at it. It's possible, in today's world of abundant tech and unlimited content, to go days or weeks or longer without ever feeling understimulated. The smartphone alone has turned every mundane task into something else entirely. On an elevator? Check your email! Waiting in line? Time for Twitter! Walking the dog? Fire up that dog-walking playlist and check your daily step count.

We've created an always-on, maximize-every-moment world, and now we're raising our kids in it. It's gotten so intense, writes David Epstein, author of *Range: Why Generalists Triumph in a Specialized World*, that in online forums, anxious parents "agonize over what instrument to pick for a child, because she is too young to pick for herself and will fall irredeemably behind if she waits."

No wonder just one in five parents think it's good for kids to get bored once in a while. How can we possibly justify boredom when there are exams to ace, pianos to play, and paychecks to earn?

"It's important to know when we need to stop, reflect, and receive," Rogers once wrote. "In our competitive world, that might be called a waste of time." However, "I've learned that those times can be the preamble to periods of enormous growth. Recently, I declared a day to be alone with myself. I took a long drive and played a tape. When I got to the mountains, I read and prayed and listened and slept. In fact, I can't remember having a calmer sleep in a long, long time. The next day I went back to work and did more than I usually get done in three days."

Wasting time, in other words, isn't *always* a waste of time. On the contrary, sometimes it's the most productive thing we can do.

Let's imagine, for no particular reason, that you're writing a book about Fred Rogers and the tools for learning. You're in the midst of the creativity chapter, and things are going well—you've got your research in front of you, you've written your outline, and you have a pretty good idea of what you want to say and how you want to say it.

But then, in the middle of a paragraph, it happens: You hit the wall. You get stuck.

You know you need an example here—one that illustrates your point and tees up the next section—but nothing comes. You stare at the cursor and force your hands to the keyboard. You type a few words and delete them.

An hour goes by. Two. You're on a deadline, damn it; you don't have time for this. Why is writing so easy for everyone else, yet so difficult for *you*? You pound your forehead and pour a cup of coffee. You consider crying but don't. Finally, resigned to failure, you give up and go for a walk.

It's only after several miles—after you've walked far enough to forget about your problem and to stop *thinking* so much—that inspiration finally hits. Suddenly, it seems so simple; you can't believe you didn't think of it before. You rush home to type your clever meta-example, overwhelmed with relief and silently thanking your brain.

Congratulations! You've just discovered your *default mode*, the network of interconnected brain structures where the muses live. The default mode network is where we go when we're really, truly bored—so bored that we jump the rails of conscious thought and let our minds wander where they will. It's where, after we've put in our 99 percent perspiration, we can stop racking our brains and listen instead for inspiration.

"Now neuroscientists know that the default mode is when you do your most original thinking," says Manoush Zomorodi, author of *Bored and Brilliant: How Spacing Out Can Unlock Your Most Productive and Creative Self.* It's where "you do your problem-solving. It's where you have imagination, where you have empathy." If we've done enough work, our default mode networks are there for us, ready to gift us creative ideas—as long as we're willing to shut up and listen. The irony, of course, is that we do everything we can to drown ourselves out.

It's not a new problem. A century ago, sociologists were already warning city dwellers about the dangers of constant stimulation, recommending "extraordinary, radical boredom" for would-be creatives. Today, as adults and kids alike fill downtime with structured activities, binge-worthy TV shows, and the infinite expanse of the internet, they visit their default mode networks less and less frequently. No wonder more than 70 percent of people have their best ideas in the shower—it's one of the few remaining places where we leave our brains alone.

Water and creativity, by the way, go way back, perhaps because water quiets our minds. Rogers himself made a point of swimming every morning, even when he was traveling. Swimming, says Maxwell King, "was a period of meditation for him. It was a period in which he could get away from organized thinking and just let his creativity flow. In the summers, when he'd go up to Nantucket, he'd swim across Madaket Harbor and then walk back to his house. He used to talk about how much he loved to do that, because swimming and walking gave him a chance to be contemplative. He'd have a lot of his ideas that way."

Rogers wasn't alone. Albert Einstein was known to stare at the sea for hours. Maya Angelou considered a midday shower essential to her work. And then there's the Japanese inventor Yoshiro Nakamatsu, a man famous for taking this just a little too far. Nakamatsu submerges himself in a pool to starve his brain of oxygen, remaining underwater until he's just seconds from drowning—at which point, he jots his ideas on a waterproof notepad. And though it's true that Nakamatsu invented the floppy disk and it's true that he holds three thousand other patents, his process isn't exactly foolproof. Nakamatsu's more-questionable claims to fame include spring-loaded shoes, a weighted wig that can be swung in self-defense, and LoveJet 69, an elixir designed to raise the Japanese birth rate.

The upshot is that boredom—or, perhaps more accurately, a period of mental quiet—contributes to creativity in a big way. "When a child has nothing to do and must fill the time, creativity can emerge," write Golinkoff and Hirsh-Pasek in *Becoming Brilliant*. "It can be right there in a file drawer or a kitchen cupboard or in those shiny new markers lying on the table." This, of course, is what Rogers was telling us each time he sang "Let's Think of Something to Do"—a *Neighborhood* staple that appears, for the first time, when Rogers' friend gets delayed.

> *Let's think of something to do while we're waiting*
> *While we're waiting for something new to do.*
> *Let's try to think up a song while we're waiting*
> *That's liberating and will be true to you.*
> *Let's think of something to do while we're waiting*
> *While we're waiting 'til something's through.*
> *You know it's really all right*
> *In fact, it's downright quite bright*
> *To think of something to do*
> *That's specific for you.*
> *Let's think of something to do while we're waiting.*

In addition to making kids feel better about boredom, the song also hints at something else. Its insistence on doing something *liberating* and *true to* and *specific for you* reflects what learning scientists have been saying all along: "When we attempt to foster children's creativity," Vygotsky wrote, "we need to observe the principle of freedom. . . . This means that the creative activities of children cannot be compulsory or forced and must arise only out of their own interests."

Creativity, it turns out, can't be imposed.

But in the right environment—in spaces where kids feel safe, relaxed, and free to follow their interests—creativity *can* be encouraged. And no one created those environments quite like Rogers.

"Everywhere You Look Here, There's Something Beautiful Looking Back"

Rogers designed every aspect of the *Neighborhood* to buoy the creative impulse. Take, for example, his TV wardrobe: a compendium of sweaters and shoes intended to put viewers at ease. Rogers emitted an aura of safety and relaxation that's essential to creativity—when kids feel rushed or intimidated or judged, experts say, or when they don't trust their surroundings, it can be difficult for them to think through their own stress.

Accordingly, Rogers slowed the *Neighborhood* to a deliberate, almost crawling pace. Each episode begins with a rush of piano notes, which decrescendo over the next few measures until the theme song sounds like a lullaby. As he enters the set, Rogers ditches the suit-and-tie uniform of the fast-paced working world. The traffic light in his living room signals yellow, telling us it's time to slow down. And the unhurried scenes that follow are almost sedating in their warmth and radical calm: In one episode, there's a minute-long close-up of an egg timer; in another, there are several shots of Rogers watching paint dry.

"I remember when we did a segment at an art museum and Fred spent almost the whole time looking at *one* painting," says Bill Isler, the longtime president of Rogers' production company, Family Communications (which later became Fred Rogers Productions). "The museum staff wanted him to feature some more. But he said, 'I want children to be able to slow down and focus so they can see all the little details in the thing this person has created.'"

Even the *Neighborhood*'s color scheme seemed optimized for mental peace. The color blue, for example, was linked by one study to an increase in creative output, possibly because we associate it with the sea and the sky and thus find it calming. And where is Rogers as he schools us on creativity? In his very blue living room, wearing a blue sweater, a blue tie, and blue shoes.*

He also made a point of always cleaning up, says Hedda Sharapan. "When he was working with crayons or paper or anything else, the last part of the sequence was always about putting things back together or putting them back in the cupboard. That helps children know that cleaning up is part of the creative process, too. You come back to an environment that's clean and inviting."

Indeed, environment matters. In 2002, Janetta McCoy of Washington State University tested the creative performance of high school students in two settings: one rich in wood and soaked in sunlight, the other comprised of sterile, manufactured materials like plastic and drywall. Though the task was the same in both environments, kids in the former setting churned out more imaginative work, suggesting that natural-seeming spaces can aid creative thought.

Of course, "rich in wood and soaked in sunlight" sounds an awful lot like Rogers' living room—his home base in a *Neighborhood* full of beautiful, bright, well-made things. It could also describe the Manchester Craftsmen's Guild, one of the most remarkable community arts centers on the planet.

---

* This might have been a coincidence—Rogers himself was partially color-blind and couldn't even see the color blue. Moreover, the study of blue's effects took place several years after his death, and the science is far from settled. Still, it seems Rogers might have been aware of the color's calming potential: X the Owl, the Neighborhood of Make-Believe's famously anxious strigiform, calls to mind the color blue whenever he needs to relax.

Located in Pittsburgh's Northside neighborhood, the guild's lobby alone contains colorful story cloths from the city's Hmong community, exquisite Japanese benches built by a famous furniture maker, more orchids and artworks than one could count, and even a kitchen that serves gourmet food (and *only* gourmet food, its chefs will tell you). The building itself—all glass, plants, and parallel lines—recalls the work of Frank Lloyd Wright, whose homes looked so in tune with nature that they seemed to sprout from the forest floor.

It looks, you might say, like an artist's retreat: a place where the leisure class might want to unwind for a few days among world-class art in a world-class building with world-class food. And that's exactly the vibe that its founder, Bill Strickland, was going for—with one exception. He built the guild not for the ultrarich but for the kids in Pittsburgh's underserved neighborhoods.

"Most of the young people we see come from environments where fear is the predominant emotion: fear of failure, of violence, of economic hardship," he says. "They're surrounded by negativity. In my view, that's the worst part of being poor: what it does to your spirit."

It's a feeling he knows firsthand. By his own account, Strickland's dreams had been dampened by the same structures and forces that surround his students today. He lived in the same neighborhood, went to the same under-resourced schools, and bumped up against the same societal barriers. As an adolescent, he says, he was aimless, apathetic, and not particularly hopeful about any sort of future.

Until one day, a high school pottery teacher invited him to shape some clay—an experience that completely changed his sense of self. "All of a sudden, I felt like I had a purpose," Strickland recalls. "I started going to that room every day, first thing in the morning. I was a Black kid who didn't know anything about pottery, but I felt, for the first time, like I had a creative side. That I could build something worthwhile."

Pottery was just the beginning. In that classroom, Strickland discovered an entire creative world. His teacher brought albums by Herbie Hancock and other giants of jazz. He brought books that kids actually wanted to read. He brought fine art. And he took students to see Fallingwater, Frank Lloyd Wright's masterpiece.

"I was blown away by that place," Strickland recalls. "Here was a house that was tranquil and peaceful and aesthetically tied to nature. It was exactly the kind of environment a kid like me needed yet never got to see. So I said, 'Someday, I'm going to build a school just like that.'"

In 1968—the same year *Mister Rogers* debuted—Strickland found a dilapidated row house in Pittsburgh's Manchester neighborhood. Living out of a sleeping bag, he installed a kiln and cleaned the place out. He had few resources and little experience, he recounts in his memoir, but he knew what young people needed: "A safe, sane, quiet environment where they could escape the madness that reigned in the streets, work on some clay, find a way to shape something personal and beautiful, and spend some time in a bright, clean, nurturing place where it did not seem pointless to dream."

The Manchester Craftsmen's Guild was born. It wasn't Fallingwater, but it would do.

As kids came in from the street, Strickland saw in them the same changes he'd seen in himself: They started showing up for school more regularly. Their grades improved. In clay, they connected with math; in glaze, they connected with chemistry. In Strickland's bright, clean, creative environment, they found the tools to shape their dreams.

Eventually, the guild attracted attention—and funding. Throughout the 1980s, Strickland raised several million dollars to build the school he'd always wanted. He hired one of Frank Lloyd Wright's students to do the job, and the result was one of the most successful community arts centers ever built. Today, the guild sees hundreds of kids each year and operates campuses around the world. A full 98 percent of its students graduate from high school on time, and 85 percent go on to college or some other sort of secondary education. Moreover, in fifty years of operation, the guild has never had an incident involving violence or drugs, and they've never called the police. It's the same story elsewhere—at the guild's location in Israel, for example, Jews and Palestinians walk side by side to their art classes every day. "Someone once asked me where the metal detectors were," says Strickland. "I said, 'Here, we call them students.'"

All of this comes down to the guild's environment, he says. "We literally create a space that says, 'We're into creativity 24-7, and you *deserve* to be here. And if you stick around long enough, you're going to start to believe that—through absorption if nothing else.'"

Strickland walks through his office, lined with nearly thirty honorary degrees and pictures of presidents and first ladies shaking his hand. He wanders the guild's hallways, which double as sunlit art galleries. "Everywhere you look here, there's something beautiful looking back," he explains. "That is *deliberate*. Kids look at orchids. They feel sunlight. They eat gourmet food and take pottery lessons from the best teachers in the world. Environments like this one erase fear. They cure cancer of the human spirit. And the kids inside them blossom."

While Strickland learned creativity's life-changing power from his ceramics teacher, his lessons on building a positive, calm, creative environment came from a different role model altogether.

"He was kind," Strickland recalls. "He was *always* kind. And he demonstrated by his life that no matter how you look or where you came from, you were a member of the *Neighborhood*. That's the reason I built this place: I wanted to give kids that same feeling. I wanted to be Fred Rogers."

Rogers himself felt the same about Strickland, featuring the guild on the *Neighborhood* more than once. In one episode from the early 1990s, Rogers brings viewers to the guild's ceramics studio, where he and Strickland conduct a master class on creativity. They start with raw clay and slowly learn to shape it. They discuss the importance of practice and patience. And they show viewers what the final product can look like, noting that children, too, can make beautiful things. At the end of the segment, Rogers muses about Strickland's talents. "My friend Bill is a good teacher," he says. "He uses clay *so well* because he's been working at it for *so long*."

But creativity, Rogers adds, is more than just work. The drive to create in the first place comes from a much deeper impulse. "[Strickland] didn't do fancy things with clay when he was a little boy," Rogers explains. "He just loved to play with it and make things—anything that he could. That's how it all began with him: playing with mud and with clay. And *now* look at the things that he can make!"

Better to Make a Cape Than to Buy a Costume

Freddy Rogers, too, was a boy who loved to play.

Born March 20, 1928, in Latrobe, Rogers grew up wealthy during the height of the Great Depression. But the wealth came at a cost. His father's silica brick business earned a fortune lining the insides of factories, and Rogers—like lots of kids in western Pennsylvania—had more than his share of health problems. The soot-induced asthma that plagued the region often kept him indoors, especially during the warmer months. He sometimes spent whole summers in his room with nothing but puppets and a piano for company.

So Rogers did what any kid would do: He played. He made up songs. He pretended. He imagined other worlds and populated them with his puppet-friends. Through play, Rogers expressed and expanded his existence, discovering the creative talents and passions that would one day turn a lonely little boy into the world's most beloved neighbor.

Though his family's wealth made him an outlier, Rogers' path from playful kid to creative adult is surprisingly well-trodden. Bill Strickland walked it, despite growing up in poverty. So have kids of every background and circumstance who've grown up to be artists, scientists, and entrepreneurs. And often, researchers think, their common thread is play.

Open-ended, imaginative play is crucial to creativity—or, as psychologists Dorothy and Jerome Singer call it, a willingness to explore the possible. In their book *The House of Make-Believe*, the Singers identify the essential ingredients of that willingness: (1) an adult who inspires, encourages, and joins in children's play; (2) a dedicated, "sacred space" for play; (3) unstructured free time; and (4) simple objects that enrich the imagination.

Rogers had these ingredients in droves. "Lots of people encouraged his creativity," says Maxwell King. "Certainly, his grandfather did. And his mother did, too. The fact that he was given a lot of encouragement to develop his capacities as a musician really helped him understand the things that mattered to him."

Over the past few decades, however, play has grown increasingly absent from children's lives. Busy lifestyles and an emphasis on academics have muscled playtime out of family and school routines. When kids *do* have time to play, they increasingly do so on electronic devices—which, though not inherently negative, aren't always as open-ended as puppets or a hunk of clay. In fact, by 2018, playtime's decline had become so severe the American Academy of Pediatrics released a "prescription" for the nation's parents: Play with your child. Every day. "Play is not frivolous," the doctors declared. "Play is fundamentally important for building 21st-century skills, such as problem-solving, collaboration, and creativity . . . skills that are critical for adult success."

Rogers, of course, knew this all along. "Play was the subject of a lot of debate in the '70s and '80s when Rogers was making the *Neighborhood*," says King. "A lot of people just wanted kids to immediately apply themselves to learning numbers and language—to cognitive learning in a very organized way. But Rogers was a great proponent of free play and creativity, not just because he wanted to give kids a chance to have fun, but because he recognized that it was essential to children's learning and to the development of their capacities for learning."

Roberta Schomburg agrees. "He knew that children start to develop initiative between three and five years old," she says. "That's why he focused so much on creativity, because initiative emerges if children are given some control over the way they play, the materials they use, and what the final outcome is. Lots of parents and teachers were focused on having children follow *their* patterns for making things and for playing a certain way. So what Fred was doing was fostering creativity and a sense of initiative by modeling something different and valuing the child's ideas."

Hence his daily invitations to the Neighborhood of Make-Believe: A bright, colorful play world where people, things, and ideas from everyday life can be customized and modified at will. It's a place where anything's possible—where a tiger can live in a clock and purple pandas can ping to other planets. And it's where, at the beginning of make-believe week, we find Lady Aberlin and King Friday XIII mixing pretend tea with real spoons.

Spoons, the king, and Lady Aberlin. *Let's make it up together.* The story expands as quickly as a five-year-old's mind: Over a warm cup of imaginary tea, King Friday XIII suddenly has an idea. Once, on the side of a mountain, he says, he had a lovely cup of *real* tea. And wouldn't it be fun to do that again—to have a tea party on a very tall mountain beside his castle?

Of course, there *aren't* any mountains in Make-Believe. But in play worlds like this one, reality—let alone the complex geophysics of tectonic shift—need not apply. And so the king makes up his mind. "I, King Friday XIII, command you both to make a mountain right beside the castle here in Make-Believe," he declares. "I'm sure you'll find a way."

Lady Aberlin and her friend Robert Troll think for a moment about the task they've been assigned. People can't make *mountains*; everyone knows that. But because they're playing, the characters don't dismiss it as impossible. Instead, they generate ideas, seek help from their friends, and even distract themselves when their thinking hits a wall. ("I think we should sing a song," Aberlin suggests. "That's a good idea—take our minds off it," says Troll.)

Through play, in other words, Make-Believe's characters leverage divergent thinking, convergent thinking, and even the brain's default mode network. They seek creative collaborators who help them think differently about their problem. And crucially, they're unburdened by self-censorship—in Make-Believe, there's no idea too strange, too nonsensical, or too implausible to consider.

Eventually, Lady Aberlin and Robert Troll devise a potential solution. Though there aren't any mountains in Make-Believe, there *is* an Eiffel Tower—and by covering it with trees that they've dug up with special spoons, they might just fulfill King Friday's command. This, of course, leads to several more adventures, until make-believe week culminates in a full-blown opera—one titled, appropriately, *Spoon Mountain*.

That's the power of play: Something simple becomes something more. A spoon becomes a mixer for pretend tea, a shovel for transferring trees, an inspiration for an opera. Play is the seed from which creativity sprouts. "You see a child play, and it is so close to seeing an artist paint, for in play a child says things without uttering a word," said Erik Erikson. So how do we encourage more of it?

For starters, we can do what Rogers did and take play seriously—that is, we can treat children's mud pies, block buildings, and made-up games and stories with respect, no matter how absurd they seem to adults. We can assign play the importance it deserves by restoring unstructured free time to children's schedules. Though modern parents might understandably balk at playtime when there are spelling words to memorize and math problems to solve, play can be every bit as effective as schoolwork—sometimes even more so. "Play is often talked about as if it were a relief from serious learning," Rogers once said. "But for children, play *is* serious learning."

We can also give kids their "sacred space," whether it's a corner of the kitchen table or a section of the backyard. ("My mother let me build a pottery shop in the basement of our funky little row house," Bill Strickland recalls. "And then I took over the laundry room and made it a photography studio. I didn't have much, but I did have a caring mother who said, 'My kid is on *fire*. I'll wash clothes somewhere else—leave the kid alone.' Without that, you don't grow up to build buildings.")

Finally, to the extent that we're able, we can give kids access to simple objects that propel their play. Mud pies and block buildings will work just fine.

Just ask Jane Werner, executive director of the Children's Museum of Pittsburgh, America's largest cultural campus for kids. Housed in an ancient post office, a once-abandoned library, and a former planetarium, the museum includes vats of mud; towers of wooden blocks; a real car for kids to play in; a climbing gym made of packing tape (fifty miles of it); and, in its makerspace, soldering irons, sewing machines, and table saws. All of this, says Werner, reflects the museum's approach to creativity: Let kids play with real stuff.

"Kids have imaginations," she explains, wading through a sea of first-graders. "They don't need manufactured fun. They don't need plastic. They don't need fake trees or fake logs or fake animals." Instead, she says, creativity comes from the stuff of real life—from "playing with real materials and using real tools and making real things."

It's a philosophy she learned from Rogers himself, with whom Werner spent countless hours designing exhibits—many of which are on tour around the country. (One of them, *How People Make Things*, spotlights the craft of making spoons.) "He was always pushing us to remember what it was like to be a kid," she says. "He'd say, 'I don't need to tell you what's right for children. Somewhere inside, you *know* what's right for children, because you were a child yourself.'"

When Werner and her team considered their own childhoods, she says, their standout moments always revolved around real stuff: playing in creeks, staging shows, and painting pretty pictures. No one had discovered his or her talents by watching TV or playing with plastic toys. "That's what Fred had been telling us all along," says Werner. "And that's what the Children's Museum tries to reflect."

To that end, the museum puts power tools and paintbrushes in visitors' hands—real things that expand children's understanding of their own capabilities. "We had a kid come in recently who'd decided he wanted to make a sign for his Wiffle ball field," she says. "We taught him how to use a table saw. He cut the wood for the sign, then cut the words into it with a laser cutter. Now he wants to make all sorts of things. When kids can act on their ideas, they tend to have another idea. And another. And another."

Likewise, when kids build with the museum's blocks or use its laser cutters for the first time, they begin to think, *I am capable. I am confident. I am creative.* Real materials and real tools help them bring their ideas to life and question their models of the world. Block buildings become prototypes. Doodles become first drafts. Werner sums it up like this: "It's better to make a cape than to buy a costume. To kids, a piece of fabric can become anything."

Research suggests she's right. Open-ended toys, like blocks and dollhouses, tend to produce more imaginative kids than manufactured toys with only one use. In the 1980s, psychologists Debra Pepler and Hildy Ross gave toddlers a set of toys that could be used as either a puzzle (by fitting the pieces into a form board) or as freestanding blocks. Then they split the kids into two groups: one group got the toys and the form board; the other got only the toys.

After giving the kids some time to play, Pepler and Ross tested each group's problem-solving abilities. They found that the kids without form boards—that is, kids who'd had to develop their own uses for the toys—came up with more creative solutions than their peers who'd played with a predefined puzzle.

That's why Rogers deployed simple objects like spoons in the *Neighborhood*. "A spoon allows you to bring whatever you are to it," says Hedda Sharapan. "Maybe you use it to feed your baby doll. Maybe you make a drum noise with it or use it to scoop up some sand. Unfortunately, most commercial toys are one-trick ponies. We want children to be able to do things that are of their own making. That's what creativity is: 'What are your ideas? What would you do? Your ideas matter!'"

At the Children's Museum, Werner sees this every day. "Kids walk into this space and think, 'I can do *anything* here,'" she says. "And that's empowering. That's where creativity comes from."

New Uses for Old Things

Suddenly, there's a knock on Rogers' door, and there stands Mary Alice Sherred—his long-delayed friend. She's finally here! Already today, we've seen several types of spoons, watched a film about how spoons get made, and made up a spoon-story in the Neighborhood of Make-Believe. Now, Sherred's here to deliver the final, most important spoon-point.

"Should I get you some spoons?" Rogers asks, leaning in expectantly.

"No," says Sherred. "I carry my ol' faithfuls with me."

She pulls two tablespoons from her pantsuit pocket and holds them back-to-back. She slaps the spoons against her hand, taps them on her knee, and claps them together. She makes *music* with those spoons— manic, beautiful, joyful music! And in doing so, she shows kids why creativity matters: Mary Alice Sherred has found a new use for an old thing.

Creativity, scientists say, is about more than drawing pictures or shaping pots or making spoons. It's about putting boards under spinning tires, turning paper cups into telephones, and—one day—meeting the challenges of climate change and poverty. It's about taking the knowledge and ideas and feelings that exist in the world already and making them more useful to ourselves and our neighbors. "Isn't that what we need to encourage everywhere?" Rogers asked. "In constant reference to the traditional, new solutions to old problems?"

Indeed. Which brings us back to one of the oldest problems of all: the fact that so many of us stop drawing, stop painting, and stop inventing stories. The fact that so many of us set down our instruments and let our music go quiet.

For more than a century, scientists like George Land have warned that the world and its pressures can crush creativity if we let it. But they've also assured us that our inner creativity never truly disappears—that it's still in there somewhere, waiting for us to wake it.

Maybe it's time we try.

Though picking up a paintbrush or sitting down at a Steinway might seem painful after a years- or even decades-long creative drought, doing so brings immediate benefits, scientists say. Adults who do something creative at least once a day have been found to be happier and healthier than their peers, an effect that sometimes lasts for days. Vonnegut was right—creating something, even when it's lousy, confers an enormous reward.

But more importantly, it models for children that creativity isn't just for kids—that even with their busy schedules and jangled nerves, adults paint portraits and shape clay and make up stories, too. It shows kids they don't *have* to give up their mud pies or block buildings, even when the world seems to scoff at them. And it shows them that the point of painting and drawing isn't to make a masterpiece or be the best at something but rather to make our souls grow—to become more fully ourselves.

The best way to raise creative kids may be to show them that we, as adults, value creativity, too. Scientists have found that imaginative kids are more likely to have imaginative parents—people who consider themselves adventurous and open-minded. This holds true even beyond the fourth-grade slump; creative older kids are more likely to say their parents told them stories or engaged in make-believe with them. In fact, parents' emphasis on imaginativeness can predict their children's creativity even years down the road.

It's not just parents. Exposure to *any* creative adult can be helpful. "Art museums, school art exhibits, community art center exhibits—all show that real people draw and express themselves [creatively]," write Golinkoff and Hirsh-Pasek. That's why the *Neighborhood*'s regulars all make a point of showing off their skills: There's Officer Clemmons, the opera singer; Bob Trow, the builder and portrait painter; Audrey Roth, the business owner and needlepoint expert; and Joe Negri, the handyman and gifted guitarist. These characters are everyday adults—people whose creative endeavors enrich not only their own lives but also the lives of the people around them. And that's not to mention the *Neighborhood*'s creative guest stars, from Yo-Yo Ma the cellist to Bill Strickland the potter to Mary Sherred the spoon player.

Finally, there's also Rogers himself, the otherwise-ordinary man at the heart of it all who sings, paints, makes up stories, and sees the limitless potential in real stuff like spoons. "Even when Rogers sits there folding a paper fan out of construction paper or using safety scissors to cut out something, he acts like he's doing something for himself as well as the viewer," notes the television critic David Bianculli. "[As] though, on a rainy day, he might amuse himself the same way even if there were no cameras to record his actions."

What a way to live a richer life.

⋯⋯⋯

The spoon concert ends, Mary Sherred departs, and we're left with Rogers in his blue sweater and his blue shirt in his blue living room. "Well," he says. "Good memories with spoons." And then he sings his farewell.

He swaps his sweater for the suit and tie he walked in with. The music speeds up until it feels almost frantic, and it's clearly time to go: back to the fast-moving place past that famous front door. Back to a world that's sometimes scary, or mean, or lonely, or sad. Back to the world where make-believe ends and a spoon is just a spoon.

But as Rogers gets ready to leave, he departs ever so slightly from his same old goodbye—the sing-smile-wave routine we've seen so many times. Today, he does something different: He grabs a fistful of spoons on his way out the door. He bangs them together and looks back at the camera. He grins as if he's pulled off a heist.

And maybe he has. Because as Rogers leaves the set, it's clear he's managed to keep something that so many others have lost. And he's shown us, in his own creative way, that we can keep it, too.

WHAT MIGHT YOU DO?

- Schedule "What now?" time. Put aside the phones, turn off the TV, and ask, "What can we do together during these next thirty minutes?" *Explore what's in your cupboards or out in the yard, and create something new. Maybe a silly game. Maybe a pillow fort or some other make-believe structure. Or, do something you haven't done before! (And show us what you end up doing, using this hashtag: #WhenYouWonder.)*

- Environment drives behavior. That's a core lesson from both the Manchester Craftsmen's Guild and the Children's Museum of Pittsburgh. Whenever and wherever possible, give children the support and the space to ask, "What might I do here, with these things?" Adults can do this, too. "I've been in professional development where [educators] pass around a paper towel tube and say, 'What could this be?'" says Hedda Sharapan. "That helped us remember that that's how children think: 'What could this be?'" *Set aside a corner in your basement, classroom, or library as a makerspace. Fill it with knickknacks from around the house or from a thrift store or a yard sale.*

- Make time for your own creative self, whether you're picking up an old hobby or learning a new one. "When was the last time you dabbled in art—painting or drawing or music or photography?" ask Golinkoff and Hirsh-Pasek in *Becoming Brilliant*. "We are often so afraid that we are not good enough that we don't even try. Who cares if our attempt at drawing that apple looks more like unidentifiable scribbles on a page?" *Let your kids see you try something that once captured your own interests. Gregg recently pulled out his old skateboard, and he made it down the street without a single bump or bruise. Six kids on the street now have their own boards. Your own creativity could inspire your kids to try something new.*

THREE

It All Works Out If You Talk and You Listen

Communication

"I have some pictures to show** you," says our man in the sweater. It's a beautiful day in Studio A, and Mister Rogers holds up an album. "This is the way my dad and mother looked when I was a little boy."

The camera moves in for a close-up. There's Fred's father, Jim Rogers, looking dapper in a three-piece pinstripe. There's Nancy McFeely, Fred's doting mother and Latrobe's beloved do-gooder. Fred has his father's fine hair and his mother's warm smile. He beams at their memory. "Very special people," he muses.

It's pure, unadulterated Rogers: a shot of hundred-proof wholesomeness you won't find anywhere else. What could be more decent, more moral, more *pleasant* than America's Neighbor fondly recalling his parents?

There's a reverent pause. The camera pans over the photos.

And then Rogers says it.

"Did you ever wish you could *marry* your mom or your dad?"

71

He gives us a moment to shift uncomfortably in our seats. Where, exactly, is this going? Just what does Mister Wholesome think he's doing?

"When I was four or five years old," he says, "I thought when I grew up that I would marry my mother."

It's a hard left turn—one that crashes through the median and into oncoming traffic—but there's an earnestness to what Rogers says. His candor disarms the topic like it disarms everything else: the first day of school, the death of a goldfish, a divorce in the family. "My mom was *very helpful* to me by what she told me then, when I was very young like you."

Somewhere off-set, a piano plays. Our host smiles his mother's smile. And then he leans in to tell us what she said.

Deep Listening and Loving Speech

It was just after 7:00 a.m. when Vaz Terdandenyan heard it: the steady, unmistakable thrum of a nearby helicopter. He went outside to look, but he couldn't pinpoint the source—the noise seemed to shift ever so slightly, always hovering just beyond his sight. As he set out from his apartment, hitting the streets in the sunny California morning, he decided to text his boss. This impromptu investigation, he figured, would probably make him late.

Terdandenyan stared at his phone as he walked. The roar of the rotors grew louder. Then, all of a sudden, the helicopter's presence made total, terrifying sense. It had been following an animal: specifically, the four-hundred-pound bear just inches from Terdandenyan's face. He'd been too wrapped up in his text message to notice.

Footage of Terdandenyan spinning around and sprinting away went viral, joining the medley of warnings about the perils of distracted texting. Not that it had any effect—years later, thousands of people annually still get hurt while walking and texting. We text while driving, too, accounting for one out of every four car accidents. We text at the dinner table, in bed, in meetings, on dates. By the time you finish this page, some sixteen million texts and emojis will have hurtled through the air.

Meanwhile, when we're not texting, we're "checking." On average, Americans look at their phones some fifty-two times a day. The average adult spends nearly four hours a day looking at a smartphone; teenagers log more than seven.

We simply can't help ourselves. Human beings are hardwired to communicate. It's fundamental to our survival and well-being; our lives are shaped by it from beginning to end. We come out of the womb and we cry. We learn to point, listen, respond, and write. When we die, we utter our famous last words. Some companies have even developed software promising a "social afterlife," posting tweets and Facebook posts from beyond a user's grave.

Though nearly all living things communicate in one way or another, humans have taken it one step further—we've developed language. Without it, we'd have to literally reinvent the wheel, perhaps for the millionth time. Language lets us pass along knowledge, build on old ideas, and deepen our connections with other people. When we lose those connections, we suffer immensely: think of the agitated toddler in time-out, the heartbroken lover in an empty house, the person in prison coming undone in solitary confinement. We need to communicate like we need water and air.

All of this explains, to some degree, the attentional black holes that spring from our smartphones. Every notification, every text, every like on your latest post sends a shot of dopamine to the brain—the same feel-good chemical released during exercise and meals. The more shots we get, the more we *want* to get, and so our phones become the first thing we see in the morning and the last thing we see at night. They promise unlimited chances to communicate—something we're programmed to crave from birth.

Unfortunately, smartphones aren't enough on their own. Despite the technology's ubiquity, nearly half of American adults say they're isolated from others. The average person hasn't made a new friend in five years. In Britain, most seniors say their primary companions are pets or televisions.

And in Japan, one survey counted half a million young people who hadn't interacted with *anyone* for six months or more.

This isn't just tragic—it's a real public health crisis. Loneliness has been linked to heart disease, strokes, and Alzheimer's. One study equated its health effects to a fifteen-cigarette-a-day smoking habit. A survey in Britain named loneliness the number-one fear among young people today, more terrifying than cancer or homelessness. The so-called loneliness epidemic has gotten so bad that some countries' responses seem torn from dystopian novels. In 2018, Britain appointed the first minister for loneliness, a government employee tasked with addressing "the sad reality of modern life."

Something is broken. We're talking and texting but not connecting. This isn't technology's fault, of course—tech is only a tool. But with smartphone-detox camps springing up around the world, it's fair to say that something needs to change. Our physical health, our mental well-being, and the strength of our relationships and democracies may depend on it.

Fortunately, a chorus of psychologists, learning scientists, and even Buddhist monks can point us toward something better. "To lead a happy and successful life," argues one team of researchers, "one must master the skills that support effective communication in the forms of communication they encounter most commonly."

In other words, the better we communicate, the better off we'll be. Researchers have found clear links between communication skills and one's relationship quality, academic success, job performance, and income. In Silicon Valley, managers seeking employees who can communicate with each other—and with customers—have begun hiring English majors alongside engineers, prompting *Forbes* to call liberal arts degrees "tech's hottest ticket."

The implication is that people who hold such degrees bring proven communication skills to the table. But what *are* those skills? Communication is a big concept, one that encompasses reading, writing, speaking, and listening. Then there's everything nonverbal: our tones of voice, our eye rolls, our embraces. When we have something to say, we have to deploy the right tools to craft the right message using the right channel, all while those channels continue to multiply. A quick scan of our office alone reveals iPhones, PowerPoints, Post-its, emails, tweets, texts, Snapchats, and WhatsApps.

In the face of so much complexity, perhaps it's best to start with something simple. In his 2013 book, *The Art of Communicating*, Thich Nhat Hanh—the Vietnamese poet, scholar, and monk—boils effective communication down to two basic elements: deep listening and loving speech. "Deep listening and loving speech," he writes, "are the best instruments I know for establishing and restoring communication with others and relieving suffering."

Fortunately for us, no one listened more deeply, or spoke more lovingly, than Fred McFeely Rogers.

Putting Feelings First

There he is in his living room: still in that sweater, still discussing that same awkward topic. "My mother told me that she was already married to my daddy," he says, "and maybe someday I would find a wife of my own."

Readers, if you were hoping for a one-off moment—an uncomfortable-but-fleeting aside—then we have bad news. Rogers even wrote a song about marrying his mom. "A rather long song," he says as the music begins to play.

> *One day I said, I'm really going to marry my mom.*
> *I told my mom, I'm really going to marry you!*
> *She smiled—didn't laugh—said, I hope you will marry.*
> *Maybe someone like me.*
> *But you see, she said, I'm already married.*
> *I'm married to your daddy.*

The first few lines of "Going to Marry Mom" look admittedly strange on paper. Of all things to sing about, why linger on a little misconception like this one? Why focus on something so mundane when the bigger problems of childhood loom so large?

Imagine, for a moment, that you're Nancy McFeely. You're sitting in your parlor in Latrobe, maybe planning a fundraiser for a neighbor who's down on her luck, when your four-year-old son bursts into the room and declares he wants to marry you.

As an adult, you have a range of responses to choose from. You could, for example, set the facts straight and get back to what you were doing: *Moms and kids don't marry one another, Freddy. Now please, I'm very busy.* You could deploy some light parental sarcasm—*I don't think so, pal*—or deny his incorrect desire: *You don't want to marry me, kiddo.* You could also play along, perhaps giving a good-natured chuckle. Such innocence is, after all, undeniably cute.

But now let's imagine you're Freddy. You've been in your room all day, making up stories with your puppet-friends. You've just staged the make-believe wedding of James Michael Jones and Betty Okonak Templeton, when all of a sudden, it hits you: One day, you're going to marry the person you love most in the world. Thrilled by this realization—and proud that you deduced it yourself—you rush to the parlor to tell her.

Songs like "Going to Marry Mom" remind us that to children, mundane moments aren't always so mundane. What might look to adults like a simple misunderstanding could, to a child, be an expression of love and the need to be loved. In that sense, Freddy's question carries unspeakable weight. Answered well, the moment can affirm the deepest human desire—to feel oneself "beloved on the earth," as the writer Raymond Carver once put it. Answered not so well, the moment can be devastating.*

---

* For the record, clinical counselor Dr. Deborah MacNamara offers a number of possible responses to a preschooler's marriage proposal on her blog: http://macnamara.ca /portfolio/my-preschooler-wants-to-marry-me-should-i-say-yes/. MacNamara suggests

If the stakes here make you nervous, you're not alone. Everyday life is full of reminders that effective communication takes practice, skill, and lots of hard work, especially when it comes to kids. "Conversing with children is a unique art with rules and meanings of its own," writes the late psychologist Haim Ginott in his bestselling classic, *Between Parent and Child*. According to Ginott, to speak well with children, it helps to learn a new kind of communication—one that helps us discipline without humiliating, criticize without demeaning, and praise without judging.

It's here that experts from different fields, places, and eras converge. Whether it's Haim Ginott of Israel or Thich Nhat Hanh of Vietnam or Margaret McFarland of Pittsburgh, psychologists, Zen masters, and child-development experts alike nearly all agree on a singular point: that effective communication, above all else, acknowledges and respects children's feelings. We don't necessarily have to *agree* with those feelings, but we *should* refrain from ridiculing or condemning them, even when we feel they're unjustified.

Which brings us back to the Rogers family living room, where four-year-old Freddy has just told his mother he wants to marry her. Of the countless ways she could have responded, we know—thanks to the song he sang some fifty years later—that Nancy McFeely not only acknowledged her son's need to be loved but also managed to teach him what marriage means without mocking him or making him feel like a fool. In fact, a few lines show how deftly she handled the whole situation.

> *She smiled—didn't laugh—said, I hope you will marry.*
> *Maybe someone like me.*
> *And as you grow more and more like your daddy*
> *You'll find a lady like me.*

---

saying something like, *Yes, this love is forever.* "We don't have to agree or disagree with their marriage proposal at face value," she explains, "but rather answer their question at the place that it matters. We need to answer the deepest hunger they have and one that can only be filled with an invitation for relationship that is unwavering."

And she'll love you as I love your daddy
And she will marry you.
And I hope you will have little children
And they will be like you.
'Cause mothers and dads have special love for children
Especially children like you.
It all works out if you talk and you listen
'Cause someone cares about you.
Yes, someone cares about you.

Rogers repeats certain lines again and again as if speaking directly to the adults in the room. Communication with children, he reminds us, doesn't come easily. It's a learning process—one to which Rogers committed himself with monk-like dedication. We'll get into that later on, but for now, a brief example to show just how meticulous our man in the sweater could be.

Hedda Sharapan remembers a taping in which a *Neighborhood* cast member told Henrietta Pussycat not to cry. "The Make-Believe scenes were tightly scripted, but now and then, spontaneous things happened in the conversations between puppets and people," she says. "When Henrietta started to cry, the actress said caringly, 'Oh, Henrietta, don't cry.' Fred stopped the taping, came out from behind the set, and said, 'When we say *don't cry*, we're really saying, *I have trouble handling that*. I wonder if you can find another way to help Henrietta?' And she did. [The actress] just comforted her."

In the *Neighborhood*, all feelings were valid; every emotion was worthy of expression. "Anything that's human is mentionable, and anything that is mentionable can be more manageable," Rogers once said. "When we can talk about our feelings, they become less overwhelming, less upsetting, and less scary. The people we trust with that important talk can help us know that we are not alone."

Listening Is Where Love Begins

Sometimes, when the weights we carry grow heavy, what we need more than anything is someone who's willing to listen. Sometimes it's an old friend. Sometimes it's a spouse, a parent, or a neighbor. Sometimes it's a professional—there's a reason Americans spend tens of billions of dollars a year on mental health treatment, including counseling. It feels good to talk, even when our listeners can't solve our problems or take away our pain. Often, we simply need to be heard. "At times of strong emotion," writes Ginott, "there is nothing as comforting and helpful as a person who listens and understands. What is true for adults is also true for children."

Rogers understood this on a level that captivated his audience, both on-screen and off. His friends and staff remember him as an extraordinary listener, someone more interested in hearing their stories than he was in telling his own. (Journalists, of course, found this tendency maddening.) His office at WQED was more living room than workspace, recalls one former colleague. Rogers refused a desk, considering it too much of a barrier between his visitors and himself. Instead, he'd sit on a couch or a reclining chair and listen.

It was the same story when he'd encounter his viewers out in the real world. Bill Isler recalls rushing through the Boston airport with Rogers when a parent stopped them to introduce her three-year-old son. "The little boy came over and gave Fred an ice cube, and Fred bent down with the ice cube in his hands and just talked to the child until the ice cube melted. When he talked to children, he was always down on one knee. He always got down to eye level—he knew how important that was, no matter what was happening around him. That always blew me away."

Despite his medium's limitations, Rogers put listening front and center in the *Neighborhood*. When he asked his viewers a question—*What do you think about when you look at this African violet?*—he left space for their answers. "He would ask a question and leave time for children to develop a response," says Sharapan. "Part of allowing children to be curious is giving them silence, trust, and space—letting them know that it's okay to still be thinking about something and to not have an answer right away."

Although Rogers couldn't hear his viewers' responses in real time, he managed to listen another way: through the mail. The Fred Rogers Archive in Latrobe houses some thirty years' worth of notes from kids and adults alike, many of whom simply wanted to thank him for his steady presence in their lives. "The mail was so important to him. That was his feedback," says Sharapan. "The first thing he did every day when he came into the office was look at the mail that was waiting for him. When you're taping in a television studio, you are talking to a camera and have no idea how people are reacting. That's why he so appreciated that people took the time to write."

He also felt that each letter deserved a meaningful response—a signal that someone was listening. "More and more," he wrote, "I've come to understand that listening is one of the most important things we can do for one another. Whether the other be an adult or a child, our engagement in listening to who that person is can often be our greatest gift. Whether that person is speaking or playing or dancing, building or singing or painting, if we care, we can listen."

This is what Thich Nhat Hanh means by deep listening: the patient act of ensuring that someone feels acknowledged, valued, and heard. Deep listening can take lots of forms, but in every case, it's rooted in compassion rather than criticism. "When we listen to someone with the intention of helping that person suffer less, this is deep listening," Nhat Hanh writes. "When we listen with compassion, we don't get caught in judgment. A judgment may form, but we don't hold on to it."

This means listening to children uncritically, at least at first. For parents, it's sometimes a tall order—we're criticizing, lecturing, advice-dispensing creatures. It's in our DNA. Though we don't always differentiate between children's feelings and children's behavior, it's possible, even *necessary*, to empathize with the former before reacting to the latter. Like everyone else, children withhold their feelings when they fear they'll be shamed, punished, or worse for expressing them. "Being supportive often means waiting and listening and more waiting, until you're better able to understand the drama that a certain child is living through at the moment," said Rogers—"something that may actually be keeping him or her from learning well."

Imagine, for example, that your fourth-grade daughter comes home from school in tears. She slams her bag on the table, sending a glass of water shattering across the floor. Before you can speak, she screams, "Ms. Appelbaum *yelled* at me today!"

Or make-believe this: It's the day of a big wedding, and Daniel Striped Tiger is refusing to get dressed. He's decided, after several practice attempts, that he can't carry the ring down the aisle without it slipping off the pillow. "I *can't* be a ring-bearer!" he cries to the adults around him. "I just *can't* be. The more I think about it, the worse it seems to me!"

In situations like these, our instinct is often to act—to ask our shaken daughter what she did to deserve her teacher's scolding or to teach Daniel Tiger how to hold the ring so he can get dressed and get on with it. As parents, teaching and fixing are major parts of the job description. We jump in with our hard-won wisdom, correcting and protecting, building up and dressing down. The internet is full of horror stories about parents who take this too far: assaulting youth-sports referees or accompanying their grown children to job interviews.

But in our rush to fix children's problems, we sometimes skip a crucial step: taking time to just listen, even when we don't like what we hear. What if, instead of reacting, we resolved to simply *receive* for a while? What if, like Rogers, we committed to listening more deeply, even when there's glass on the floor or we're going to be late for a wedding? We might be surprised what we learn.

Consider our daughter in distress. If we begin by accusing her of deserving Ms. Appelbaum's wrath, we're not going to get very far, even though we suspect she's in the wrong. Feelings are far stronger than logic, and they have to be dealt with first—that is, they have to be heard by someone who'll listen without critiquing. "If we try to interrupt or correct the other person, we will transform the session into a debate and it will ruin everything," writes Nhat Hanh. "After we have deeply listened and allowed the other person to express everything in his heart, we'll have a chance later to give him a little of the information he needs to correct his perception—but not now. Now we just listen, even if the person says things that are wrong."

This is easier said than done, especially mid-meltdown. But we can take a moment to acknowledge our daughter's feelings, perhaps by saying, "You sound very upset! You must have had a really difficult day." This tells her we're listening and that it's safe to say more. Maybe she *did* deserve her teacher's wrath, but perhaps she acted out because she's being bullied, or because she's struggling with math, or because she can't see the blackboard from her seat. The bottom line is that we can deal with misbehaviors later. Right now, it's more important to hear what our daughter is telling us.

"When I'm upset or hurting, the last thing I want to hear is advice, philosophy, psychology, or the other fellow's point of view," explain Adele Faber and Elaine Mazlish, authors of *How to Talk So Kids Will Listen & Listen So Kids Will Talk*. (Unlike your present coauthors, Faber and Mazlish use the singular *I*.) "But let someone really listen, let someone acknowledge my inner pain and give me a chance to talk more about what's troubling me, and I begin to feel less upset, less confused, more able to cope with my feelings and my problem."

And what of Daniel Tiger? In this particular episode, another puppet, Betty Okonak Templeton, jumps in to fix his ring problem, using a little Scotch tape to keep it on the pillow. And yet Daniel *still* won't get dressed. It's the kind of scenario that vexes parents everywhere—the issue gets resolved, but the reaction doesn't change. Daniel's still terrified, and now everyone's going to be late. Frustration builds and builds.

Perhaps, by jumping in too quickly with the Scotch-tape solution, the adults around Daniel missed his underlying concern. Kids, after all, tend to speak in code; sometimes, their fears take a bit of deciphering. Roberta Schomburg of the Fred Rogers Center recalls when her young daughter had a difficult time accepting a baby brother. "She'd painted a picture of the baby at school, and I told her it was beautiful," she says, laughing. "Then her teacher showed me the caption on the painting. She had named it 'The Hand of the Monster,' and had painted a blue blob hanging over the baby's head. I thought, 'Oh, dear.'"

Sometimes, in other words, it's not *really* about carrying the wedding ring. And in fact, when Betty Okonak Templeton approaches Daniel a second time, giving him space to speak, she eventually learns that he's misheard *ring bearer* as *ring bear*.

"I'm a tiger!" he cries. "And I don't want to be a bear!"

No wonder Daniel wouldn't get dressed—the task had threatened his entire identity. It's only when an adult was willing to listen that his real concern could be discovered, discussed, and resolved. "Fred recognized that children have underlying motivations for the things they say and do—motivations that they probably aren't even aware of themselves," says Schomburg. "And those motivations can come out in odd ways, like in the titles of children's paintings. And so we have to listen for that."

Indeed, when we make a point of listening more than we talk, we'll sometimes find that listening is enough on its own. We don't always have to act or give advice or have something meaningful to say. When your daughter's upset or Daniel Tiger won't get dressed, they're not necessarily seeking solutions. Sometimes, they just want someone to hear them.

"When your loved one is suffering," writes Nhat Hanh, "your impulse may be to want to do something to fix it, but you don't need to do much. You just need to be there for him or her. That is true love."

Simple Interactions

In the early 1980s, Rogers released a series called *Mister Rogers Talks with Parents*. Though largely forgotten now, these programs did for adults what the *Neighborhood* did for kids: They provided a framework for talking through difficult topics like day care, divorce, and school. Though Rogers largely avoided prescriptive advice, "the major messages to parents stayed constant," writes author Ellen Galinsky: "Take the time to listen to and understand your children and yourself, and the appropriate solutions to problems will become evident; you are the expert, so have confidence in yourself."

It's easy to forget amid parenting's complexities and frustrations, but each of us is, like Rogers' mother, an expert. We're all capable of a well-timed embrace, a supportive smile, or something else that makes children feel valued. We might not know it or think about it or even be able to name it, but when it comes to communicating with kids, we all have strengths that ought to be recognized.

It's something that Dana Winters knows better than anyone. A professor of child and family studies at the Fred Rogers Center, a large part of Winters' career has involved filming children's helpers: educators, caregivers, parents, and anyone else who works with kids. "I spent six months filming the crossing guards of Pittsburgh," she says, laughing. "You'd be surprised—what crossing guards can do for children in very small moments is just amazing."

Winters directs Simple Interactions, a strengths-based approach to noticing and affirming exactly the sorts of moments that Rogers described in "Going to Marry Mom"—the tender moments of closeness that form the building blocks of loving relationships. They happen every hour of every day among every kind of person, says Winters, and by learning to notice them, we can learn to make more of them.

It works like this: Winters and her team film unscripted, almost random interactions among children and helpers. It doesn't necessarily matter what gets filmed—"I could show up and film for two hours on any given Tuesday and have enough material to do this for years," she says—though they tend to gravitate toward routines. Small, seemingly unimportant moments like feeding or changing a diaper happen all the

SIMPLE INTERACTIONS TOOL

Noticing and Appreciating Human Interactions Across Developmental Settings

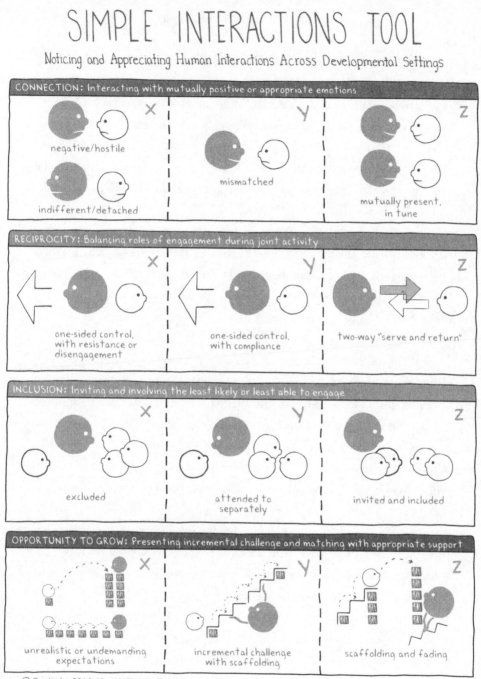

CONNECTION: Interacting with mutually positive or appropriate emotions

X — negative/hostile; indifferent/detached

Y — mismatched

Z — mutually present, in tune

RECIPROCITY: Balancing roles of engagement during joint activity

X — one-sided control, with resistance or disengagement

Y — one-sided control, with compliance

Z — two-way "serve and return"

INCLUSION: Inviting and involving the least likely or least able to engage

X — excluded

Y — attended to separately

Z — invited and included

OPPORTUNITY TO GROW: Presenting incremental challenge and matching with appropriate support

X — unrealistic or undemanding expectations

Y — incremental challenge with scaffolding

Z — scaffolding and fading

© Junlei Li, 2014. Updated with Tom Akiva and Dana Winters, 2018. Illustration updated by Kate Luchini.

time, says Winters, "so what might we do in those moments to elevate the interaction?"

Afterward, Winters and her team play the videos back for the helpers, using the Simple Interactions Tool (see page 85) to describe specific moments. In each interaction, how did the helpers forge connections with children? How were they present in the ways they communicated—in the ways they received and responded to the kids in their care? Did they make children feel included? Valued? Loved?

"Overwhelmingly," says Winters, "we hear two things when we play back the videos. The first is, 'I don't remember that moment,' which shows just how ordinary these moments really are. The second is, 'I don't even know what I was doing,' which I think speaks to helpers having a lack of confidence in their practice and a lack of awareness of how much *good* they're really doing."

The Simple Interactions approach helps create that awareness. As a group, the helpers identify moments of connection and reciprocity, as well as opportunities for kids to belong and grow. And because the point of the program is to help adults learn from what they're already doing well, the helpers focus on each other's strengths. "It's a deeply reflective process," Winters explains. "It's not evaluative. It's not scored. It simply helps us describe these moments so we can be more intentional about how and when they happen."

Picture Nancy McFeely scooping up Freddy in her parlor, explaining that moms and dads have a special love for their kids. How could we describe that moment using the Simple Interactions Tool? Certainly, it's one of connection, of mutual presence, of being "in tune" with Freddy's emotions. And it's certainly a two-way "serve and return" conversation, with Freddy proposing marriage and his mother responding and expounding in a loving way. (There's evidence that engaging in back-and-forth conversations like these can boost children's language skills.) And it's unquestionably a moment of growth.

Of course, Freddy's mother wasn't thinking about any of this when he burst into the room. More likely, she was simply reacting—the same thing most of us do when caring for kids. But when we have the language, tools, and space to think about interactions like this one, we can become more intentional about the ways we approach them. The next time Nancy McFeely hears a surprising question from Freddy, she'll likely remember the comfort she brought him when she smiled, but didn't laugh. And she'll know to react accordingly.

First developed by Winters' colleague, Harvard University lecturer (and former codirector of the Fred Rogers Center) Junlei Li, Simple Interactions has reached more than twenty-five thousand helpers in classrooms, orphanages, libraries, and museums around the world. And because it's freely available online, it's increasingly used by parents and families working to understand their own interactions with kids.

"I've had parents come to me and say, 'I'm making a decision for my child right now, and something doesn't feel right,'" says Winters. "And then they go to the tool and say, 'Oh, what I'm doing actually doesn't encourage, enrich, and empower human relationships. *That's* why it doesn't feel right.'"

Winters pauses, then laughs. "I even had a woman tell me that she uses the tool to understand her relationship with her mother-in-law. That's when I knew it can really work for anyone."

In classrooms, Simple Interactions has been shown to reduce teacher depression and increase psychological safety—that is, teachers' willingness to experiment and try new things, despite the risk of failure. It's also been shown to improve relationships and communication among adults and kids, and Winters thinks she knows why. "We push back against the idea that either you can interact with people or you can't," she says. "The best communicators and best interactors got that way by working at it and developing their craft. Fred Rogers used to say that there are no shortcuts to building a relationship. And we don't take shortcuts. Every day, we're focused on those basic building blocks."

Many Ways to Say I Love You

If simple interactions are the building blocks of human relationships, then deep listening and loving speech are the double helix that holds them together. It's by listening deeply that we help alleviate other people's suffering, and it's by speaking lovingly that we express *ourselves*, whether we're communicating affection, anger, or anything else in between.

Loving speech comes in countless forms and can convey almost anything. Thich Nhat Hanh writes that speech is loving when it communicates our presence to others and lets others know that their presence matters to us. It doesn't always mean saying, "I love you," though that's certainly part of it. An arm around the shoulder can be loving speech. So can a protest. So can a phone call or a text message or a business presentation. When babies cry, our blood pressure spikes and our heart rates rise, prompting a response. That's loving speech, too.

Rogers himself wrote an ode to this. Here's a snippet of "Many Ways to Say I Love You":

> *Cleaning up a room can say I love you.*
> *Hanging up a coat before you're asked to*
> *Drawing special pictures for the holidays and*
> *Making plays.*
> *You'll find many ways to say I love you.*
> *You'll find many ways to understand what love is.*
> *Many ways, many ways, many ways to say*
> *I love you.*

The *Neighborhood* was, in a sense, a thirty-year sermon on loving speech's value—on its importance in a world where reserves of it seem to be dwindling and where speech that demeans and humiliates has become the new normal. It might seem quaint in a time when the meanest tweets get the most attention, but for all the acrimony that's crept into our discourse, loving speech remains the most powerful communication tool we have. It's one that works in every setting, from the classroom to the board-room. "All of us long to hear that we are accepted as we are," said Rogers. "That kind of message can draw the world together."

It's this longing that turned Rogers' chance encounter with a television into a sort of conversion experience. In 1951, during his final year as an undergraduate at Rollins College in Florida, Rogers returned to La-trobe for a short break. His parents, he discovered, had recently bought a strange glowing box—an invention that was still relatively rare at the time, but which would soon transform American life like little else had before it.

Throughout most of the 1940s, just a few thousand households owned televisions. By the time Rogers first saw one, that number had soared to about 3.8 million—a figure that would multiply twelvefold within a de-cade. In a striking example of the new technology's influence, officials in Toledo, Ohio, announced in 1954 that they'd discovered a strange phe-nomenon: The city's water use was surging at regular intervals each night, as if everyone in town was running their faucets at once. An investigation eventually revealed that television had synchronized Toledo's residents. Families all over town were flushing their toilets during the same commer-cial breaks.

It was in that enchanting machine that Rogers glimpsed his future for the first time. He didn't like what he saw.

"I saw people throwing pies at each other's faces," he told a reporter a half century later. "And that, to me, was such demeaning behavior. And if there's anything that bothers me, it's one person demeaning another."

Rogers knew at once what he had to do. He postponed his plans to enter the seminary and went instead to New York City, where he learned the nuts and bolts of television production. Upon returning to Pittsburgh in 1953, he worked for WQED, the country's first community-sponsored television station. During his lunch hours, he worked toward his master of divinity degree at what is today the Pittsburgh Theological Seminary, which connected him to McFarland and his studies in child development.

After a brief detour to Canada, he eventually returned to Pittsburgh and began creating the *Neighborhood*: a beacon of loving speech that would—as Rogers once put it—broadcast grace through the land.

As a communicator and television host, Rogers held his responsibilities sacred. "The space between the television screen and whoever happens to be receiving it—I consider that very holy ground," he told an interviewer. "A lot happens there."

That's why he went to such extraordinary lengths to ensure that the *Neighborhood* spoke lovingly to viewers—that it affirmed their dignity and humanity and self-worth. A typical scriptwriting session required hours of consultation with McFarland. Then came several rounds of revision as Rogers made change after exacting change. Even after all of that, Rogers would sometimes stop a shoot—"a cardinal sin in the highly expensive world of television production," notes Maxwell King—and go back to McFarland for advice.

To outside observers (and sometimes to Rogers' own staff) this all seemed a little extreme, especially for a program that spent half its time in a make-believe puppet-world. But Rogers had good reason to take such care: He knew how thoroughly children absorb the speech they hear, regardless of whether that speech is loving. And he knew that to counter the tsunami of advertising and negativity and dehumanization that threatened to drown out everything else, he'd have to speak relentlessly, unfailingly lovingly, no matter how many times it meant trudging the half mile between his studio and McFarland's office.

Of course, most of us can't spend hours crafting our lives in twenty-eight-minute segments. Things go wrong: a parent gets sick, a creditor calls, a car breaks down. The pressures and heartaches of everyday life can shake even the strongest commitment to loving speech. So where does that leave us?

The first thing we can do is cut ourselves some slack. Learning to speak lovingly is a lifelong process, one that even Rogers had to work at. He consulted with McFarland until her death in 1988 and relied on a team of child development experts until the very end of his career—a team that continues his work today at Fred Rogers Productions. The difference between Rogers and everyone else wasn't that he'd been gifted some special, saintly capacity for loving speech. It was that he committed himself to speaking more lovingly every day of his life, even when doing so seemed futile.

And it seems futile more often than we'd like to admit. Consider all the times you've heard someone demean or hurt another person: the spouses who take shots at each other over dinner; the stranger who berates a bus driver; the boss who rules by insults and threats. It's easy to think that we ourselves would never do such things, but the truth is that all of us speak less than lovingly at times, especially when dealing with kids.

"We would like to believe that only a disturbed parent responds in a way that is damaging to a child," writes Haim Ginott. "Unfortunately, even parents who are loving and well-meaning also blame, shame, accuse, ridicule, threaten, bribe, label, punish, preach, and moralize."

He gives a startling—but relatable—example:

What do we say to a guest who forgets her umbrella? Do we run after her and say, "What is the matter with you? Every time you come to visit, you forget something. If it's not one thing, it's another. Why can't you be like your younger sister? When she comes to visit, she knows how to behave. You're forty-four years old! Will you never learn? I'm not a slave to pick up after you! I bet you'd forget your head if it weren't attached to your shoulders!"

We do this in subtler forms, too. Imagine a colleague complains that your office is too warm and starts to take off his sweater. You wouldn't respond by saying, *No, it's not too warm—put that sweater back on, mister.* Or imagine you're at the movies and your date, clearly moved, quietly starts to sob. You wouldn't look over and say, *I'll give you something to cry about.* But with children, we're sometimes more than willing to deny their emotions and tell them that their inner selves can't be trusted.

These habits are passed down from our parents and teachers and from *their* parents and teachers and so on. Among adults' most common refrains, we'd be willing to bet *I sound just like my mother* ranks somewhere near the top. And while there are certainly some advantages to this—at some point, for example, we all need to hear that money doesn't grow on trees—these patterns can lead us to speak to kids in ways we wouldn't dream of speaking to anyone else.

Especially, it must be said, when we're angry. It's a cruel irony that loving speech seems most difficult when it's also the most needed—that is, when emotions are already running hot. But anger and loving speech aren't mutually exclusive. Anger can and should be expressed in healthy ways—ways that don't hurt yourself or anybody else, as Rogers often put it. Parents can do this by following a simple rule: "Except for one safeguard, we are entitled to express what we feel," writes Ginott. "We can express our angry feelings provided we do not attack the child's personality or character."

Again, the Simple Interactions Tool can be useful. Consider your interactions on any given day and describe where they fall on the spectrum. That moment we sat down with our upset daughter, empathized with her frustration, and lovingly asked her about what's going on at school? That was squarely in the Z zone—a moment of mutual presence and conversation and growth. That moment we berated her for forgetting her umbrella? That was more along the lines of X or Y. It was hostile and one-sided, and it attacked her character instead of offering support.

Most of the time, our interactions will span the tool's spectrum, and that's okay. Moments of Z aren't *always* better than moments of Y—there are times when X or Y moments are appropriate and necessary. (Winters gives the example of a shop class, where kids could get hurt if they're not listening and complying.) The point is that by describing and becoming more conscious of the ways we speak to kids, we can be more deliberate about speaking to them lovingly, regardless of the patterns we've absorbed over time. And when we do that, we start to forge new patterns—patterns we invariably pass on to others.

The Legend of Kung Fu Joe

If every town has its characters, Pittsburgh has an ensemble cast. There's Burgh Man, the amateur superhero who wanders the city donning a mask and cape. (His superpowers? Battling bullies, pollution, and negativity.) There's Rachel Ann Bovier, Pittsburgh's self-proclaimed "premier poetess," whose motivational verse graces our billboards and classifieds. And then there's Andrew Anthony, better known to Pittsburghers as Kung Fu Joe.

A second-degree black belt in Shaolin kung fu, Kung Fu Joe's kicks and chops have made him a minor local celebrity. Passersby give high fives, toss coins in his "tip jar," and generally wish him well. He's the friendly neighborhood mainstay whom people like but don't deeply *know*—the kind of guy whose backstory gets written by everyone else. The kind of guy who, as happened in 2016, sometimes gets stabbed in the middle of the night, sparking rumors and hearsay and speculation that's taken as fact.

Or at least he was, until he shared his story with a teenage TV crew called *The Reel Teens.*

"The kids had the idea," says Wendy Burtner, sitting in her South Side office. "They said, 'We want to go find Kung Fu Joe and figure out who he really is.' So we talked about what their story line might look like and how they might approach him and what kind of message they might want to send. The documentary they made has, at this point, been in three or four different film festivals now."

Burtner is president and CEO of Steeltown, a nonprofit that trains teenagers in film and digital media arts. "Basically," she says, "we take kids with a passion for digital media and help them follow that to what we hope is a profession. If they want to go work on big Hollywood movies, we'll help them figure out how to do that. If they want to do their own documentaries or go work at WQED, we'll help them do that, too."

Founded in 2003 by Maxine Lapiduss, Ellen Weiss Kander, and Carl Kurlander, kids in Steeltown's film academy develop their skills by taking on real-world work for paying clients. They also write, shoot, edit, and host *The Reel Teens*, a documentary TV series that airs on local stations and YouTube. Every year, the nonprofit's teaching artists lead thirty to forty teens through more than one hundred hours of technical training, teaching them the basics of storytelling, camerawork, audio recording, and lighting. Kids learn what a close-up is and how a boom mic works. They learn to write for a wide audience. And because film captures things that they might not otherwise think about, such as body language and tone of voice, Steeltown's students become better communicators in every sense of the word.

These skills are relatively straightforward and can be taught by almost any competent filmmaker, says Burtner. The trickier part is helping kids bridge that "holy ground" between viewers and a screen—helping them captivate an audience and prompt a response like Rogers did. "You have to teach kids to think about how they're going to make people *feel*," she says. "And that's a lot more difficult than teaching them to hold a camera."

Filmmaker Ian Altenbaugh agrees. A teaching artist at Steeltown since 2016, Altenbaugh gives students two rules, whether they're crafting something for a client or producing a *Reel Teens* episode. The first has to do with intention—kids communicate well when they know what they're trying to say and why they're trying to say it. "They don't have to have a profound reason for it," he says. "If their purpose is just to make some people laugh, then that's awesome. They're bringing joy to people's lives. But they have to be able to articulate that."

The second rule springs from loving speech. "It's okay to tell stories about something that's weird or goofy or silly, but you have to do so with respect," he says. "There's no punching down. Your subject is a human being, so let's celebrate what makes them unique or different, not isolate them or turn them into an 'other.'"

The result is programming like the Kung Fu Joe documentary: television that humanizes and uplifts rather than ridicules and demeans. Programming that, as Rogers might say, broadcasts grace through the land.

Over the course of just six and a half minutes, *The Reel Teens* show how a childhood marred by bullies and poverty led Kung Fu Joe to the martial arts. We glimpse his prior life as a bodybuilder, then as a panhandler, and then—as he puts it—a legend. We see the stab wounds on his face and neck, and we learn, for the first time, what happened that night in 2016.

Kung Fu Joe, it turns out, had intervened to stop an attempted rape. He nearly died in the struggle, but the victim made it to safety—a fact Joe credits to God and the martial arts. Now he sees himself as the South Side's protector. "A lot of people depend on me," he tells the teens. "I can't let them down."

The program ends with Kung Fu Joe on the street, telling his neighbors he loves them. It feels, in many ways, like the *Neighborhood*'s spiritual sequel—a portrait of fearless authenticity, produced by people determined to speak lovingly through a screen. Perhaps it's no wonder that Steeltown shares a building with Fred Rogers Productions.

"Teenagers could have made a very different movie about someone like Kung Fu Joe," says Altenbaugh. Instead, they made a film that shows the world that "he's this really wonderful person who cares about his neighbors and their well-being. And in turn, I think the film shows the world that it ought to care about *him*."

⁘

Back in Studio A, Mister Rogers stands at his fish tank. It's the same fish tank he's stood at a hundred times before, the place where he talks and he listens one last time before he leaves.

We've learned a lot about love today, he tells us. We've learned a lot about marriage and ring bearers and the special kind of love that moms and dads have for their kids. And we've learned that no matter what we feel inside—whether we're sad or we're scared or we want to marry our moms—it all works out if we talk lovingly and listen deeply. And even if questions and feelings remain, that's okay. Questions and feelings are how we know we're growing.

"Do you sometimes wish that you could be the bride or the groom in a wedding?" Rogers asks. "It seems like a long time to wait until you're grown up enough to be a *real* bride or groom."

Mister Rogers waits for our answers in silence. Though he can't hear us, he listens. He wants us to know that whatever we say—and whoever we are—there's someone out there who wants to know how we feel. There's someone out there who knows how deeply we want to be heard.

WHAT MIGHT YOU DO?

- Talk to your kids about "the mad that they feel," as Rogers put it, or about their disappointments. Ask lots of open-ended questions when something's not going right or not going well. "Sometimes the best thing to say is, 'Can you tell me about it?'" says Hedda Sharapan. We adults want to solve problems and avoid tears, but we might not know whether we're solving the right problem. Who would have guessed that Daniel Tiger was frightened about being something other than himself? *How many times have you later learned that your child confused something like being a "ring bearer" with being a "ring bear?" Listening is sometimes enough.*

- Tell your child ways that *you* express your anger or disappointment—ways that don't hurt yourself or anyone else. Let them know that sadness isn't forever. Even though we feel overwhelmed and frightened by our negative feelings, those feelings will always change with time. *"Almost everybody gets angry once in a while, and certainly I do,"* Rogers once explained. *"But do you know what I do when I'm angry? I like to swim, and so I swim extra hard when I'm angry."*

- Experiment with Simple Interactions and practice using the tools. Maybe even pull out your smartphone and ask someone to record ten minutes of your morning routine or your afternoon playtime. Then, watch yourself and notice which moments are special, or instructive, or give you pause. *Ask yourself how you might practice the simple interactions that will help you be more deliberate and conscious of contributing to loving moments.*

- Make up a story with your child, perhaps as part of your bedtime routine. Practice creating patterns by using storyboarding techniques. Gregg's daughter wrote a whole week's worth of stories about just the lawn sprinkler by first drawing the elements of her story. *Come up with a list of characters. Think about when and where they are. Identify a problem they're trying to solve. And figure out a solution—or, better yet, many solutions. When it's finished, give it a title and add your names.*

FOUR

Appreciation Is a Holy Thing

Working Together

Ah . . . summertime in Make-Believe.

On the castle balcony, King Friday XIII stares at the sun, marveling—perhaps a little jealously—at its withering power. Daniel Striped Tiger lounges beneath an umbrella, half asleep in the heat. Even Mister McFeely, the speedy deliveryman himself, isn't so speedy today. It's just too *hot*.

But there's good news afoot: Make-Believe has a surplus this year. After all the road repairs and school upkeep and everything else needed to keep a community functioning, the Neighborhood still has some money to spend. And King Friday has an idea.

"I'm planning a spectacular addition to our Neighborhood," he tells his sweltering subjects. "One that may even cool us off."

The news breaks like a wave over Make-Believe: King Friday is building a pool! An honest, real, filled-with-water community swimming pool! Ellen Paterson of Paterson's Pools surveys the land and draws up an estimate.

Relief seems imminent at last. "A cool pool," Paterson says, "for a hot Neighborhood."

That's when the trouble begins.

Maybe it's the heat. Or maybe it's the fact that not everyone *wants* a community swimming pool. Or maybe it's just inevitable when groups of people and puppets work together. Whatever the case, disagreements and disengagement threaten the pool from the get-go.

First, Paterson's estimate comes in higher than Friday had hoped. Then, when the sire asks his subjects to dig the pool themselves—thus saving on labor costs—Daniel Tiger refuses to help. He's worried the work will be hard and the hole will be scary and dark. Lady Elaine complains, too, saying she needs new paintbrushes more than she needs a pool. And when the digging finally gets going, the denizens find that the pipes beneath Make-Believe have burst, sapping the Neighborhood's water and causing a very complicated, very expensive Make-Believe headache.

"I need the telephone *immediately!*" King Friday cries as his half-dug hole fills with wasted water. "Paterson's Pools? This is Friday XIII," he thunders into the receiver. "I wish to report water ahead of schedule. No, it cannot be stopped by us. We need professional assistance!"

....

We all need help sometimes.

In 2006, Felix Warneken and Michael Tomasello—two researchers at the Max Planck Institute for Evolutionary Anthropology in Leipzig, Germany—were studying altruism, the selfless concern for others that drives some of us to extraordinary acts. Hoping to glean some insight into this strange and wonderful impulse, Warneken and Tomasello recruited three young chimpanzees and two dozen eighteen-month-old humans. By comparing the two species, they thought, perhaps they could learn something about where altruism comes from and the role that it plays in nature.

The scientists presented each of their subjects with a problem. A stranger—usually Warneken himself—would enter the room and appear to struggle with something. He'd "accidentally" drop a clothespin, for example, and signal that he couldn't reach it himself. Or he'd struggle to open a cabinet while his hands were full.

Although they'd never met Warneken, nearly every human baby sprang to his assistance, "and they did so basically immediately," Tomasello writes in his book, *Why We Cooperate.* But when Warneken would appear to throw his clothespin on purpose, or when he'd bump a cabinet without trying to open it, the infants did nothing. Fetching objects or opening cabinet doors, it turned out, held no intrinsic appeal. The infants only acted when they sensed their help was needed.

In follow-up studies, children as young as fourteen months proved so eager to assist adult strangers that Warneken and Tomasello had to deploy a distraction activity to keep the babies occupied. But it didn't work; in the vast majority of cases, the babies "pulled themselves away from this fun activity—they paid a cost—in order to help the struggling adult."

As for the chimps, they helped, too, but not nearly to the same degree. Warneken and Tomasello concluded that humans are unique among animals in the ways they help and cooperate with one another. And their drive to work together appears at an impossibly early age.

That's good news for the species. More than almost anything else, our capacity to work together has catapulted human beings to our highest heights.* It's how we put a man on the moon, brought him back alive, and even made time for a little lunar golf. Collaboration built the internet and the International Space Station. It developed democracy and wiped smallpox off the planet. It's responsible, in one way or another, for almost all our modern comforts—and it gave us *Abbey Road* to boot. We owe it a good deal of thanks.

---

* And also, it must be said, to our lowest lows. There's a reason "collaborators" were shunned and shamed in post–World War II Europe. Collaboration gets things done on a grand scale—for better and for worse.

In his 2004 book, *The Wisdom of Crowds*, journalist James Surowiecki explores the power of working together. Under the right conditions, he argues, groups of people tend to make better decisions than even the brightest individual experts. "With most things," Surowiecki writes, "the average is mediocrity. With decision-making, it's often excellence. You could say it's as if we've been programmed to be collectively smart."

Perhaps it's no wonder, then, that crowds—or, more precisely, teams—have largely replaced the kind of old-school pecking orders where one person called the shots. Today, nearly nine out of ten workers spend at least a third of their time in teams, and in survey after large-scale survey, employers consider the ability to work with others a top qualification. Some companies have even hired chief collaboration officers, while others are finding new ways to reward their top team players. The glass-and-ceramics manufacturer Corning, for example, names select employees "fellows," guaranteeing them jobs for life. To become a fellow, employees have to not only author a multimillion-dollar patent—they have to help their colleagues do the same. As Rogers himself once said, "What really matters is helping others win, too, even if it means slowing down and changing our course now and then."

Predictably, people who work well with others tend to punch above their weight. You can be the most curious molecular biologist or the most creative jazz drummer on the planet, but if you can't collaborate, you're not likely to get very far.

The same thing goes for kids. Learning scientists have long known that something powerful happens in social, collaborative settings, partly because hearing and generating language helps forge new neural pathways. The very act of discussing ideas, articulating difficult concepts, and hearing other people's perspectives can rewire children's brains and deepen their understanding. In one study, scientists randomly assigned students to complete a science unit in groups or on their own. After a few weeks, kids who'd gone through the unit in groups outperformed their peers on every single assessment. Even better, the students who'd scored lowest at the unit's outset showed the greatest gains by the end.

But despite the proven benefits of working together, doing so doesn't come easy. In 2015, the Programme for International Student Assessment, or PISA, decided to test teenagers' collaborative skills for the first time, asking fifteen-year-olds around the world to lead computerized bots through a group activity.

The results were bleak. On average across participating countries, fewer than one in ten students maintained an awareness of group dynamics, resolved interpersonal conflicts, and led their bots to triumph. Worldwide, just 8 percent of students qualified as top-level collaborators. Girls scored significantly higher than boys.

To be sure, it's difficult for a test to capture something as complex as collaboration. There are so many ways of working together, and plenty of people have criticized PISA and its methods. However, as anyone who's worked on a dysfunctional team can tell you, good collaborators can often be hard to find.

This worries more than classroom teachers and project managers. Even Congress has taken note, despite a track record of its own that doesn't exactly inspire confidence in its ability to work together. In 2017, the body's Joint Economic Committee released *What We Do Together*, a report chronicling the decline of American social life. Since the 1970s, the report explains, Americans have become less likely to spend time with their neighbors or to see their colleagues outside of work. Likewise, we've drifted away from the meeting places and institutions that used to bring us together. Mixed-income neighborhoods are largely a thing of the past. More and more, our social lives are defined by an ever-shrinking circle of close family members, friends, and people who are just like ourselves.

This might seem like an unusual concern for a congressional committee, especially one whose primary charge is tweaking economic policy. But our inward turn has come with real costs: "We no longer relate to each other so easily beyond our inner circles," the report argues. "The connective tissue that facilitates cooperation has eroded, leaving us less equipped to solve problems together within our communities. So, too, are we less able to collaborate across communities."

The result is a fractured society in which people have largely lost faith in one another. Less than a third of Americans now think most people can be trusted, and young people are far and away the most suspicious of others. No wonder collaboration has suffered—you don't have to *like* other people in order to work with them, but it helps if you trust that they're not out to get you. Sadly, that's not so simple anymore, and it only takes a glance at the headlines to understand why.

Restoring trust on a grand, democracy-fixing scale certainly won't be easy. But if we start small—that is, if we show kids what working together can look like and give them the tools to try it themselves—then perhaps we'll have a chance. "Social research has gathered impressive evidence to show that when people work together for group goals, there are a number of desirable effects on people's feelings for one another," write Rachel Lotan and the late Elizabeth Cohen, two Stanford University professors whose book, *Designing Groupwork*, made them experts on classroom collaboration. "When groups engage in cooperative tasks, they are more likely to form ties, to trust one another, and to influence one another than when the task stimulates competition among members."

Fortunately for us, cooperative tasks are a daily occurrence in the *Neighborhood*, whether we're building a swimming pool in Make-Believe or behind the scenes in Studio A. Day in and day out, we're immersed in a world where people and puppets of every stripe work together for common goals. It doesn't always go well, but in every case, the *Neighborhood*'s denizens make good-faith efforts to resolve their differences and search for solutions.

It's a higher-minded idealism, perhaps, than the program's production values let on. Though it's mostly puppets and papier-mâché, the

Neighborhood is also a small civil society, writes psychologist Lynette Friedrich Cofer—"one in which people work to discover truths about themselves as individuals and truths about the ways in which they are interconnected and can realize shared ends or civic goods."

These are the same truths, experts say, that we're most at risk of forgetting now. And in that regard, the *Neighborhood* has plenty to teach us. The best model for twenty-first-century living and working, it turns out, came together a half century ago in a tiny TV studio in Pittsburgh.

Greater Than the Sum of Its Parts

Mister Rogers enters the living room, donning his usual suit and tie. He changes his shoes as usual, zips up his sweater as usual, and sings his usual song.

But today is no usual day.

"We've been thinking a lot about work," Rogers tells us. "So, I thought I'd like to tell you about some of the work that I do."

The camera cuts away from the living room, revealing the hanging lights and coiled cables of Studio A. We see, for the first time, the men and women behind the scenes directing and filming and pushing the cameras. There's the famous model neighborhood from the title sequence, with its little houses and tiny trolley. There's Johnny Costa at the piano, playing "Won't You Be My Neighbor?" What little existed of the program's fourth wall comes irreparably crashing down.

"It takes a *lot* of people to make television programs," says Rogers, stepping off the set. "A lot of people. And all those people care about you!"

This week's theme—"Mister Rogers Talks About Work"—has taken us to Washington, D.C., to see how people make stamps. We've gone to the *Neighborhood* dairy farm to see where milk comes from; to the *Neighborhood* workshop to learn how people fix things; and to the *Neighborhood* grocery store, where we took a riveting tour of the stockroom. In the Neighborhood of Make-Believe, we've watched people and puppets plan a community swimming pool. We've learned about all kinds of work, and we've seen that no matter what we grow up to do, we won't be working alone. It takes a lot of people to make stamps or stock a grocery store. It takes a team to dig a swimming pool or to make a children's TV program. Whether we grow up to be dairy farmers or grocers or the postmaster general, we can work with and help our neighbors.

And that can be such a good feeling.

In 2012, Google gathered its top statisticians, engineers, psychologists, and others for a singular mission: to build the perfect team. The company had long been interested in using data to improve collaboration, but it had yet to discover a formula that could send its teams to the stratosphere. Project Aristotle—code-named for the philosopher who once called the whole greater than the sum of its parts—aimed to change that.

The project team began by studying fifty years' worth of scientific literature about collaboration, leadership, and more. Then they analyzed data from about some two hundred Google teams, searching for patterns that could help explain why some teams thrived while others crashed and burned.

It didn't go very well. "Some groups that were ranked among Google's most effective teams, for instance, were composed of friends who socialized outside work. Others were made up of people who were basically strangers away from the conference room," writes journalist Charles Duhigg in the *New York Times Magazine*. "Some groups sought strong managers. Others preferred a less hierarchical structure. Most confounding of all, two teams might have nearly identical makeups, with overlapping memberships, but radically different levels of effectiveness."

The company with a better grasp on the world's information than any other entity had been stumped by collaboration. And it might have stayed that way, had Project Aristotle not discovered the work of Amy Edmondson, a professor at Harvard Business School. In 1999, Edmondson had pinpointed an invisible fuel that helps power top-performing teams. The same concept crucial to curiosity, creativity, and communication, it turned out, was also crucial to collaboration: psychological safety.

On many teams, writes Edmondson, "people tend to act in ways that inhibit learning when they face the potential for threat or embarrassment." Where asking for help, admitting mistakes, or disclosing one's ignorance invites ridicule or rejection, team members will generally refrain from doing so—often with disastrous results. In 2005, for example, one survey found that health care workers regularly saw colleagues taking shortcuts or "appearing critically incompetent." At the same time, fewer than one in ten felt safe enough to speak up about it. Perhaps it's no surprise that according to some estimates, medical errors are the third-leading cause of death in the United States.

But on teams that have established psychological safety—that is, "a sense of confidence that the team will not embarrass, reject, or punish someone for speaking up"—team members feel safe to ask questions and admit mistakes. They feel safe to be *themselves*: to voice dissent, seek clarification, and ask for help when they need it. And the learning that results almost always boosts outcomes for everyone.

This takes far more than trust. Psychological safety has to be earned; it cannot exist where members see others as less human, less capable, or less worthy of inclusion. It cannot exist where members sacrifice one colleague's safety for another colleague's comfort, allowing racism or homophobia or hate to fester unchallenged. It cannot exist where even one team member feels that he or she doesn't belong. Psychological safety only takes root where deep trust and mutual respect coincide.

Perhaps you've been fortunate enough to be a part of such a team, where you felt free from the pressure to be flawless, where you could ask for help, admit mistakes, and even express self-doubt. And if you haven't had the luxury, perhaps you've had the feeling. Psychological safety is the difference between a tough job interview and dinner with your closest friends. It's the difference between speaking in public and speaking to your spouse.

Psychological safety can have profound effects on how teams and their members perform. At Google, teams that lacked psychological safety missed their sales targets by an average of 19 percent. By contrast, teams that felt safe *exceeded* their targets by almost the same amount. Googlers on psychologically safe teams were less likely to leave the company, better able to harness creative ideas, and twice as likely to be rated "effective." Without psychological safety, the company concluded, effective collaboration simply doesn't happen.

We've seen this phenomenon elsewhere. When the PISA exam tested students' ability to work together, it also asked about students' well-being. How often, for example, had they felt threatened by their peers, insulted by their teachers, or made to feel otherwise unsafe at school?

The correlations were stunning. On average, kids who had *not* been threatened scored eighteen points higher than kids who had. Those who felt respected by their teachers scored twenty-three points higher than their peers who'd been insulted. The more students felt safe in a given school, the better that school performed overall. When we work with people who make us feel safe and respected, it turns out we learn better—both individually and collectively.

We should note here that psychological safety does not mean the absence of conflict. On the contrary, psychological safety can make conflict *more* likely, because team members feel free to voice dissent. Properly handled, however, conflict can improve the final outcome.

Just ask fans of rock and roll.

Throughout the genre's history, dozens of so-called supergroups have come and gone: Cream, SuperHeavy, and the Hollywood Vampires, just to name a few. At best, some of these groups have managed a catchy song or a half-decent album. At worst . . . well, let's just say there's a reason you've never heard of SuperHeavy. In fact, after fifty-plus years of disappointments, duds, and disasters, it's become a rock-and-roll truism that supergroups rarely work.

But one group managed to buck the trend. In the 1980s, George Harrison assembled the Traveling Wilburys, a band comprised of himself, Roy Orbison, Bob Dylan, Tom Petty, and Jeff Lynne. Perhaps as a result of his time in the Beatles—when he'd been overshadowed by his more-famous bandmates—Harrison knew that for the Wilburys to work, they'd have to address Dylan's near-mythical status. What musician would dare disagree with rock's most revered songwriter?

Harrison came up with a plan. On day one of the supergroup's recording sessions, he turned to his bandmate. "We know that you're Bob Dylan and everything," he said in front of everyone, "but we're going to just treat you and talk to you like we would anybody else."

And Dylan replied, "Well, great. Believe it or not, I'm in awe of you guys, and it's the same for me."

Talk about feeling safe, respected, and fairly treated. Even the band's name reflected an openness to errors and risk. When a band member played a wrong note, Harrison would tell them not to worry. "We'll bury 'em in the mix," he liked to say of mistakes. Hence, the Traveling *We'll-burys*.

The group recorded its first album over the course of a week. *Traveling Wilburys Vol. 1* went triple platinum, earned rave reviews, and even won a Grammy. The band had broken the supergroups' curse.

The Uniqueness and Worth of Every Human Being

Concluding our tour of Studio A, Rogers walks back to his TV living room and pulls out some sheet music. "Another thing I do for my work," he says, "is write songs and then sing them for you. This is a song that I wrote that I like to sing to people that I really care for. Maybe you know it."

Over the course of his career, Rogers wrote some two hundred songs and a dozen operas for the *Neighborhood*, which were arranged and played live by the gifted jazz pianist Johnny Costa and his trio. Nearly all the program's music, Rogers said, sprang from the same underlying goal: "All these songs are really songs about how we feel about ourselves," he explained. "If we can help our children feel accepted and valued when they are small, they'll have a better chance of growing into adults who can feel good about who they are, too."

The song Rogers sings now appeared more frequently than almost any other. It's an affirmation—an assurance that someone out there likes us exactly as we are.

> *It's you I like*
> *Every part of you.*
> *Your skin, your eyes, your feelings*
> *Whether old or new.*
> *I hope that you'll remember*
> *Even when you're feeling blue*
> *That it's you I like,*
> *It's you yourself*
> *It's you*
> *It's you I like.*

It's a message Rogers reinforced for thirty years, deploying the song at every conceivable turn—from quiet moments in his *Neighborhood* living room to his moving duet with Jeffrey Erlanger. And it's no coincidence that he deploys it now, capping off his week of discussing work. Rogers understood then what scientists, educators, and employers are rediscovering now—that when we feel accepted and valued as we are, we're more likely to accept and value others. "How each of us comes to feel about our individual uniqueness has a strong influence on how we feel about everyone's uniqueness," Rogers once said—"whether we grow into adults who rejoice in the diversity of the world's people or into adults who fear and resent that diversity."

In the early 1970s, Lynette Friedrich Cofer, then a young psychologist at Penn State University, set out to study the effects of violent television.

Although she hadn't planned on including the *Neighborhood* in her experiment, she'd recently noticed some changes in her young son. He'd grown more patient and more expressive. He'd been getting along better with his playmates. And perhaps not coincidentally, he'd started watching *Mister Rogers*. "If my child could find such meaning in the program," she thought, "why not include it in our design to see if other children would respond in similar ways?"

She split Penn State's nursery school students into three groups. One watched violent cartoons, another watched neutral films (such as nature documentaries), and another watched the *Neighborhood*. "We selected several sequences of *Mister Rogers* programs in which dilemmas arose and were resolved, focusing on themes such as the uniqueness and worth of each person," she writes.

Each group watched their programs for four weeks. Afterward, Friedrich Cofer found that while children who'd watched violent cartoons displayed a decline in self-control, kids who'd watched the *Neighborhood* showed the opposite. They grew more patient with each other. They were more willing to wait for and help their peers. And just as Friedrich Cofer had seen in her son, the quality of the group's play improved. They became more cooperative, more expressive of their feelings, and more sympathetic toward the feelings of others.

Friedrich Cofer was thrilled. She headed east for Philadelphia to lead follow-up studies with a larger and more representative sample, including children from different races and socioeconomic classes. Though the impact of watching the *Neighborhood* varied from school to school, Friedrich Cofer found that when she paired the program with a teacher who could explain and elaborate upon its themes, kids of every background and circumstance started getting along better with their peers.*

---

* Friedrich Cofer even noted changes among teachers themselves. Watching and talking about the *Neighborhood*, it turned out, made them more enthusiastic and more confident in their ability to work with kids.

The key, she writes, is that "in the *Neighborhood*, feelings, beliefs, and opinions are listened to with respect. Often neighbors are puzzled or don't understand views that are different from our own. In some instances this calls for reassurance; in others it means a series of questions or challenges. But in every case, what is common to each situation is the careful progression and clarification of ideas and feelings that includes all participants."

In other words, problems get solved when everyone talks and everyone gets to be heard, regardless of what they look like or how different their ideas might be. When Daniel Tiger refuses to dig, he's not ridiculed for being scared of a hole. Instead, his friends step in to reassure him. The work will be hard, Lady Aberlin tells him, but also rewarding. As additional challenges present themselves—the broken pipes, the rising water—Make-Believe's denizens have to come to a consensus and decide, together, what they want to do.

The process unfolds over multiple episodes—a deliberate choice, says Bill Isler. After airing single half-hour programs for several years, Rogers "eventually learned that it takes more time to work through problems and ideas. In the real world, problems don't get solved in half an hour, and he wanted viewers to see that. So in 1979, he started doing those five-episode theme weeks."

Research suggests it was the right call. While there's evidence that programs such as the *Neighborhood* can help teach young children how to work together, single episodes aren't typically enough on their own. For viewers to grasp the scope of a program's conflict and make sense of its resolution, repeated exposure is probably necessary, experts say. Collaboration, after all, is complicated and difficult to model, especially for young children. That's why having a caring adult—whether it's a teacher, a parent, or someone else whom a child knows and trusts—can be so helpful. Just as Friedrich Cofer discovered in Philadelphia, subsequent studies have found that adults can enhance a program's benefits by watching alongside children, explaining the program's messages and lessons, and even role-playing similar scenarios.

Anyone, it seems, can become a good collaborator. It takes modeling, practice, and guidance from a caring adult, but the skills required to be a good teammate can be taught like anything else. And often, the best teams are the ones that have figured this out already.

Something Sacred

Just a short walk from Rogers' Studio A, a group of girls gathers in a highbay warehouse on the campus of Carnegie Mellon University. Huddled over wires, wheels, and circuits, they're building a machine that, if all goes well, will crush their competitors and carry the girls to a world championship.

Welcome to Girls of Steel, an all-female competitive robotics team that's become an unstoppable force in the world of FIRST Robotics. An international league based in New Hampshire, FIRST pits student-built robots against one another in matchups that look, to spectators, like part science fair and part science fiction.

Founded in 2010 to get more girls into STEM, Girls of Steel recruits members from elementary, middle, and high schools throughout Pittsburgh, whether they're public or private, well-resourced or low-income. Working with volunteer mentors, the girls learn the fundamentals of building robots, from wiring and coding to meeting the specs handed down by the league. The girls also run the team itself, planning fundraisers, maintaining the website, and handling media outreach and marketing. From the first meeting at Carnegie Mellon in the fall to the first day of competition in the spring, the Girls of Steel have just weeks to build a winning robot—and a winning team.

It's a tall order. The Girls of Steel come from every kind of background; they bring different beliefs, different knowledge, different experiences. When they first arrive on campus, they're not a team at all but rather a group of disparate individuals with no connections to one another and no particular reason to feel safe. "A lot of the girls are nervous when they first get here," says program manager Terry Richards. "They're intimidated by coming to a prestigious university. They don't know anybody. And often, they feel like they don't know *anything*."

It's not exactly a recipe for cohesion—nor, for that matter, for winning a championship. That's why the Girls of Steel developed structures and norms designed to build a sense of psychological safety. For the team to collaborate, Richards explains, "Every girl needs to feel like she's making a contribution. Every girl needs to know that her ideas matter, and that when she speaks, her team is going to listen. Her idea might not work for whatever reason, but we emphasize that that's okay. The important thing is that she puts her voice out there and helps her team coordinate and create something."

At each week's "all-hands" meeting, Richards and the team's other mentors present scenarios drawn from real life—from real problems the girls are grappling with, but fictionalized to be made less personal. (This, of course, is exactly what Rogers did when he deployed his *Neighborhood* puppets.) "We ask them, 'What would you do when you encounter such-and-such situation?'" Richards says. "Each scenario has to do with the team's core principles—integrity, teamwork, safety, communication, respect, and inclusion—but they're not scripted. They're not something the girls read on a screen."

Instead, they're rehearsals for the messy reality of working with other humans. The girls discuss their potential responses and even act them out, giving each other feedback and building a working awareness of how their actions and reactions affect the team as a whole.

It's the kind of preparation, experts say, that's crucial to collaboration. When conflict is handled poorly, it can lead to disengagement, defensiveness, and a team's eventual downfall. It doesn't take much—the human brain tends to treat even slight conflicts as life-or-death threats. When disagreements flare, "the amygdala, the alarm bell in the brain, ignites the fight-or-flight response, hijacking the other brain centers," writes Laura Delizonna, an author and consultant who's worked with teams around the world. "This 'act first, think later' brain structure shuts down perspective and analytical reasoning. Quite literally, just when we need it most, we lose our minds."

That's especially true in adolescence: that anxious and confusing country that's bordered, roughly, by the ages of ten and twenty-five. Despite their reputation for recklessness, adolescents can think and reason just as well as adults do during moments of "cold cognition"—that is, during moments that are free of passionate emotion or peer pressure. In states of cold cognition, adolescents are surprisingly good at predicting consequences and assessing risk, often making far better decisions than adults might expect. (It's adolescents, after all, who've taken the reins on issues from gun violence to racial equity to climate change.)

But as anyone who's been rejected at the middle-school dance can tell you, moments of cold cognition can be fleeting. And because children's brain structures have yet to fully develop, "hot cognition" sometimes poses a problem. When young people are nervous or heartbroken or feeling pressured to look cool, they're far less capable of reasoned judgment. Common sense goes out the window. And when we—their dumbfounded parents—ask whether they've lost their minds, we'd do well to remember that the answer, in a very real sense, is yes.

The good news is that practicing collaboration during cold cognition can help kids work together during hot cognition. That's why exercises like those at Girls of Steel are so valuable. Thinking through conflict in a pressure-free environment can help build safety and respect among team members, who gain a better idea of where their colleagues are coming from. The next time they disagree or find themselves arguing, they'll be less likely to shut down or dissociate from the group altogether.

It's an approach that echoes the *Neighborhood*. "The program modeled the social interactions and the conflict resolution and the everyday decisions it takes to get things done collaboratively," says Roberta Schomburg. "Rogers showed children that things break—things fall apart—but it isn't the end of the project. There was always a way to figure out how to bring it together. Maybe there were some changes in the expected outcome, but people never just threw up their hands and walked away."

Of course, some conflicts defy rehearsal or reason. For particularly difficult cases, some experts suggest exercises that ask quarreling colleagues to consider the following:

> *This person has a body and a mind, just like me.*
> *This person has feelings, emotions, and thoughts, just like me.*
> *This person has experienced physical and emotional pain and*
> *suffering, just like me.*
> *This person has felt unworthy or inadequate, just like me.*
> *This person worries and is frightened sometimes, just like me.*
> *This person has longed for friendship, just like me.*
> *This person wishes to be loved, just like me.*

Reflecting on statements such as these can help team members recognize each other's humanity and approach conflict as collaborators, rather than as opponents who have to be vanquished. "I believe that appreciation is a holy thing," Rogers once said—"that when we look for what's best in a person we happen to be with at the moment, we're doing what God does all the time. So in loving and appreciating our neighbor, we're participating in something sacred."

The Girls of Steel do this by turning to a series of questions, many of which build on the statements above. The questions, says Richards, help team members approach disagreements with compassion and mutual respect.

They begin by grounding girls in a sense of common purpose: *What are the goals of Girls of Steel? What did you hope to achieve by joining?* Then they help the girls express their feelings and needs: *What is your issue, and how do you feel? What would you like to happen?* Next, they push the girls to stretch their perspectives and imagine the feelings of others: *How do you think the other side sees the situation? How do you think the other side feels?* And finally, they give the girls a voice in potential solutions, allowing them the autonomy to work toward consensus—and, if needed, to ask for extra help. *What are your recommendations to solve the issue? What are the recommendations of the other parties involved? Do you need to meet with a mentor to moderate a discussion?*

The result is a team that's both sensitive to its members' feelings and safe enough for girls to speak up. "That's really the key to making Girls of Steel work," says Richards. "They can say what's on their mind. They don't have to be afraid because they don't know something. Instead, they ask questions, because they're around people who aren't going to judge or intimidate them. It takes time, but they develop into these incredible leaders who run the team themselves."

And by any measure, they're running it well. On competition day, the girls—all dressed as Rosie the Riveter—set their contraption loose in the ring, where its mechanical arm grasps at the basketballs that litter the floor. The Girls of Steel shout directions to one another, steering their robot from one place to the next in their drive toward the opposite goal. The other team's robot tries—and fails—to intercept it.

"Whoa!" shouts the announcer. "A little too much pepper on that salad!"

A buzzer blares. The crowd roars.

The Girls of Steel have taken the playoffs.

The Radical Mister Rogers

The Neighborhood of Make-Believe has no choice, King Friday announces: It's no use building a pool if there's no water to fill it. The underground pipes will have to be fixed—and paid for, sadly, with Make-Believe's surplus. There will be no cool pool for this hot Neighborhood. "It will be good to have running water again," the king asserts, doing his royal best to mask his disappointment. "Even if we can't have the community swimming pool."

Ellen Paterson of Paterson's Pools calls in her backup business: Paterson's Pipes. Half of Make-Believe converges on the hole, helping Paterson lug shiny bronze tubes into the hollowed earth. They set the pipes and twist the screws. They wheelbarrow dirt from one pile to the next. They shout instructions and questions to one another, and at one point, they even break for jazz (that most collaborative of genres).

It's a colorful crew. King Friday has arrived on-site, as has Ellen Paterson. There's Lady Aberlin and Lady Elaine, Daniel Tiger and X the Owl. People and puppets—some Black and some brown, some white and some felt—all show up to help. A few, like Ellen Paterson and Handyman Negri, clearly know what they're doing. Others know nothing of municipal water, yet clearly want to help. It takes a lot of people, after all, to do important work.

It takes a team to make the Neighborhood better.

Which brings us, readers, to collaboration's other component. The more a team reflects the world's diversity—in terms of race, gender, ethnicity, experience, culture, and more—the richer and more original and more enduring its output tends to be, whether the team works in a classroom, a corporate office, a government, or a half-dug hole in the *Neighborhood*. On one hand, teams that mirror the world's realities perform better simply by virtue of variety. As Surowiecki notes in *The Wisdom of Crowds*, adding new members almost always makes a team smarter, because the knowledge the new members bring "is not redundant with what everyone else knows."

On the other hand, that new knowledge isn't much use if it isn't heard or it's not taken seriously. Diversity's real potential lies not in simply bringing more members to the table, but in sharing with those members the power to make decisions, allocate resources, and determine the team's direction. And though this tends to frighten rulers like King Friday—born as they were into power and the systems built to sustain it—the *Neighborhood*'s characters discover, again and again, the mutual benefits of true solidarity.

In Make-Believe, characters' differences are treated as unique assets for learning. "Each neighbor is a distinct individual with different strengths and weaknesses, preferences, limits, and possibilities. Each has dignity and worth and something to contribute," Friedrich Cofer writes. And from those contributions come the ideas that move the *Neighborhood* forward—often in unexpected ways. "There are always surprises about which member of the community will come up with the insight that moves others to find middle ground."

In this scene, "middle ground" is more than a metaphor. The crew working in the hole finally fixes the pipes, restoring water to Make-Believe's faucets. But with its surplus spent on repairs, the community's swimming pool remains a distant dream.

Until a new team member steps in.

In many ways, Mayor Maggie of nearby Westwood is King Friday's polar opposite. For one, she's a human—one who governs her community not by fiat but through conversations with advisors and input from her constituents. Where Friday once built a wall along Make-Believe's borders, Mayor Maggie builds bridges. When she heard that Make-Believe needed help with its pipes, she volunteered without delay. And now she has an idea.

For a long time, the citizens of Westwood have tried to think of a way that we could have a community swimming pool. We've even had drawings made by Paterson's Pools.

Now, we have the money for such a pool, but we don't have the water. We've never had a large enough water supply in Westwood for such a venture. Just today, one of our friends suggested that we build the pool midway between this Neighborhood and Westwood. You provide the water, we'll provide the pool, and everyone from both neighborhoods will swim in it. A double community pool!

King Friday thinks for a moment, taken aback by Mayor Maggie's proposal. Here, on one hand, is a chance to build a pool—to make the community better and escape the withering heat. On the other, it's an idea that wasn't *his*. King Friday won't get the credit or the praise or the naming rights. He won't get to make the pool's rules, and he'll have to share it with people outside of his Neighborhood.

And though King Friday has lived his life making laws that suit himself, it's clear that such an approach cannot sustain a community. It's clear that kings alone can't build a Neighborhood that works for everyone—that in order to form a more perfect Make-Believe, the people themselves have to have a voice. And so King Friday does what he's never done before—he gives up some of his power.

"Well," he says, "all in favor of providing water for the midway pool, say aye."

The measure passes democratically. Cheers ring out through the Neighborhood. The midway pool will be built after all—a testament to what's possible when people and puppets bring their unique perspectives to bear on a problem that touches them all. "Each person is in some way different from everybody else," writes Friedrich Cofer, "but similarities bind all human beings together."

For young viewers, it's an indispensable lesson, especially in a country that's more interconnected than ever before. Already, the generation born after 1996 is the most racially and ethnically diverse in U.S. history. Meanwhile, new neighbors continue to arrive from every part of the world: In 2017, some forty-four million foreign-born people called the United States home, the highest share in more than a century.

That's a lot of new and valuable perspectives. And yet you wouldn't necessarily know it from the media we consume. For several years, researchers at UCLA have tracked how well—or how poorly—American media reflects the country's population. Though the statistics have improved slightly since the initiative began, women and people of color remain underrepresented in every conceivable role, even though content that's more representative of the country typically does better by every measure, including ratings, reviews, and revenue.

Children's media is no exception. One analysis found that among children's television programs, female characters were no better represented in 2017 than they had been in 2007. Racial representation fared a bit better, but the bar was outrageously low to begin with. In 1983, about a year before the *Neighborhood*'s swimming-pool episodes aired, a sample of some eleven hundred children's TV characters found just eighty-nine who weren't white. Of those, just forty-two were Black.

Media representation can have real-world effects on children, scientists say. One survey of some four hundred kids, published in the journal *Communication Research*, found that watching television boosted self-esteem—but only for children who were white and male. For white girls, Black girls, and Black boys, self-esteem tended to drop as television consumption climbed, an inverse relationship ascribed to homogenous TV casting. If you can easily see yourself in a program's heroes, the logic goes, then you're more likely to feel good about yourself and your place in society. Conversely, if your TV counterparts—assuming you have them at all—are consistently the sidekicks, the scolds, or even the villains, then you might start to wonder about your own self-worth.

Aisha White directs the P.R.I.D.E. (Positive Racial Identity Development in Early Education) Program, an initiative of the Office of Child Development in the University of Pittsburgh's School of Education. Through training and support sessions, P.R.I.D.E. helps parents, educators, and caregivers learn to counter harmful messages and help Black children feel good about themselves, their heritage, and their race.

If that strikes you as a Rogers-like mission, it won't surprise you to learn that White spent several years working with Rogers himself, directing a program that helped childcare providers use the *Neighborhood* more effectively in their classrooms. Today, in addition to leading P.R.I.D.E.,

White consults for *Daniel Tiger's Neighborhood*, helping animators ensure that the program's characters and scripts are culturally affirming and relevant.

It's important work, says White, in a world where children's media still tends to present white as the norm—as the *preferred* color. Though she's seen books and television and movies grow slightly more reflective of reality over the years, "a lot of kids still don't see themselves or their families in the things they're watching and reading." And given the sheer amount of time that kids spend consuming media—about six hours' worth per day among eight- to twelve-year-olds, according to one survey—"it just makes sense that they should see people who look like them, particularly in important roles."

Kids and families themselves have made this loud and clear. White cites the runaway success of *Black Panther*, the 2018 film praised for its Black superheroes. Not only did *Black Panther* quickly become the first-ever superhero film to receive a Best Picture nomination, it also outearned every solo-superhero film ever made. But more important than its critical acclaim or its box-office success is what *Black Panther* provided for families. "Black parents were so grateful to finally see a film with Black superheroes—superheroes who looked like their children," says White. "It's not that their kids couldn't imagine themselves as superheroes before, because they always have. But kids get so much more from a film when there's someone in it who looks like them. It makes it more personal. It's like an extra gift."

And when it helps kids see themselves in a more positive light, it's a gift that keeps on giving. According to research compiled in a report that launched the P.R.I.D.E program, when Black children feel good about themselves and their identities, it can lead to better academic achievement and better problem-solving skills. It's been linked to lower stress, greater self-esteem, and better health outcomes. And perhaps not surprisingly, it's also been linked to prosocial behaviors—helping, cooperating, and working together.

In fact, it's important for kids of *every* race to see diverse characters portrayed positively in the media, experts say. "If our brains are presented with many images of certain groups of people posing as threats (for example, shown as criminals or terrorists), our brain almost always treats those images as memories," writes Britt Andreatta, author of *Wired to Connect*. As those "memories" accumulate, they can start to intrude on reality, affecting the ways that children perceive, interact with, and ultimately treat their peers.

That's one reason Rogers was so intentional about the images the *Neighborhood* conveyed. Much has been made of the program's civil rights undertones. In one scene from 1969, Rogers invites François Clemmons—the opera singer, actor, and gay Black man who played Officer Clemmons on the program—to join him in cooling their feet in a plastic swimming pool. At the time, pools were proxies for Jim Crow; where Black bathers gathered, white supremacists left nails on pool floors, poured bleach in the water, or closed public pools altogether. By contrast, Rogers stakes an undeniable position in front of the camera. "Cool water on a hot day," he muses, helping Clemmons dry his feet.

The *Neighborhood* is full of pointed affirmations of humanity—an aspect of the program that Maxwell King traces in part to Rogers' time as an undergraduate in Winter Park, Florida. "In one sense, Florida was more diverse than Latrobe in that there were a lot more people of color in his life when he was down there," says King. In another sense, however, it was *less* diverse because of Jim Crow. "And I think Fred, in his own way, took that in and internalized it as something that he wanted to be in a position to do something about."

To that end, Rogers introduced Mayor Maggie of Westwood in the 1970s, bringing a Black woman in a position of power to the *Neighborhood*. The Puerto Rican actor Tony Chiroldes owned the *Neighborhood*'s book-and-toy shop, where he taught his neighbors Spanish words and phrases. The program's guest stars, meanwhile, spanned the full spectrum of abilities, identities, and beliefs. There was Jeffrey Erlanger showing off his wheelchair; Dolly Naranjo crafting Pueblo pottery; Suzie McConnell, the women's basketball legend; and Maya Ying Lin, the architect who designed the Vietnam Wall. Day in and day out, viewers saw every kind of person excelling in every kind of role.

"It's important for children to experience lots of options in terms of who they can be or what they can be, rather than accepting views of their abilities based on what they look like—on one piece of their identity," says White. When Rogers published *First Experiences*, for example—a series of books written to help children face new, often frightening early childhood experiences such as going to the doctor or getting on an airplane for the first time—he ensured that the books' illustrations defied stereotypes and sent children the message that all people grow up to do all kinds of things. A growing list of contemporary children's books aim to teach the same.*

Seeking out such books is a good first step toward raising collaborative kids. But experts caution that it's only a start. Kids *also* need caring adults who can help them make sense of what they're seeing and reading, and who can answer the natural questions that come up when kids notice human differences. And though adults may shirk these questions, preferring instead a "color-blind" approach that downplays differences, such an approach is squarely at odds with the realities children observe. Studies have shown, for example, that kids recognize racial differences at just three months old. By the time they reach preschool, race becomes a factor in who they decide to play with. This happens regardless of parents' self-proclaimed color blindness. Whether or not adults are willing to talk about it, their children are noticing race and striving to make meaning of it.

---

* Lists of these books—including, in some cases, specific recommendations about what parents can look for and discuss with children—are available here:
https://www.naeyc.org/resources/pubs/yc/may2016/culturally-responsive-classroom
https://www.commonsensemedia.org/lists/coretta-scott-king-book-award-winners
https://www.embracerace.org/resources/20-picture-books-for-2020
https://news.harvard.edu/gazette/story/2020/07/antiracist-baby-helps-kids-and-adults -learn/

That's why avoiding the topic won't alleviate racism. On the contrary, color blindness leaves kids to their own devices, signaling that innocent questions are off-limits or unworthy of answers. Without a caring adult to turn to, children develop ideas about race based on their own observations, input from their peers, and the media. This doesn't exactly set them up for success, especially when it comes to a fraught and complicated topic. Instead, experts say, it's better to discuss our differences head-on, even when we find it difficult.

"Lots of adults find it uncomfortable," says White of talking about race with kids. "At P.R.I.D.E., we have a number of things that we suggest for people." First and foremost, she says, "is for adults to respond to questions about race the same way they'd respond to any other kind of question. You don't want to signal to kids that they're doing or saying something wrong when they question racial differences." Likewise, "the conversation should be calm, just like it would be in any other case. And adults should be honest about what they know and what they don't know. If a child asks a question that they don't know the answer to, they can say, 'Well, I don't know, but maybe we could find a book that would help us answer that question together.'"

White and her colleagues also encourage parents and caregivers to be proactive guides when consuming media with their children, asking questions that promote awareness of—and inquiry about—the various ways that stories and characters are presented. "If you're reading a book together," says White, "you might ask, 'Why do you think they drew this person to look this way? Is there another way the author or illustrator might draw this person? What does the author look like? Does the author look the same as the characters?'" Often, these are things that children notice anyway; by asking proactive questions, adults can model that it's good to wonder and ask.

The important thing, says White, is to not avoid the topic when it comes up—and that includes glossing over it under the cover of kindness. While kindness is undoubtedly important, dismissing questions of race and representation with phrases like *We're all equal* or *We're kind to our friends* can deny kids the teachable moments that allow them to grow. Such phrases don't help kids who've been harmed by racism, says White; nor do they help kids understand when they've said or done something hurtful. "I think we can help kids think about [race] in terms of fairness and respect instead," she says. "We can help them understand what it means to be human and to show humanity toward someone." We can show them, in other words, what kindness and caring *really* mean, rather than deploying those words to duck a hard conversation.

Together with this kind of guidance, media that portray characters working together across racial and ethnic lines can positively impact children's attitudes toward people of different groups. The more children see others accepting and celebrating and working across their differences, the more likely they are to do so themselves. We know from the PISA exam that kids in diverse classrooms tend to be better team players. We also know that collaborating across lines of difference can strengthen young people's intercultural ties—ties essential for building healthier schools, communities, and democracies.

Community Weavers and Leaders

Taylor Allderdice High School is a hulking, beige-gray building on a sloping green lawn in Pittsburgh's Squirrel Hill neighborhood, a bustling mashup of cultures, traditions, religions, and food. Its students come from some of the poorest parts of Pittsburgh as well as some of the wealthiest, converging on streets lined with synagogues, churches, Chinese restaurants, specialty shops, and leafy trees that shade the wide boulevards.

It's an idyllic couple of miles—the kind of place you'd picture when you hear the word *neighborhood*. No wonder Rogers made Squirrel Hill his home: The lifelong Presbyterian felt a spiritual kinship with his predominately Jewish neighbors and their concept of *tikkun olam*, or "repairing the world." For much of his adult life, Rogers lived just a few blocks from Allderdice—the school where, in 2016, a first-year student named Peyton Klein looked around and saw that something was wrong.

"I was sitting in homeroom," she remembers, "and I realized I knew everybody's name except for one. I'd grown up in a Jewish household and I believed all these things about being welcoming and understanding, but I wasn't really *living* those values. So I turned and said hello."

The stranger's name was Khwala.

Although Khwala was still learning English—it was only recently that she'd fled her home in Syria—she and Klein managed to bond. The girls shared, after all, something that transcends the limits of language, of borders, and of childhoods spent an ocean and a scripture apart. "We both really, really hated biology," says Klein. "We talked about it every day."

The friendship gave Klein a glimpse into the challenges faced by English language learners. Things that native speakers take for granted, such as meeting with a guidance counselor or getting a schedule changed, become orders of magnitude more difficult. So do everyday things like making friends and doing homework. And then there's the added challenge of prejudice—of being teased on one end of the spectrum and being called a terrorist on the other.

The insight led Klein to launch the Global Minds Initiative, an intercultural organization run entirely by youth. At its core, Global Minds is part conversational English practice and part cultural bridge—a place where students' voices matter, whether they're from Squirrel Hill or Syria. "We always say that diversity is a fact, but inclusivity is a choice," says Klein. "At Global Minds, we make the conscious choice to be inclusive."

What began with Klein and Khwala quickly grew to ten members, then twenty, then one hundred. By the end of its first year, Global Minds took up a whole floor after school. Students came for conversations about diversity and human rights and inequality, says Klein, but they stayed for community—for fellowship and mutual exchange. "At Global Minds, my friends from Ecuador might help me with my Spanish homework, and I might help them with history or math," says Klein. "No one is saving anyone. We're all cocreators. We're all building a community together."

Over time, Klein and her peers developed a curriculum for building positive, diverse communities: a series of exercises and activities that help members discover their similarities and embrace and celebrate their differences. Each week, members start by sharing their name, their hometown, and their answer to "some silly question," says Klein. "It sets a precedent for the way we interact with each other. We're really specific, for example, about name pronunciation and knowing everybody's name. That might sound trivial, but by having everyone share their name and share something about them, it sets a norm: 'We value one another. We value your voice.' It sets the tone for some really great conversations."

Another activity asks members to write down and share four things they bring to the Global Minds community, showing the group that each member has something to contribute. Still another asks members to choose a word that describes them from any language. Students draw a picture of that word, then use their pictures to form a mural. "It's really cool to see how we all have some of the same words, like *family* and *community* and *funny* and *intelligent*, but in different languages. It shows that we have these common bonds."

And discovering those bonds, says Klein, allows for deeper, more meaningful discussions about differences. "So you can ask those questions that you might think are stupid. You can ask those questions you're scared to ask in other spaces. Because here, we're all humans first. Here, we're all community weavers and leaders."

The community they've woven has spread well beyond Allderdice. It's even spread beyond Squirrel Hill. Today, Global Minds boasts some two-dozen chapters across the United States and Canada, comprising more than 3,500 members from fifty countries. It has a staff of high school students who hail from all over the world, an office in Pittsburgh, and a growing list of programs that includes a conference series and a summer leadership academy.

Klein credits the organization's success to its multinational makeup. "You want people who can check your privilege, who can build on each other's ideas, and who can contradict each other in productive ways. That's why we've set the norm that Global Minds leadership should always be 50 percent English language learners and 50 percent native speakers. We want to keep diversity front and center."

Despite the Initiative's growing reach, Klein says she's most proud of the effect that it's had at home. Global Minds has helped change the culture at Allderdice. Classrooms and lunchrooms are less divided; English language learners access far more support; and students form friendships across lines that hadn't historically been crossed. "We've become known for this project of inclusion," she says. "We've become known for being changemakers. We don't ask ourselves, 'What do I want to do when I grow up?' Instead, we ask, 'What can I do *right now?*'"

It's a question that's grown more pressing—and more personal—than Klein and her peers ever imagined. On October 27, 2018, a gunman walked into Tree of Life, a synagogue just up the street from Allderdice. He'd been ranting online that morning about a Jewish nonprofit that provides humanitarian aid for immigrants and refugees—"invaders," the man had called them. Armed with three pistols and an assault rifle, he opened fire on the congregation, killing eleven people and injuring several more.

It was the deadliest attack on Jews in U.S. history. Among Tree of Life's surviving congregants is Peyton Klein herself.

"I think Tree of Life was an awakening," she says, looking back on that morning. "Here's what happens when someone falls victim to stereotypes and doesn't see the glory of humanity. Here's what happens when someone doesn't have the sort of bountiful empathy that we'd been working so hard to cultivate."

For members of Global Minds, the massacre only amplified the importance of their work. It only made that "holy thing," as Rogers once called it, more sacred. After the final shots were fired; after the smoke cleared and the first responders hung their heads; after thousands of strangers stood vigil on a Squirrel Hill street corner; after the city's Muslims raised enough money to cover the victims' funeral costs; what Tree of Life made clear was this: It's the appreciation of one's neighbor that makes the *Neighborhood* real.

Now the young people of the Global Minds Initiative want to take that message to the world. "Listen," says Klein. "We're not going to be discouraged by an act of terror. We're going to use this as an impetus to rise up, move forward, do better, and grow faster. We're going to work against this type of hate. We're going to keep it from taking root. And we're going to do it together—every single day."

WHAT MIGHT YOU DO?

- Help kids team up. "Many creative scientists and writers report collaboration promotes creativity," writes Kyung Hee Kim. "Homes and schools should provide opportunities for students to develop teamwork skills, methods for fairly evaluating peer and self-performance, and mechanisms to accept and incorporate criticism." *Encourage the kids on the street to stage their own musical or launch their own weeding company. Among friends, kids will experiment with negotiation and compromise. Rather than stepping in with rules, encourage them to ensure that everyone gets to be taken seriously and everyone gets to be heard.*

- Model psychological safety by asking for help, expressing your self-doubts, and admitting your mistakes. At Gregg's local school, a teacher and her students created an after-school club, originally designed for girls to tinker, create, and invent. That atmosphere of risk-taking and embracing failure led one student to speak up and raise the issue of bullying. Her words sparked the #BeTheKindKid movement, which has now spread well beyond her school. *How might you, too, create conditions where children feel safe enough to express their fears, misgivings, and concerns?*

- When difficult conflicts arise, let children know that there are ups and downs in every friendship. "Fred used to say, 'It's the people we love the most who can make us feel the gladdest *and* the maddest,'" says Hedda Sharapan. "He wanted children to know that it takes work to repair a relationship, but it's the repairing that really strengthens it." *Speak honestly with children about times when you struggled with friends. What did you do to repair that relationship? How was that relationship stronger in the end?*

- Talk to your kids about the collective effort required to make their favorite TV shows, toys, or desserts. Rather than ruining the magic, you'll be showing them that they, too, can create such things with the help of others. *"Do you know how I made this unicorn cake? Well, yes, I made it right here in our kitchen, with your grandma's help; but I couldn't have done it without the ingredients. And I had to go to the store to get the ingredients, and the people who work there helped me find the right things. Of course, they didn't make the flour; that came from a mill. Oh, and before I did anything, I watched that Nerdy Nummies video on YouTube. . . . "*

- Talk to your kids, also, about what and who they're seeing in the media they consume. When the topic of race or human differences comes up, discuss it as calmly and honestly as you'd discuss anything else. *"We recommend to adults that they practice,"* says Aisha White. *"We recommend that they practice having these conversations with adults before they have conversations with children. Because otherwise, adults will be uncomfortable if it's something that's unfamiliar to them."*

FIVE

It's You Who Have to Try It and It's You Who Have to Fall (Sometimes)

Learning and Growing

Mister Rogers comes through the door with a leather-bound book and a legal pad. He's got that look in his eye—that look that tells us he's learning. He's launched a new project, maybe, or he's had a new idea. Whatever it is, we've seen that look before—when he brought us the player piano; when he took us along to the shoe store; and when he found his childhood ventriloquist dummy, Hischer Booptrunk, and showed us how it works.

There are so many things to learn about, he always likes to say. And today it's clear that he's learning something new. "Yes," he says, "I'm trying to learn the Greek language. And I have a *really* splendid teacher."

On his legal pad, he writes a few letters—first, the letter *A* from the Greek alphabet, then a *G*, then a *P*. Pretty soon, we've guessed the word's meaning before he even says it aloud. (Mister Rogers may have many interests, but he's nothing if not consistent.)

"*Agape!*" he says. "That's one way you say 'love' in Greek. In fact, there are so many ways of saying and expressing love in this world."

He starts to sing a song about that very idea when suddenly the sound of a whistle whips through Studio A. Mister McFeely is here, and he's brought with him Eileen McNamara, a professional singer and whistler. McNamara whistles some birdcalls and a happy improvised tune, and Rogers leans in to listen, clearly in awe of her skill. "Who taught you to whistle?" he asks.

The whistler replies that as a little girl, she'd asked her father to teach her. "I was fascinated when I was little, listening to him [whistle] all the time," she says. "I'd watch him and I'd listen. And I'd try to imitate it."

At first, the point of the scene seems clear: With a splendid teacher or a patient father, it won't be long before you're speaking Greek like Rogers or singing with the birds like McNamara. It almost sounds *easy.*

And so what Rogers says next feels, in many ways, like a confession.

"That's something I've tried and tried to do, but I just never learned very well," he tells McNamara. He purses his lips to whistle, but instead there's only silence. Mister Rogers—the TV neighbor who can play the piano, paint pictures, sing songs, and make Hischer Booptrunk talk—has done what we rarely see him do.

Mister Rogers has failed.

In 1868, an obscure writer hit it big with his fourth novel, *Ragged Dick.* An instant bestseller, the book told of a shoe shiner whose virtue, work ethic, and sheer determination helped lift him from poverty and into the middle class. Remaining in print for forty-plus years, Horatio Alger's book tapped—and perpetuated—the seductive idea that all people, with enough hard work, can succeed in their chosen endeavors.

They simply have to persist.

We can't get enough of stories like Alger's. You've probably heard, for example, that before he changed our understanding of the universe, Albert Einstein flunked math. Likewise, before becoming a basketball legend, Michael Jordan claimed he was cut from his high school team. And Oprah Winfrey was fired from her first job in television, deemed unfit for the medium. Each of these icons suffered a serious setback, yet each persisted until they dominated—and even defined—their respective fields. What's more American than that?

"Nothing in the world can take the place of persistence," said Calvin Coolidge, the nation's thirtieth president. "Talent will not; nothing is more common than unsuccessful men with talent. Genius will not; unrewarded genius is almost a proverb. Education will not; the world is full of educated derelicts. Persistence and determination alone are omnipotent."

It's an ethos that's built into everyday life. Schools are plastered with quotes from Winston Churchill ("Never, ever, ever give up") and Vince Lombardi ("Winners never quit, and quitters never win"). Some have taken to measuring and even grading students' "grit," a term for passion and perseverance coined by author and psychologist Angela Duckworth.

Meanwhile, stories of persistence-despite-the-odds are grist for the media's mill. How many times have you encountered a headline like these?

- Beating the odds, more than 100 homeless students in New York City graduate high school (CNN)
- 9-year-old sells $6K worth of lemonade to help sick brother (Associated Press)
- Man walks 15 miles to work every day: "No excuses" (*The Today Show*)

Stories like these are our modern-day Alger novels, harkening back to America's original promise—that no matter who you are, the only thing standing between you and success is dogged determination. The only difference between the people at the top and everyone else is that the

Einsteins, Jordans, and Winfreys of the world tried harder or sacrificed more or walked more miles to work. Above all, they resolved to never, ever, ever give up.

It's a fundamentally American myth. And like most American myths, there's a kernel of truth to it. Perseverance is, without a doubt, an essential part of success. No one does anything great by throwing in the towel at the first or the fiftieth sign of trouble. Without perseverance, we wouldn't have WD-40 (which takes its name from the number of attempts required to perfect the solvent's formula) or Dyson vacuum cleaners (which came on the heels of some 5,200 failed prototypes).

Nor would we have lifesaving antibiotics. As author Bill Bryson writes in *The Body: A Guide for Occupants*, scientists searched for two years to find a mold strong enough to produce commercial penicillin. And they might have given up, had a lab assistant not brought in a cantaloupe to share with her colleagues for lunch. After scraping some mold off the rind, the scientists found it was two hundred times more powerful than anything else they'd found. The fruit was eaten, Bryson writes, "but the mold lived on. Every bit of penicillin made since that day is descended from that single random cantaloupe."

Perseverance, in other words, certainly has its place.

But there's more to success than simply sticking with it. Horatio Alger, of all people, struggled to support himself financially, despite writing dozens of rags-to-riches books. Albert Einstein never flunked math—his grades were exceptional, and he was baffled by rumors that he'd been a poor student. Michael Jordan was never cut from his high school team—he was assigned to junior varsity, as was every other sophomore except for one, who happened to be six foot seven. In fact, of all the icons mentioned above, only Winfrey's story hasn't been stretched.

Winston Churchill never said, "Never, ever, ever give up," Vince Lombardi quit job after job, and Calvin Coolidge never uttered a word about persistence. The quote attributed to him—and slapped on posters, greeting cards, and coffee mugs ever since—predates him by half a century and doesn't mention persistence at all. Instead, in its original form, it emphasizes *purpose.*

The distinction cuts to the heart of a modern debate about learning. While nearly everyone agrees that perseverance counts, a growing chorus of scientists, educators, parents, and others are calling for a more balanced approach to helping kids succeed. Perseverance alone, they argue, doesn't necessarily predict a person's success. Nor is it particularly easy to teach; most of the programs that claim to boost it hold "limited value," writes Marcus Credé, a psychologist at Iowa State University.

Instead, if we want to help kids do difficult things, it helps to consider the *conditions* that make perseverance possible. It helps to admit that the zealous pursuit of a singular goal—memorizing facts or formulas, or playing piano at Carnegie Hall—might work for some children, while a more meandering path will likely work better for others. In fact, "eventual elites typically devote *less* time early on to [the] activity in which they will eventually become experts," writes David Epstein, author of *Range.* Instead, they go through what researchers call a "sampling period"—they try out lots of different things, many of which have little or nothing to do with their eventual vocation. They grow successful not because they've persevered toward an immutable goal but because they've been given the permission and the privilege to go out and discover their purpose.

Rogers himself experienced such a period. "Throughout his life, he developed all these different interests," says Maxwell King. "At one point, he was going to be a French teacher. Then he was going to be a diplomat. Then he was going to run some sort of institution for very young children who needed help. Then he was going to be a Presbyterian minister, which of course he did later become. And then he decided to go into television." Rogers knew that a large part of his success had come from pursuing different interests without having to worry about where they led or whether they'd become a career.

Hence the sheer variety of *Mister Rogers' Neighborhood.* A single episode might span the letters of the Greek alphabet; several types of whistles; visits from various professionals; a meditation on wind mechanics; and much, much more. At no point are viewers pressured to take to something; the goal is simply exposure and sampling. If viewers find themselves drawn to whistling, that's wonderful. If not, that's okay, too—even Mister Rogers moves on to other things. He asks only that viewers try.

"Life is marked by failures and setbacks and slip-ups as much as by hard-won satisfactions and sudden discoveries of unexpected strength," he wrote. "We need to help children understand that for us, as for them, life is made up of *striving* much more than attaining."

That's as true now as it's ever been. Attainment matters, but it's also temporary. In a fast-changing world, a skill that's useful today can be automated tomorrow. "[People] can expect to switch jobs, see whole sectors disrupted, and need to develop additional skills as a result of economic shifts," notes a report by the Brookings Institution. "The type of work they do at age 30 likely will be substantially different from what they do at ages 40, 50, or 60."

The people themselves will be substantially different, too. Despite the belief that we get stuck in our ways as we age, the process of personal growth never actually stops, no matter how old we are. As Epstein puts it, "The precise person you are now is fleeting, just like all the other people you've been." That's why *striving* counts as much as attaining. If we design our lives around getting that dream job or achieving a certain social status, we risk unhappiness and even disaster.

In 1958, a young writer named Hunter S. Thompson penned a letter to a friend who'd asked for life advice. Though Thompson was just twenty-two years old at the time and still a decade away from finding his own purpose—redefining American journalism—his words proved remarkably prescient.

When you were young, let us say that you wanted to be a fireman. I feel reasonably safe in saying that you no longer want to be a fireman. Why?

Because your perspective has changed. It's not the fireman who has changed, but you. Every man is the sum total of his reactions to experience. As your experiences differ and multiply, you become a different man, and hence your perspective changes. This goes on and on. Every reaction is a learning process; every significant experience alters your perspective.

So it would seem foolish, would it not, to adjust our lives to the demands of a goal we see from a different angle every day? How could we ever hope to accomplish anything other than galloping neurosis?

. . . The goal is absolutely secondary: It is the *functioning* toward the goal which is important.

What is it, then, that allows a child to strive—to function toward a goal or a purpose of his or her choosing? What is it that drives kids to keep growing and learning, even when it's difficult? And how do they develop the trust and confidence they need to persevere—or, when necessary, to take a risk and pivot?

Fortunately, Fred Rogers left us some answers.

Love, or the Lack of It

"Ohhhhhhh, me. Ohhhhhhh, my."

In the Neighborhood of Make-Believe, H. J. Elephant III speaks his magic words—the droning incantation that precedes his vanishing act. As he explains to the children at the Neighborhood school, speaking these syllables summons a rush of wind that will carry him off in an instant, only to bring him back a few moments later to the exact spot where he stands. It's a trick he calls *boomerang magic*, and sure enough, a gale kicks up in the classroom.

It's a complicated, fantastical act, and H. J. Elephant has been honing his skills for weeks. A friendly puppet whose favorite color is that of his own skin ("pinkish-yellowish-brownish-orange"), H. J. prepares to boomerang up to the clouds when a soft-spoken pupil timidly raises her hand.

It's Ana Platypus, and she'd like H. J. to stop, please. She likes it when he boomerangs back to the classroom, but it scares her when the wind comes to whisk him away. "When he said, 'Ohhhhhhh, me. Ohhhhhhh, my,' I thought *I* was going to blow away, too," she tells the class.

H. J. stops what he's doing—the last thing he wants is to scare anyone. The wind in the classroom dissipates. H. J.'s lesson on boomerang magic will have to wait.

But then Ana has an idea. She looks at Daniel Tiger, the classmate who sits to her right. "Maybe," she asks, "I could hold Daniel's paw?" The classmate to her left volunteers as well. "I would like to hold Ana's hand," says Prince Tuesday. The three of them link their arms and paws, forming a windproof puppet-chain to withstand the boomerang's breeze.

Ana asks H. J. to try his trick again. This time, with support from her friends, she's not so scared. On the contrary, she feels safe. She feels steadied. And now she feels ready to learn.

There's a reason Rogers launched this five-part series, dubbed "Mister Rogers Talks About Learning," with *agape*. The *Neighborhood* hinged on his long-held belief that learning and love are linked—that "love is at the root at everything," as he once said in an interview. "All learning. All parenting. All relationships. Love, or the lack of it."

It's a lesson that lingers in every part of the *Neighborhood*. In the scene above, Ana Platypus feels threatened—both physically and psychologically—by H. J. Elephant's boomerang magic. The wind seems as if it can blow her away; the speed at which H. J. vanishes feels sinister. But with the love and support of her friends, she finds the strength she needs to forge ahead.

In another scene from the "Learning" series, Rogers plays viewers a video montage: There's a mother teaching her son to roller-skate, a coach teaching a girl to play basketball, and friends teaching one another how to pot a plant. "There are so many ways—*so many ways*—of learning things," Rogers explains. "And do you know what the best way is? To have somebody you love help you."

It sounds unscientific, but scientists today will largely tell you the same. Jo Boaler is a professor of mathematics education at Stanford University, where her efforts to make math more accessible to students around the world have garnered international renown. In Boaler's view, the reason so many people shy away from math isn't a lack of intelligence. It's anxiety—the very same anxiety that Ana Platypus felt in the *Neighborhood*.

"Anxiety in any subject area has a negative impact on the functioning of the brain," Boaler writes in her book, *Limitless Mind*. Neuroscience has shown that when we're anxious or stressed or scared, several changes occur in our heads. Our working memory—the cognitive system that lets us juggle data and use it to solve problems—short-circuits. Our performance takes a nosedive, and because we've done poorly, we're even *more* anxious the next time around. A vicious cycle commences, "a pattern of harmful beliefs soon follows," and before we know it, we're giving up on math (or music, or science) altogether.

If we want kids to stick with something, experts say, we need to take a different approach at the beginning—one that reduces the stress and anxiety that we seem to insist on inflicting. How many times have children heard that half their class will fail, or that no one ever earns an A from a particular teacher? How many times have they been rushed through assignments and tests, told that time matters more than their learning? Tactics like these might aim to convey difficulty and inspire hard work, but they also provoke anxiety, reduce psychological safety, and push promising young people away. The less a child perceives a sense of love, the less likely she is to learn.

Love or the lack of it, indeed.

By contrast, the *Neighborhood* helped kids do hard things by making them feel safe and nurtured enough to be able to push *themselves*. Despite the widespread misbelief that he'd served in Vietnam, Rogers is no drill sergeant—he never tells viewers that half of them aren't good enough. He never injects unneeded stress by scolding kids for their speed or shaming them for making mistakes. The *Neighborhood* recognized that learning happens best *without* the extra anxiety that's often heaped on by adults.

"Children always knew, for example, what they were going to see and where things were," says Roberta Schomburg. "He didn't just randomly move things into different places. They could really trust that things would be where they ought to be, and if something was out of order, there was a reason and a conversation about why it had been moved. For so many kids, that's very important, because their lives can seem chaotic to them sometimes."

We see this in action at the Neighborhood school, where H. J. Elephant's boomerang magic—and all its chaotic wind energy—overwhelmed Ana Platypus. It's a scene that, for all its whimsy, reflects real life: When learners are faced with a threat, their bodies release stress hormones. Adrenaline and cortisol make their hearts pump faster and their muscles tense. Their bodies prepare to run, fight, or freeze.

In small doses, responses like these can be good things. Stress can motivate us. It can help us rise to difficult challenges and—if necessary—escape danger. When our stress-response systems are working like they're supposed to, stress hormones dissipate after the threat has passed. Our muscles and minds relax, and our bodies go back to baseline. Over time, we learn to take on bigger and bigger challenges, managing healthy levels of stress along the way.

But what happens when the threats keep coming and there's no one to turn to who makes us feel safe? What happens when we can't relax and can't get back to baseline? What happens when stress *is* the baseline? Suppose Ana Platypus hadn't been supported that day at school—that her classmates had ignored her or even bullied her. And suppose she'd gone home to an empty house with no food and no one to ask how she's doing. Suppose her parents work multiple jobs just to keep the lights on. Suppose there's an eviction notice on the door.

It's far-fetched in the *Neighborhood*, but it's something close to reality for countless American kids. When adversity becomes the norm and daily existence is a fight to survive, the cumulative stress of it all can wreak havoc on bodies and brains. Our stress-response systems work overtime, blaring warnings even after an immediate threat has passed. The constant presence of stress hormones disrupts digestion, sleep, memory, and more, increasing the risk of every imaginable calamity. It's a state researchers call "toxic stress," and its effects on kids can be catastrophic.

Toxic stress has always been with us, but our ability to quantify its effects is relatively recent. Throughout the mid-1990s, researchers from the Centers for Disease Control and Prevention (CDC) collected survey responses from some seventeen thousand adults. How often, the surveys asked, had the adults been abused physically or emotionally as children? How often had they felt loved, hated, or neglected? Had their childhood homes been dysfunctional or violent? To what degree, in other words, had they experienced toxic stress as kids?

When the researchers compared the survey data to respondents' outcomes as adults, they were shocked by what they found. Nearly two-thirds of adults reported at least one Adverse Childhood Experience, or ACE. Nearly a quarter reported three or more. The more ACEs a person reported, the higher their risk for heart disease, depression, addiction, and more. Compared to people who reported zero ACEs, adults who reported four or more were twice as likely to have had cancer and seven times more likely to struggle with alcoholism. People with six or more ACEs were thirty times more likely to have attempted suicide.

Recent studies have shed even more light on ACEs.* One found that people with six or more ACEs die, on average, nearly twenty years earlier than their peers. Another found that while ACEs affect people from every

---

* The term itself has expanded to include experiences outside the home—things like violence in a child's community, being suspended or expelled from school, or experiencing racism—because the body's stress-response system reacts the same way regardless of the source of a threat.

walk of life, people of color, LGBTQ populations, and people with annual incomes of less than $15,000 tend to have higher ACE counts than others. Yet another found sobering links between ACEs and incarceration: Four out of five young people who'd been arrested and detained in Chicago reported childhood physical abuse. Even years after their time in detention, their risk of dying young was more than quadruple that of their peers.

Through no fault of children's own, toxic stress takes a devastating toll on learning and growing. Kids whose inner alarms are constantly going off—whether due to hunger, racism, a pending eviction, a loved one's lack of health care, or any other combination of traumas—can get caught in a cycle that's hard to escape. According to author Paul Tough:

> Students don't learn to read on time, because it is harder for them to concentrate on the words on the page. They don't learn the basics of number sense, because they are too distracted by the emotions and anxieties overloading their nervous systems. As academic material becomes more complicated, they fall further behind. The more they fall behind, the worse they feel about themselves and about school. That creates more stress, which tends to feed into behavioral problems, which lead to stigmatization and punishment in the classroom, which keep their stress levels elevated, which makes it still harder to concentrate.

The systems in which children find themselves are rarely designed to support them through toxic stress. In fact, young people (particularly Black students) are often punished or pushed out of their learning environments for expressing the very challenges that keep them from learning. This can lead to a child's first contact with the juvenile justice system and a damaging criminal record—a cycle known as the *school-to-prison pipeline*.

The consequences are beyond costly. Experts call toxic stress a national public-health crisis that dwarfs even the opioid epidemic. The problem is so severe and so rampant that Dr. Nadine Burke Harris, a leading researcher in the study of ACEs and the first surgeon general of California, has called for screening every student for childhood trauma. As she envisions it, "A school nurse would also get a note from a physician that says: 'Here is the care plan for this child's toxic stress' . . . Instead of reacting harshly and punitively, every educator is trained in recognizing these things. Instead of suspending and expelling or saying, 'What's wrong with you?' we say, 'What happened to you?'"

Preventing and healing ACEs, experts say, would avert some two million cases of heart disease and twenty-one million cases of depression. An extra 1.5 million students would stay in school instead of dropping out, and communities would collectively save hundreds of billions of dollars a year. Of course, prevention and healing would require a shift in the country's priorities—one that marshals our resources to meet every child's needs. "By ensuring that all children have access to safe, stable, nurturing relationships and environments," writes a team of researchers from the CDC, "we can prevent or alleviate the effects of ACEs."

Study after study has shown that nurturing relationships and environments can act as a buffer against toxic stress. In his book *How Children Succeed*, Tough cites a study in which baby rats who'd been licked and groomed by their mothers excelled in every regard. They were better at mazes and lived longer, healthier lives. Remarkably, it didn't matter *which* mother had shown them love and care. "When a pup received the comforting experience of licking and grooming as an infant, it grew up to be braver and bolder and better adjusted than a pup who hadn't, whether or not its biological mother was the one who had done the licking and grooming," writes Tough. The implication is that every adult—whether a parent or not—has a role to play in helping children thrive.

In 2019, researchers from Brigham Young University found that so-called counter-ACEs could set people up for long, healthy lives, even if they'd experienced toxic stress. Among the study's small sample, participants who'd endured four or more ACEs turned out to be just as healthy as those who'd experienced none—but only if they *also* reported counter-ACEs, such as positive relationships with neighbors and friends, attention from trusted caregivers, and predictable routines at home.

A separate study, published in *JAMA Pediatrics*, came to a similar conclusion. Its authors calculated a "positive childhood experiences" score for each participant, asking how often they'd been given space to discuss their feelings when they wanted to, how often they'd felt supported by their friends, and how often a nonparent adult had taken a genuine interest in them. The higher their positive childhood experiences score, the more they flourished as adults, even if they'd experienced ACEs.

When it comes to doing difficult things, it's important to remember that plenty of kids are doing difficult things already. Many have endured far more than their share. To succeed in their chosen endeavors, they need a sense of persistence, yes—but they *also* need relationships that help them weather life's tempests. They need safe, affirming environments that meet their basic needs, letting them relax, learn, and be themselves in full. And they need opportunities to sample life's flavors while they search for their purpose—the thing that makes them tick, even when that thing gets tough.

That's the idea behind Remake Learning Days, a family-friendly festival billed as "the world's largest open house for the future of teaching and learning." First launched in Pittsburgh in 2016, the festival—comprised of hundreds of events held over several days—brings families and kids together to sample new ways of learning in comfortable, low-stakes environments. In an old theater, for example, kids and families might build robotic replicas of their favorite movie characters. Or they might learn how to spot invasive plants and turn them into paper. Whatever the focus, each event does what Rogers did in the *Neighborhood*: provides opportunities for "sampling" in families' own neighborhoods and on their own terms, with an emphasis on discovery, community, and joy.

Dorie Taylor is a mother and connector who works with arts and education organizations to strengthen their engagement and community-building efforts. She's also the festival's producer, and the many hats she wears reflect the variety of Remake Learning Days. "We have more than two hundred events in southwestern Pennsylvania every year, and they're organized by lots of different themes: the arts, making, outdoor learning, science, technology, and youth voice," she says. The events take place everywhere from museums and parks to community centers and schools, and more often than not, they blend those themes together. "There's one event in particular that my family goes to every year," says Taylor. "It's held at an art museum, but you spend your time outside making paint out of leaves. So it's this great mashup of art, science, and nature where you get a little bit of everything."

Learning, says Taylor, isn't limited to the classroom or the school day. It's something that can happen in any place at any time in any community, and Remake Learning Days honors and uplifts that learning. Kids and families are drawn to the festival because "there's no pressure. You don't have to know or have the answers. You're just learning and discovering, and you're doing that with the people you care about."

Each event is designed to be fun—they *have* to be fun to draw families on weekends and after school—but also to give kids a glimpse at the hobbies, activities, and even potential careers that they might not encounter during the course of a typical school day. Taylor recalls one event at Schell Games, a Pittsburgh-based video game company that hosts an annual open house during Remake Learning Days. "Hundreds of families showed up," she says, "and they got to meet the people who make video games and even the people who make the music for video games. So if your kids are interested in technology or music or digital media, this was one more place where they could learn more about it, and maybe dig deeper if that's what they decide to do."

This sort of exposure is also important for parents and caregivers. When adults sit side by side with children in a robotics lab, or when they navigate a homemade video game for the first time, they walk away with a deeper understanding of what and how young people want to learn. They see up close the things that make their children light up—an insight that they can then use to support their children's learning. "It was during a Remake Learning Days event," says Taylor, "that my kids interacted with robots for the first time." Seeing how *into it* they got led her and her husband to look for similar opportunities as a family. "We said, 'Wow, our kids really liked this thing, so let's look for more ways we can do that thing in the community.' We even bought a robot that they could tinker with at home."

Research suggests that opportunities like these contribute to positive childhood experiences by bringing kids and their caregivers closer together. According to data collected by the Global Family Research Project, young people who attend Remake Learning Days with a parent or another family member are far more likely to say they "loved" the experience than their peers who attend alone. Although adults tend to assume that kids don't want us around, that hasn't held true at the festival. "Once adults are engaged in what's happening, children have a better experience *because* their parents or grandparents or caregivers are there," says Taylor.

To that end, the festival's organizers have worked to make Remake Learning Days more accessible, more welcoming, and more joyful every year. Many event hosts provide food and childcare, reducing families' barriers to attending. They've also deliberately clustered events in rural areas and in neighborhoods that have long been underserved. "Innovation happens everywhere, and we want to lift that up and showcase it," Taylor explains. "Kids and families don't need to leave their neighborhoods and drive across town to a museum or institution. Remake Learning Days happen in *your* community and *your* neighborhood. They happen in places that are close and comfortable, like the library across the street. We try to make that the case in as many neighborhoods and communities as possible."

So far, it seems to be working. Remake Learning Days drew more than ninety thousand families in its first few years, earning accolades from the World Economic Forum and drawing interest from India, New Zealand,

Spain, and beyond. Remake Learning Days Across America has since taken root in more than a dozen cities and regions from coast to coast. In eastern Kentucky, for example, "one business in particular—a sewing store—opened its doors to families during the festival. The owner set up a table and chairs, invited families in, and taught them how to make things," says Taylor. "Now she does it all the time. Remake Learning Days was the impetus for that." Other regions have hosted events in senior centers, giving kids and older adults the opportunity to learn from and with one another.

The festival, she says, can happen in "any city, any region, any country." And while organizing anything that comprises multiple days and events will take time and money, the festival's core idea is timeless and free.* "Here's what Remake Learning Days is," says Taylor. "It's going somewhere in your community or in the community next door. It's gathering with other people from multiple generations. It's learning by doing—it's hands-on. That can look a lot of different ways, but it's always valuable. Nothing can replace that kind of learning experience. Nothing."

Effort Plays a Part

"There it goes *again!*" Lady Aberlin shouts, dashing across the Make-Believe street. "Now where is that high wind coming from?"

She's been chasing it now for two episodes, holding a purple-and-orange contraption at various heights. With her "wind machine," she checks for wind at King Friday's castle and along the trolley's tracks. She checks at the Neighborhood museum and looks beneath a Neighborhood tree. It's a slow, painstaking experiment. Sometimes, the machine's tiny blade picks up a breeze and spins. Sometimes, it droops like a flag on a still summer day. And other times, it spins and stops without any obvious cause.

---

* The Remake Learning Days organizers have created a virtual tool kit for people who are interested in hosting the festival where they live: https://remakelearningdays.org/acrossamerica/.

Lady Aberlin sighs. She's worked so hard on her research, but the wind source still seems elusive. She checks her notes and checks them again. Finally, she decides to visit the Neighborhood school, where H. J. Elephant is getting ready to blast off.

"Ohhhhhhh, me. Ohhhhhhh, my."

A gust of wind whooshes through the school, lifting the blades of the wind machine. "That's it!" Lady Aberlin cries. "Just what I needed! Oh, thank you—I must report my data!"

She rushes off, ecstatic, and pretty soon we're back in Rogers' living room, where he's waiting to explain what happened.

"Lady Aberlin," he tells us, "worked and worked and finally found out where that extra wind was coming from. Sometimes, it takes a lot of trying to learn something. The important thing was that she *kept on* trying."

Indeed, nothing comes easy to the *Neighborhood*'s characters, whether in Make-Believe or the "real" world of Studio A. Lady Aberlin's wind research takes time and meticulous effort. H. J. Elephant's boomerang magic takes lots of practice and several stalled attempts. Even the professionals to whom we're introduced—Eileen McNamara the whistler, Bill Strickland the potter, and Mary Sherred the spoon player—all explain to viewers the labor it took to develop their skills. No one in the *Neighborhood* is a "natural" or a "genius." Some might have aptitudes for one thing or another, but their worthwhile achievements always come down to effort.

By showing this again and again, Rogers helped to lay the foundation for children's sense of industry—the feeling that they can use their skills to do and make important things. "If we see kids who don't have that sense of industry by the time they're teenagers, it's hard to go back and foster it," says Schomburg. "Once children have an attitude about working and being productive, it's easier to keep it going by showing them that some things are never finished—that you have to keep working at it if you want to make it better. Of course, there are also times when a task is complete and children can take pride in work well done."

It's a lesson that Rogers embodied in his own life from high school onward. As a classmate remembers in King's biography, Rogers was "head and shoulders above everybody else in terms of the fine arts, poetry, [and] reading." At the same time, he was also sickly, shy, and frail, with a notable lack of athleticism—traits that might not matter in adulthood, but that don't always make for a happy, confident high school student. "[I] was scared to death to go to school," Rogers recalled. "Every day, I was afraid I was going to fail."

But instead of withdrawing, Rogers made a concerted effort to keep trying. When he gave a school speech, his classmates laughed at his high, squeaky voice, but Rogers "plowed right through it," a friend told King. When an injury sent the school's star athlete to the hospital, Rogers—at his mother's behest—went to his classmate's bedside and helped catch him up on schoolwork. The two kids couldn't have been more different, but their friendship helped Rogers come out of his shell. More than anything, says King, it gave Rogers a sense of social acceptance—something he'd never really known. And his confidence began to blossom.

By the time Rogers graduated, he was "almost as much of a star" as his football-player friend, says King. He'd written for the school newspaper and become president of the student council. He'd found a door to the Ivy League in his admission to Dartmouth College. And he'd done it all thanks to two things: support and encouragement from his family, and his willingness to keep trying in the face of adversity.

It's the kind of story we tell ourselves we like—in the home of Horatio Alger, hard work and effort mean more than anything else. But evidence suggests that deep down, we actually believe the opposite. Writing in the *Atlantic*, journalist Jerry Useem describes the work of Chia-Jung Tsay, a psychologist and professor at University College London. "Tsay asked professional musicians to listen to audio clips of two pianists, one described as a 'natural,' the other as a 'striver,'" Useem writes. "Despite the fact that the two pianists were really one pianist playing different sections of the same composition—and in flat contradiction to the listeners' stated belief that effort trumped talent—the musicians thought the 'natural' sounded more likely to succeed than the 'striver,' and more hirable."

Indeed, the notion that success is a product of fixed, innate talent is more pervasive than one might think. One survey of academics from thirty different disciplines found that the more a field valued "natural brilliance," the fewer women and Black people that field included. Beliefs about natural brilliance—about who has it and who doesn't—had manifested as messages, inviting some people in and telling others to keep out, regardless of their *actual* brilliance.

Those messages affect little kids in big ways, argue Andrei Cimpian and Sarah-Jane Leslie, two researchers involved in the survey. Adults, they say, can broadcast negative messages to kids even without meaning to—indeed, even without believing the messages themselves. Parents are more likely to Google whether their sons are geniuses than to ask the same about their daughters. Teachers, too, are more likely to perceive innate ability in boys, even though girls tend to do better in school.

Kids, of course, pick up on this. In one study, Cimpian, Leslie, and psychologist Lin Bian told kids about a "really, really smart person." Then they showed the kids four pictures—two males and two females—and asked them to guess which one the story had been about. "At age five," they found, "boys and girls were equally likely to associate intelligence with their own gender, but that changed quickly." By age six, girls were far less likely to say the "really, really smart person" in the story had been a female. Likewise, when six- and seven-year-olds were shown an unfamiliar board game for "really smart kids," girls showed less interest than boys did.

As Jo Boaler writes, "[Far] too many of us have been conditioned to believe that we don't have the capacity to learn. Once people get this terrible idea in their heads, their learning and cognitive processes change." In Britain, for example, it's been estimated that 88 percent of students assigned to ability-based groups will *remain* in those groups for the rest of their school careers. In other words, it's likely that a child placed in a low-scoring group because of poor performance on one exam will also score poorly on the *next* exam, and not necessarily because of the child's intelligence. "Once we tell young students they are in a lower-track group, their achievement becomes a self-fulfilling prophecy," Boaler writes. They lose confidence in their own abilities, and adults hold them to lower expectations.*

Researchers have also documented a different (but related) phenomenon called *stereotype threat*. In a series of experiments, psychologist Claude Steele and his colleagues told Black college students—who had long been aware that others saw them less adept at standardized tests—that a difficult exam was a test of their ability. As Steele and his colleagues expected, "Black students performed dramatically less well than white students, even though we had statistically matched the two groups in ability level," he writes. However, when the researchers presented the same test as a study of how certain problems get solved (as opposed to a measure of students' intelligence), both groups did equally well. Steele concluded that performance suffers when students feel they'll be judged on the basis of stereotypes.

These findings have been replicated among other groups, too. In some cases, simply checking a box to indicate one's gender, or adding more males to a classroom, can depress women's math scores—an effect that disappears when no stereotype is evoked. "In another study, women were asked to take a notoriously difficult math ability test," writes Britt Andreatta in *Wired to Connect*. "Participants were randomly assigned to one of

---

* We should note that some researchers have found positive benefits to grouping children by ability, particularly high-achieving or "gifted" students. However, the science is hotly debated, and several organizations—including Scholastic and the National Education Association—advocate against grouping learners by ability. The answer to whether grouping is "good" or "bad" may come down to how educators implement groups and whether those groups are flexible or rigid.

three groups, labeled as women, residents of the Northeast, or students at an elite private college. The third group (elite college) consistently performed the best on the exam, even though all the labels were true of all women."

Steele and his colleagues found they could even *induce* stereotype threat among groups who don't typically experience it. In one study, they gave a group of white males a difficult math test, noting that Asians generally outperform whites. Sure enough, the group did worse than white students who'd taken the same test without such a caveat.*

All of this can contribute to what scientists call a "fixed mindset": the idea that some people can't learn and won't grow, and that they'll never be able to do what their supposedly more-brilliant peers seem to accomplish with ease. Through no fault of their own, kids can come to believe that their traits and intelligence are preordained: When they succeed, it's because they've been given the "gift." When they fail, it's a reflection of them; they fail *because they are failures*. People with fixed mindsets understandably see little point in doing difficult things—in learning to whistle or write the Greek alphabet or discern the source of the wind. Why bother with anything if you haven't been given the talent?

Growing the Garden of the Mind

Eileen McNamara stands in Rogers' front yard, whistling an improvised tune and mimicking various birdcalls.

At first, she tells Rogers, the skill seemed almost impossible. She hadn't been a natural—as a little girl, she'd heard her father whistling and decided to learn for herself. But whistling is more than a matter of pursing one's lips and blowing a gale through the mouth. It takes muscles moving in synchrony. It takes a tongue placed *just so*. Whistling well takes hours

---

* This isn't necessarily a matter of self-confidence. Even students who believe in their own abilities can be harmed by stereotypes, which are external threats that trigger stress and anxiety responses.

and hours of practice—sometimes even more. It's a skill so difficult to perfect, in fact, that some people decide they simply can't do it.

McNamara was almost one of them. "I started at first, and it just didn't come out right," she says. "But you know, if you continue to try over and over again, eventually, you might get a small sound that's very simple. And then it can become fancier."

This, scientists say, is the fixed mindset's opposite. Rather than believing that skills and success stem solely from mysterious, innate gifts, the "growth mindset" holds that our abilities improve with effort. It argues that the world's great geniuses (and great whistlers) are made, not born. And it means, as the educational researcher Benjamin Bloom once put it, that "what any person in the world can learn, almost all persons can learn, if provided with the appropriate prior and current conditions of learning."

Perhaps no one on Earth knows more about this than Carol Dweck, a psychologist and professor at Stanford University who has spent her career exploring the growth mindset's power. "The 'growth mindset' is based on the belief that your basic qualities are things you can cultivate through your efforts, your strategies, and help from others," she writes in her book *Mindset: The New Psychology of Success*. "Although people may differ in every which way—in their initial talents and aptitudes, interests, or temperaments—everyone can change and grow through application and experience."

On one hand, this can be daunting, because the growth mindset removes the crutch that so many of us depend on. If great whistlers are made, not born, then we non-whistlers can't fault our genetics or some other innate barrier. Perhaps we never had a patient, loving teacher like McNamara did. Or perhaps we never put in the effort that's required to develop a skill. Regardless, our potential as whistlers has been left unexplored and unfulfilled, and that can be a difficult fact to face.

On the other hand, the growth mindset can free us. If great whistlers are made, not born, then almost all of us can learn how to whistle if that's what we choose to do.* We don't have to be ashamed when we try and we fail. We fail not because we are failures but because we're not experts—*yet*. We're all on a journey of learning and growing—of *striving*—whether in whistling or science or art.

"This is the mindset that allows people to thrive during some of the most challenging times in their lives," writes Dweck. In a study of struggling college students, Dweck and her colleagues compared the coping mechanisms of students with fixed mindsets versus those with growth mindsets. Both groups were stressed out, overwhelmed by schoolwork, and worn down by winter weather, she writes. "And here we saw something really amazing. The *more* depressed people with the growth mindset felt (short of severe depression), the *more* they took action to confront their problems, the *more* they made sure to keep up with their schoolwork, and the *more* they kept up with their lives. The worse they felt, the more determined they became!"

We should note here that adopting a growth mindset only lets us improve from where we are. It does *not* mean that we can all be the next Michael Jordan or the next Albert Einstein. Perhaps we'll never whistle quite as well as Eileen McNamara, but that's okay. "We all need to accept some of our imperfections, especially the ones that don't really harm our lives or the lives of others," writes Dweck. That's why Rogers doesn't spend the "Learning" episodes desperately trying to whistle. Although he did attempt to learn, he's since moved on to the things he cares about more. Pivots like these are sometimes necessary, and the growth mindset can make them easier. We move on with the knowledge that we can grow and improve in whatever we tackle next.

Under the right conditions, the growth mindset has been found to increase GPAs and even mitigate the damage done by negative beliefs about learning. Remember when researchers showed children the board game for "really smart kids," and fewer girls felt like playing? Well, when

---

* "Having a growth mindset doesn't force you to pursue something," writes Dweck. "It just tells you that you can develop your skills. It's still up to you whether you want to."

researchers described the *exact same game* as being for "kids who try really hard," girls were every bit as interested as boys.

The good news is that growth mindset can be quickly, easily, and cheaply taught. David Yeager, a psychologist at the University of Texas at Austin, has teamed up with Dweck, Boaler, and others to develop a free program (available at perts.net) that teaches kids that their intelligence is malleable. A 2019 evaluation in *Nature*—one that included some twelve thousand ninth-graders across the country—found that the program boosted grades, increased enrollment in advanced math classes, and reduced the number of students earning Ds or Fs in core courses. Though the effects were small in some cases, in others, they were significant and long-lasting. All thanks to an online program that could be completed in less than an hour.

There is, however, a catch, cautions Yeager: "It turns out students don't find the growth mindset to be valid or actionable until the teacher's behavior makes it true." A survey of the schools involved found that when teachers had fixed mindsets, their students didn't benefit. The program only worked in supportive, caring environments where *adults* had growth mindsets, too. Kids learn and grow, it turns out, when the adults around them believe that they're able, and when adults *convey* that belief in ways that kids understand and trust.

In his studies of stereotype threat, Claude Steele and his colleagues gave students an essay assignment: Write about your favorite teachers. They asked students to include a picture of themselves, thereby making it clear that the essay graders would know the students' race. White students, the researchers found, took the feedback they received at face value—in a predominately white institution, they saw little reason not to trust it. But Black students were left to wonder whether their feedback was rooted in stereotypes. It was only when the essay graders explicitly communicated their high standards—and their belief that students could *meet* those standards—that students saw their feedback as trustworthy and unbiased. In fact, when this happened, Black students became even more likely than other groups to revise their essays, even though they weren't being graded for credit.

The bottom line is that when it comes to growth mindset, adult behavior matters. It's adults, after all, who create the environments in which young people learn—environments that communicate love and respect on one end of the spectrum, or prejudice and low expectations on the other. It's adults whose job it is to build trust. If we want kids to persevere, we have to show them that we not only believe in them but that we're also here to support them, even if they stumble and fall.

The Importance of Making Mistakes

"How we deal with the big disappointments in life," Rogers wrote, "depends a great deal on how the people who loved us helped us deal with smaller disappointments when we were little."

As any parent knows, those disappointments can be legion. There's so much to learn when we're little. In the span of a few years, we walk, talk, tie our shoes, take baths, use a toilet, start school, and more. Almost everything we do involves intricate processes and unspoken rules. Almost everything involves lots and lots of mistakes.

Mistakes, after all, are the things that power our learning. In fact, at the biological level, that's what learning *is*: a series of new neural pathways born of silent (and sometimes not-so-silent) struggle. Making mistakes— and then correcting them—is how we grow our brains and make new connections.

Very young children seem to get this. They struggle to walk for weeks or months, getting up, falling down, and trying again unfazed. They're relentless to the point of recklessness, sometimes to their own delight and their parents' dismay. They're simply doing what they're designed to do— explore the world's surprises with wonder and joy, mistakes and bruises and scrapes be damned.

But as children get older, learning tends to lose some of its luster. Mistakes become hazards. Struggles become wellsprings of disappointment.

As kids develop self-consciousness and start comparing themselves to others, they often become less willing to take on difficult challenges. It's not that they're afraid of difficulty—they've been doing difficult things from the moment they entered the world. Instead, writes Dweck, "they become afraid of not being smart."

It's easy to understand why. We live in a world that rewards the good report card but not the work required to earn it. We praise the first-place finisher but not the practice it took to win. We want our kids to be smart, but often, we punish or penalize the very things that *make* them smart: their setbacks, struggles, and mistakes.

Imagine a fourth-grader trying to learn long division. He has a test coming up, and so far, it's not going very well. He struggles with the steps and forgets what to do with remainders. Homework is a nightly battle of frayed nerves and fresh tears. When division doesn't come easily, he starts to hear the messages: *Your sister got this right away. Why can't you?* Or, *What's so hard about four simple steps?* Or even, *Math just isn't your thing.* Of course, none of these messages tell our fourth-grader that mistakes are a sign of learning. On the contrary, they suggest that if he has to struggle, then perhaps he lacks innate talent. Perhaps he's not smart.

Kids who hear such messages do what anyone would do: They protect themselves. They lash out, shut down, and stop trying. They sometimes turn to bullying or other acts of cruelty in an attempt at self-defense. If they don't make an effort, they reason, then they won't make mistakes. And if they don't make mistakes, they won't be judged as *not smart.*

Unfortunately, they won't learn, either, and the cycle that follows is brutal. The good news is that parents and teachers can break it by making it clear that struggles and mistakes can be *good*—that setbacks ought to be investigated and put to maximum use. Stephen Chew, a psychologist at Samford University, demonstrates this by giving his students some two dozen words on a sheet of paper. He asks one group to count the number of times that specific letters appear on the sheet. Meanwhile, he asks the other group to evaluate the "pleasantness" of the words. Students in the latter group endure some extra struggle—their task is trickier, more sub-jective, and more cognitively demanding than simply counting letters. But on tests of recall, they reliably outperform the first group, remembering up to 40 percent more words.

The effects of struggle on learning have been well documented. "Being forced to generate answers improves subsequent learning even if the gen-erated answer is wrong," writes David Epstein in *Range*. "It can even help to be wildly wrong. . . . The more confident a learner is of their wrong answer, the better the information sticks when they subsequently learn the right answer. Tolerating big mistakes can create the best learning opportunities."

It can also create learners who are more willing to stick with difficult challenges. When kids see mistakes and struggles as markers on the path toward mastery, learning becomes more exciting than scary. Setbacks be-come more intriguing than disappointing.

Of course, even kids who *like* to struggle will still find themselves frustrated. Making and accepting mistakes is one thing; learning from them is something else entirely. For that, kids need loving adults who'll talk to them honestly about their shortcomings and failures and who'll help them determine what it will take to succeed. "It can be really help-ful when you talk about your own mistakes openly," explains Hedda Sharapan. "For example, when you've accidentally spilled something, like the glitter, or forgotten something that you promised a child, like a turn at the easel the next day. Let the children know that you learned from your mistake—that you need to check to make sure the lid is tight on the glitter jar, or that next time you'll write yourself a note so you don't forget."

Likewise, it's important to value the process *and* the outcome and to show kids that they're inextricably linked. When we want a child to swim, we don't just drop her in the deep end and hope for the best. Nor do we give her a trophy for simply getting into the pool. Instead, we stand at her side and support her unconditionally as she tries different ways of keeping afloat. "Learning from mistakes takes persistence, and one of the best ways to encourage that is to comment on *how* children are working on something, not just *what* they're making," says Sharapan. "Think about how helpful it can be when you say things like, 'I saw that you were upset when the blocks fell over, but you waited a few minutes and then you built them up again!' or 'I noticed how you kept on trying.' When you applaud their trying, they're more likely to keep trying the next time things go wrong."

And in fact, that's exactly what we see in Eileen McNamara, the professional singer and whistler. Thinking back on how she learned to whistle, she tells Rogers how her father helped her try again and again. "I asked him to keep trying to show me until I would get it," she says, and her father agreed. Had he shamed her for making mistakes or suggested that whistling wasn't for her, it's doubtful she would've bothered. But with his support, she found the strength she needed to keep trying—to keep learning and growing.

Rogers captured this philosophy in "You've Got to Do It," a song he debuted in 1969 and sang for the next thirty years.

> *If you want to ride a bicycle and ride it straight and tall,*
> *You can't simply sit and look at it 'cause it won't move at all.*
> *But it's you who have to try it, and it's you who have to fall*
>   *(sometimes)*
> *If you want to ride a bicycle and ride it straight and tall.*
> *If you want to read a reading book and read the real words,*
>   *too,*
> *You can't simply sit and ask the words to read themselves to*
>   *you.*
> *But you have to ask a person who can show you one or two*
> *If you want to read a reading book and read the real words,*
>   *too.*
> *It's not easy to keep trying, but it's one good way to grow.*

It's not easy to keep learning, but I know that this is so:
When you've tried and learned you're bigger than you were a
  day ago.
It's not easy to keep trying, but it's one way to grow.
You've got to do it.
Every little bit, you've got to do it, do it, do it, do it.
And when you're through, you can know who did it.
For you did it.
You did it.
You did it.

Rogers sometimes told a story about a musician he admired deeply, Bill Isler recalls. "The musician would say, 'If I don't practice one day, I know. If I don't practice for two days, the conductor knows. If I don't practice for three days, the audience knows.' And telling that story was Fred's way of saying, you always have to practice your craft, no matter what it is or how talented you are. You have to keep that discipline. You have to continually keep after it."

Breaking Down Barriers

With his aviator sunglasses, his headphones, and his hair tied back in a ponytail, Eric Kloss looks a lot like a jazz musician. And in fact, that's exactly what he is. After discovering the saxophone in fifth grade, Kloss immersed himself in music, sitting in with some of the greatest players in jazz before he even entered high school. By age fourteen, Kloss had met John Coltrane, who gave him a piece of advice: "If you're a musician, don't waste any time." By which he'd meant, "Practice. Write. *Do.*"

Kloss took this advice to heart, releasing some two dozen albums over the course of his career, a few of which critics have called among the best in modern jazz. He toured the world and shared the stage with legends before finding his way home to Pittsburgh, where he sits now at a book-strewn table with one of his biggest, most famous fans.

"Glad to be with you, Eric," says Mister Rogers.

We're here, Rogers explains, so that Kloss can show us the special reading machine he uses at the library. Blind since birth, Kloss reads with the help of a humming, gray contraption called the Kurzweil Personal Reader—a combination scanner/computer/speaker that converts printed text to speech. Kloss toggles the machine's different voices: Perfect Paul, Frail Frank, Whispering Wendy, and more. He puts a book on the scanner and listens as it reads the contents aloud. The machine, he says, "certainly does help me—and also other blind people—read."

Rogers sits transfixed, leaning in with that look in his eye. "You must have had some wonderful teachers in your life," he says. Kloss agrees, saying he had wonderful teachers indeed—that they, too, read books to him aloud and that the stories they told eventually led him to jazz and his remarkable life in music.

Appearing toward the end of the "Learning" series, the scene with Kloss highlights an important caveat. When it comes to learning and growing, everything conveyed in the *Neighborhood*—loving relationships, growth mindsets, the embracing of mistakes and struggles—can still fall short in the face of external challenges. Yes, you've got to do it, as the Rogers song goes. You've got to ride the bicycle and read the reading book. It's you who have to try it and it's you who have to fall (sometimes). But what if, in Benjamin Bloom's words, "the appropriate prior and current conditions of learning" haven't been met? What if, like countless American kids, the streets aren't safe for you and your bike? Or what if you're blind and you don't have an adult who can make a book accessible? Some challenges can't be solved through effort and mindset alone. Personal attitudes meet societal limitations; what's within bumps up against what's without. And it's not always a fair fight.

As Bettina L. Love, author of *We Want to Do More Than Survive: Abolitionist Teaching and the Pursuit of Educational Freedom*, puts it, "There is no amount of grit that can fight off the intersections of living in poverty, being pushed out of school, facing a world full of patriarchy and racism, and suffering toxic stress." To suggest otherwise, Love contends, is disingenuous and even harmful.

Remember those headlines from the beginning of the chapter? The ones about homeless students beating the odds, or selling lemonade to pay for chemotherapy, or walking fifteen miles to work? They're headlines because they're *exceptions*—in these cases, to the inhumane conditions that keep kids and their families from thriving. They might make us feel glad for the people involved, but they don't ask *why* students are homeless, or *why* lifesaving drugs can bankrupt a family, or *why* a resident of the United States of America would have no other option but to walk a few hours to work. They imply that society's problems are no match for an individual's bootstraps and that kids and families who *don't* beat the odds have simply failed to apply themselves—a grossly unfair and easily refuted assertion.

"[No] mindset is a magic elixir that can dissolve the toxicity of structural arrangements," argues the author and activist Alfie Kohn. "Until those arrangements have been changed, mindset will get you only so far." That's why a growing number of parents and educators are teaching kids not only to recognize and acknowledge the arrangements that shape their lives but also to organize and advocate in pursuit of something better. They're helping kids leverage their inner worlds—where perseverance and growth mindset live—in pursuit of change in the outer world.

A self-described "artist/activist," Heather Arnet started out as a theater director. She wanted to use the theater to tell topical stories that impacted women and sparked audiences to action. With her goals clearly laid out (and a hefty tuition bill to pay), the drama student at Carnegie Mellon University sought a work-study job that would relate to her major and teach her the nuts and bolts of storytelling and production. That's how she found herself in the Neighborhood of Make-Believe, crouched behind a set piece with Rogers himself.

"It wasn't part of my normal job," she says, laughing. "Mostly, I helped with the viewer mail and eventually worked with Mister Rogers and

Hedda Sharapan on a book collection of fans' letters.* I don't know who was supposed to be there turning the pages for him that day while he worked the puppets, but for whatever reason, that person wasn't around. So they asked me to do it. And it was this really wonderful moment. While I'd interacted with him a great deal in the office, I hadn't yet glimpsed the Mister Rogers I knew from TV. But on the production stage, underneath the Museum-Go-Round, with each of his two hands in a puppet, I saw that while Fred was doing that kind of work, he was most *himself*. He was his most animated, present self."

The memory stuck with Arnet when she left Pittsburgh for New York, working various jobs in theater and advertising. It stuck with her when she came back to the Steel City to raise money for a local theater. And it stuck with her when she applied to run a newly created nonprofit: the Women and Girls Foundation.

Established in 2002, the foundation fights for gender equity through advocacy, grantmaking, and programming, including GirlGov—an initiative designed to equip high school students with the tools for changing societal structures. In GirlGov's early days, Arnet explains, "it was mostly about encouraging girls to think about elected office. We'd take them to Harrisburg, and they'd shadow elected officials—you can be it if you see it, right? But at the same time, because of their age, the girls can't run for office for ten or fifteen years. And so we started to think about how we could show them that they could make a difference *today*."

Their first opportunity came in the form of a T-shirt. In 2005, Abercrombie & Fitch—a clothing retailer then at the peak of its popularity— released a line of shirts for young women that included slogans such as, *Who needs brains when you have these?* The shirts had been fodder for heated discussion at GirlGov's first-ever fall retreat, where girls spent the weekend getting to know one another and learning the basics of civic engagement. "We were doing an exercise about grantmaking," Arnet recalls,

* That book became *Dear Mister Rogers, Does It Ever Rain in Your Neighborhood?: Letters to Mister Rogers* (New York: Penguin Books, 1996).

"and we had these mock 'projects' that the girls could give their Monopoly money to. One of them was a fake protest against Abercrombie & Fitch. We'd included it because they'd been talking so much about it. There were three or four other ideas, but no one even remembers what they were, because everyone put their money toward the protest. They were all saying, 'Ms. Heather, I know this is made up, but those T-shirts are real. So we should do something. We should really do something.'"

The conversation turned to what it would take to plan a successful protest. The girls would need more than markers, signs, and megaphones: Where would they go? Who did they want to reach? If they needed a permit, what would it take to get one? "The questions were just as important as the answers," says Arnet. "We were teaching the girls the building blocks they'd need not just for *this* protest but to organize any protest they might want to lead as savvy, skilled organizers later in life."

By the end of the day, the girls had a plan. A few weeks later, they held a press conference announcing their "Girlcott" of Abercrombie & Fitch.

By a stroke of luck, *The Today Show* caught wind of it, and soon the girls were on national television. "Abercrombie didn't respond until after we'd been on *Today*, CNN, and Fox News, and in newspaper articles and on NPR," says Arnet. Eventually, the company agreed to meet with the girls at their corporate headquarters to hear the girls' demands. In addition to telling the company to stop selling the T-shirts in question, the girls also presented designs that they'd developed on their own—T-shirts with slogans like *Your future boss* and *That's Madame President to you*.

In the end, the company agreed to pull the offensive T-shirts, says Arnet, though it rejected the girls' alternatives. "Abercrombie's loss in the long run," she says, noting that similar T-shirts now sell well in other stores. "The girls were, as always, leading the way. If only the men in the room had had the wisdom to listen."

Still, the early victory transformed the foundation's programming, and today it sets its sights higher: on changing the policies that prevent women and girls from thriving. Each year, about one hundred girls from across the Pittsburgh region enroll in GirlGov, which receives twice as many applications as it can accept. The girls self-select into four commit-tees: racial justice, health and the environment, education justice, and freedom from violence. GirlGov then helps each committee develop a policy agenda, which includes public-awareness campaigns and legislative advocacy. The girls meet with lawmakers, attend and lead protests, testify before city councils, and recruit their peers for their causes. GirlGov's racial justice committee works to eliminate over-policing in schools and change the policies that push Black students into the school-to-prison pipeline. The education justice committee pressures lawmakers to secure funding for students' mental-health counseling. And the freedom from violence committee works to keep immigrant families together.

"You talk about 'doing difficult things'—that's what our girls do ev-ery single day," says Arnet. "Public policy is a hard thing, and it can be a thankless thing. It would be easy for our health and environment commit-tee, for example, to plant an urban garden. Planting a garden is a perfectly valuable thing to do; it helps your environment and your community. But does it really change things in the long run?"

Instead, the young women in GirlGov push for systemic solutions to problems, even though such solutions are exponentially more difficult—and far less certain—than doing a one-off project. "We might work all year on a bill and it won't get passed," she says. "But GirlGov isn't *just* about passing a bill. It's about girls becoming informed activists. It's about the process of working with girls from other communities, other schools, other socioeconomic classes, other races, and other religions and coming together to change a policy."

Because GirlGov's high school students come from so many back-grounds and experiences, finding common ground and coming to con-sensus can be difficult, says Arnet. "The environment" might mean hiking to one girl and fracking pollutants to another. To launch an effective campaign, the girls have to know and trust each other deeply. They have to establish a sense of safety.

That's where the fall retreat comes in. "We barely even talk about policy work during that first weekend," says Arnet. It's really about getting to know people who are different from you. It's a lot of team building and mixer-type stuff."

On Saturday night, the girls stage their main event: a "Revolutionary Show-And-Tell." At the beginning, says Arnet, only one or two people sign up to perform. "But it *always* ends up becoming this four-hour marathon. By the end of it, they're all onstage singing. There are girls from different communities lip-synching and dancing to Beyoncé. There are girls doing really complicated and beautiful ethnic dances. They perform poetry that they've written, and a lot of it's about how grateful they are to be in a place where they can feel safe to be themselves."

It's this kind of community that enables difficult work. The relationships the girls form give them the confidence to keep going, whether they're meeting with corporate executives, testifying before state representatives, or cohosting events and teach-ins with other youth-led groups in Pittsburgh. "Young people have this amazing power in them and an ability to do something even though they're young and small," she says. "And to take them seriously and speak to them seriously—that's something Fred Rogers did. He took their concerns seriously. He took their *dreams* seriously. And that's what we do with teens and what our teens do with each other. We believe not just in what they can do later but in what they can do today. We believe in what they can do right now."

Mister Rogers gathers the models that he's spread out on his table: the tiny trolley, the tiny castle, the tiny Neighborhood tree. He gathers the tiny clock for a tiny Daniel Tiger. He gathers all his tiny figures, remembers all their tiny struggles, all their tiny mistakes. Don't they teach us a lot?

Aren't Ana Platypus and H. J. Elephant and Lady Aberlin always learning and growing, just like *we're* learning and growing?

"Some people can do some things, some can do others," he says. "I can't whistle, but I can clean up a room!"

Rogers stands up and sets the figures on his kitchen shelf. He's got that look in his eye again—that look that tells us he's learning. That he has a particular project in mind. That he's thinking about *agape*.

"Do you ever think of the many things that you've learned to do since you were a tiny baby?" he asks. "Whenever you see a tiny baby, do you ever think, 'I was like that baby one time, and now I'm not a baby any-more. I'm really growing a *lot*!'"

And with that, our TV neighbor changes his shoes and smiles. He hasn't learned to whistle, but he hasn't failed, either. Instead, he's made today a special day by *striving*, as he always does, toward his purpose: help-ing us discover our own.

"It always gives me a good feeling when I see people growing and learn-ing wonderful things," he says. And then the piano plays, and Mister Rog-ers starts to sing.

WHAT MIGHT YOU DO?

- Schedule what David Epstein calls "Saturday experiments": deliberate yet pressure-free opportunities to try something new. Remind kids they don't have to be good at this strange new thing. Talk about why it might feel strange. Talk about why it's important that they try. Sample lots of activities; kids can't develop an interest in something if they don't know anything about it. *"Hey, let's skip this stone across the pond."* Or, *"Have you ever seen the garden over in the neighbor's yard?"* Or, *"I have this glue gun up on this shelf, and you have lots of empty cereal boxes. . . . "*

- Notice what lights a child up. Every child has an interest, a fascination, or something that they want to figure out and improve. Pay attention, and figure out what you can do to nurture that interest, however unfamiliar it might be to you. Approach it with enthusiasm and without judgment. *"I don't have a clue why my daughter is fascinated by Paris. We've never been there, and I can say only, 'Bonjour.' But maybe we can figure out how to make croissants. And maybe we can start to learn French by doing online lessons together. And maybe we can go to the museum and see those impressionist paintings. . . . "*

- Be by your child's side. Not just at the game, or the recital, or the moment. If you can, be there at the practice, too. Be there to talk about how hard practice was, or to hear about the problems she had while coding her robot. If you give your child feedback, be sure it's specific, clear, and focused on improving the task instead of changing the person. *Remark how difficult it was for you to learn how to play the piano or how hard it was to start a new job. Talk about your own frustrations or mistakes, and mention how you moved forward.*

SIX

Such a Good Feeling

Connection

"**There are more important things** to do than having *fun*," King Friday thunders, casting a glare from the balcony.

He's been angry—no, *wounded*—for several episodes now, baffled by Make-Believe's denizens. First came their frivolous hats: His wife, Queen Sara Saturday, had declared a "hat day" for no other reason except that wearing hats can be *fun*. Worse, she'd held a whole hat party at the castle. ("I find my fun in *other* things than hats," the king had said indignantly.)

Then came soccer: the simple, silly game that Prince Tuesday has taken to playing. Lately, there's been talk of forming a team—talk that appalls our solitary king. And now, to Friday's great vexation, his subjects have gathered near the castle to sing each other a song—something about going around a mulberry bush. There's Lady Aberlin and Bob Dog and Handyman Negri and others, joining hands and spinning around in a circle.

They're smiling. Laughing. Jumping around without including *him*, their benevolent monarch, who makes their decisions and issues their rules and even—on occasion—treats them to sounds from his bass violin.

Well, no more. King Friday XIII has finally had it with *fun*. For him, *fun* means making pronouncements: "Long ones," he says, "when short ones would do." He leans over the balcony to make a pronouncement now.

But before he can speak, one of his subjects—the earnest, ever-excitable Bob Dog—looks up and sees him. And Bob Dog asks an innocent question: "Would you like to play 'Here We Go 'Round the Mulberry Bush,' King Friday? We have lots of room."

The canine's question stuns the moody sovereign. King Friday XIII isn't one to receive invitations—if anything, he's more likely to *stop* fun and games than he is to join in himself. Friday, perhaps for the very first time, doesn't know what to say. "Um, well, uh, I don't think, uh . . . Does it take a great deal of expertise?"

"Oh, try it, King Friday!" says Handyman Negri.

"We'll be glad to show you how!" barks Bob Dog.

King Friday looks around at his perch, which suddenly strikes him as lonely. He decides to join his subjects after all, and as they dance and sing and spin around the Make-Believe mulberry bush, something changes in the king. He starts to have—he won't call it *fun*—but "pleasant moments, perhaps." He lets down his royal guard, if only for a song with the people and puppets who, in another kind of life, he might have counted as friends.

And then, his voice beginning to break, King Friday starts to tell them something—something he's never told anyone else.

·········· ⋮ ·················

In the spring of 2020, as a deadly coronavirus spread across the planet and kept countless people sheltered in place at home, a curious phenomenon surfaced in the nightly news: Around the world, balconies and front porches and rooftops suddenly became stages. In Italy, quarantined residents sang operas from their windows and staged complicated, choreographed dances that included whole apartment buildings. In the United States, musicians stepped to their front porches with trumpets, guitars, and yes, even bass violins. And in Pittsburgh, neighbors came out to sing—what else?—"Won't You Be My Neighbor?"

The outbreak of COVID-19 revealed a few things about humanity. Perhaps the most poignant, however, was the extent to which it reminded us of our most basic human need—the need for connection.

No matter how solitary or self-reliant we are, we all require relationships with other people. In fact, a growing body of research suggests that the need for human connection is more than a warm, nice-to-have feeling—it's a biological imperative. "Quite simply," writes Dr. Vivek Murthy, the former surgeon general and author of *Together: The Healing Power of Human Connection in a Sometimes Lonely World*, "human relationship is as essential to our well-being as food and water." Our very survival depends on it.

In the 1940s, Austrian psychologist René Spitz followed two groups of children from infancy through the first few years of their lives. The first group grew up in an orphanage—one that, like many in the aftermath of World War II, was overcrowded and under-resourced. The nurses did what they could, caring for up to seven infants at once, but the shortage of adults meant that babies spent most of their time alone in their cribs. Sheets hung to prevent the spread of disease meant they couldn't even *see* their infant neighbors. The second group was raised in a prison nursery, where their incarcerated mothers were at least allowed to visit with and hold them throughout the day.

Although the infants' development began on the same trajectory, differences emerged as the two groups approached their first birthdays. Babies who'd been raised in the orphanage appeared less curious and less playful than their peers in the prison. They were also less physically healthy, even though the orphanage was far more sanitary. Over time, the differences between the two groups grew steadily starker. The children raised by their mothers in prison learned to walk and talk in ways comparable to their peers on the outside. After five years, all were alive and healthy. Among the kids who'd been raised in the orphanage, however, only a few could walk or talk. Most knew just a handful of words. And although all ninety-one children had been well cared for physically, within two years, thirty-four had died. "The high mortality," Spitz wrote, "is but the most extreme consequence of the general decline, both physical and psychological, which is shown by children completely starved of emotional interchange."

Spitz's work helped show the world just how essential human connection can be. Not long afterward, the American psychologist Harry Harlow removed any doubt that remained. In a series of cruel experiments that remain controversial, Harlow separated baby rhesus monkeys from their mothers to study the effects of isolation. In one instance, he raised monkeys in solitary confinement for several months or a year—an experiment that wrought bizarre behavior and seemingly permanent psychological damage. (The monkeys screamed, tore their hair out, bit themselves, and generally came undone.) In another, Harlow gave baby monkeys a choice between two artificial "mothers": The first, made of wire, contained bottles of milk that the monkeys could use to feed themselves. The second, made of cloth, contained no food at all, and yet the baby monkeys overwhelmingly preferred it. The infants chose, in other words, the surrogate who brought them comfort over the one who gave them food.

Harlow's findings suggest an evolutionary component to our human need for connection. Our early ancestors, experts say, banded together to protect themselves from starvation and attack. Raising children in hostile, unpredictable environments really did take a village—and before that, it took a tribe. Early humans who could bond with potential helpers lived longer and reproduced more, passing their wiring down to us. Even today, when we're faced with isolation, our bodies react like we're alone on the savanna, ancient predators prowling in the grass.

For most of human history, our safety depended on our security within the group. As a result, we're almost always thinking about other people. Remember your brain's default mode network from Chapter 2—that place you go when you're bored and running on autopilot? It's programmed, scientists say, to prepare you to connect with others, whether you realize it or not. You're thinking about other people even when you're not thinking at all. You've been doing this since you were two weeks old, and you'll do it for the rest of your days. Humans are *that* social.

When we feel secure within a group, we call the feeling *belonging*. Belonging is the sense that we're safe to be ourselves without the risk of exclusion. It's psychological safety on steroids, the feeling that you're part of an "in" group. Belonging has long been linked to psychological and even physical benefits, from a sense of serenity and increased well-being to better health and a longer life. In an ideal world, we'd "belong" wherever we went and bond with whomever we met, forming close, nurturing relationships across every line of difference.

But as we're constantly reminded, we're a long way from that world. Even before the COVID-19 pandemic, public health experts had been sounding the alarm about a rise in "deaths of despair": deaths due to suicide, alcoholism, drug addiction, and more, all of which have roots in a lack of belonging. Then, of course, there are the man-made pandemics of racism, sexism, xenophobia, and political toxicity, all of which thrive on disconnection and exclusion. Belonging may be a fundamental human need, but it's by no means a guaranteed part of our existence. And we suffer tremendously in its absence.

In some ways, we're victims of our own design. "It is in our DNA to want to bond deeply with some people and not others," writes Howard J. Ross, author of *Our Search for Belonging: How Our Need to Connect Is Tearing Us Apart*. As a species, we've spent most of our time in tribes—small groups of about 150 people at most, nearly all of whom were exactly like ourselves. Survival was mostly a matter of knowing who was a threat and who wasn't, who was "in" and who was "out." This tendency toward tribalism might even account for language. According to one theory, humans learned to talk not so we could cooperate or discuss our plans for hunting big game, but so that we could whisper behind each other's backs.

"It is not enough for men and women to know the whereabouts of lions and bison," explains Yuval Noah Harari in his epic account of our species, *Sapiens: A Brief History of Humankind*. "It's much more important for them to know who in their band hates whom, who is sleeping with whom, who is honest, and who is a cheat." Knowing who could be trusted and who couldn't gave early humans a huge advantage, allowing tribes to expand and setting the stage for society as we know it. "The gossip theory might sound like a joke," Harari admits, "but numerous studies support it. Even today the vast majority of human communication—whether in the form of emails, phone calls, or newspaper columns—is gossip."

For better and for worse, we've inherited our ancestors' need to prejudge others as friends or foes. On one hand, this means it's generally pretty easy to connect with people who strike us as similar to ourselves, whether in terms of appearance, attitudes, or political beliefs. When people discuss the bliss of "finding their tribe," they're tapping something ancient and real. On the other hand, humans have a long history of avoiding, disliking, and even annihilating dissimilar others. We've been quick to make others the targets of our anger and our insecurity and our ignorance, often with disastrous results.

This "us versus them" mentality appears in humans at a shockingly early age. University of Toronto professor Kang Lee has found evidence of racial bias among six-month-olds, when babies begin to associate faces from their own race with happy music and faces from other races with sad music. Another researcher, J. Kiley Hamlin of the University of British Columbia, asked nine-month-olds and fourteen-month-olds to choose which food they liked best: graham crackers or green beans. The infants then watched a series of puppet shows in which characters declared their like or dislike for the same two foods. The fourteen-month-olds not only preferred characters who had similar tastes, Hamlin found—they also preferred characters who *harmed* puppets with different tastes. Even the nine-month-olds preferred characters who harmed dissimilar "others." Babies, it seems, like to see their snack-time rivals punished.

This isn't to say that kids are born spiteful—far from it. As we've already discussed, very young children also show altruism. The point is that we're wired for both connection and cruelty, and the ways we deploy them often depend on who we see as "in" and who we see as "out." In children, those distinctions are fairly flexible, though they tend to grow more rigid with age. When children reach adolescence, for example, their brains prioritize their peers and the "in-group," which is why teens become so famously self-conscious and concerned with popularity.

While humans' ability to sort for threats has undoubtedly helped us survive, our tribalism also limits us. When we feel threatened, we sometimes revert to counterproductive, even harmful instincts. We withdraw or lash out, especially if we haven't learned to *reach* out. (Or if reaching out has proven dangerous.) We've yet to develop reliable ways of connecting across distances, whether we measure those distances in miles, years, appearances, bank accounts, or other forms of invented allegiance. According to the late author Audre Lorde, "We have *all* been programmed to respond to the human differences between us with fear and loathing and to handle that difference in one of three ways: ignore it; and if that is not possible, copy it if we think it is dominant; or destroy it if we think it is subordinate. But we have no patterns for relating across our human differences as equals. As a result, those differences have been misnamed and misused in the service of separation and confusion."

This separation spills over into everyday headlines; we see it in hate crimes and war. It spills over, too, into everyday lives: In racism, brutality, and indifference. Tribalism may have helped build our modern society, but somewhere along the line, it stopped serving us. We're too interconnected, too dependent on one another. Even if you *wanted* to avoid the "other"—the person from the other country, the other race, the other snack-food preference—today's world makes doing so impossible.

To discover and sustain a sense of belonging, then, we have to forge it even beyond our tribes. We have to build new connections, new relationships, and new spaces to meet each other as humans.

We have to build a neighborhood.

Exclusion Hurts—Literally

"This is quite difficult for me to talk about," says the emotional King Friday, his voice shaky and hesitant. Today, he confesses, was his first time going around a mulberry bush. Before now, he'd never been invited.

"Uncle *Friday*!" Lady Aberlin cries. "I didn't know that."

It's true. "When I was a young prince, I was not very fine at playing games," explains the sullen king. "So when it came time for people to choose their teams, nobody ever . . . "

He trails off, doing his best to collect himself. So much of King Friday XIII suddenly makes sense—his moods, his obstinance, his drastic changes of heart. It had all seemed so arbitrary before. But now, as he tries not to weep before his Make-Believe subjects, it's clear that King Friday's in pain. "Sometimes it makes people sad when nobody chooses them," he says.

His subjects nod. "That's for sure," says Bob Dog. An outsized canine from Westwood, Bob Dog knows what it's like to be the "other"—to feel unwanted by a team. "I was all paws," he says. "I really didn't play very well."

"You either?" King Friday asks.

"Me either," Bob Dog responds.

In the distance, a piano plays a sorrowful chord.

⋯⋯⋯⋯⋱⋰⋯⋯⋯⋯

A lack of belonging hurts. Although it's something that most of us already know, admitting it isn't easy, as King Friday could tell you. We need human connection like we need water and food, yet "hunger and thirst feel much more acceptable to acknowledge and talk about than loneliness," writes Dr. Murthy. "To combat this silencing effect, then, we need to more deeply appreciate the relationship between loneliness, social connection, and physical and emotional health."

Thanks to advances in science, that relationship has grown increasingly clear. Loneliness and exclusion, researchers say, inflict more than sad feelings—they influence our decisions, diminish our cognitive capabilities, and keep us from thriving in every conceivable way. Students from schools with high rates of bullying tend to do worse on standardized tests than kids in kinder, more inclusive classrooms. Likewise, a study in New York City found that when neighborhoods gentrify, the low-income kids who were born there face higher rates of anxiety and depression. According to one researcher, the changes wrought by a sudden influx of wealth make original residents "feel like they no longer belong in those neighborhoods, which makes kids feel uncomfortable and anxious. That is something to watch out for."

It's not just kids. Adults, too, feel the powerful effects that stem from a lack of belonging. In 2002, psychologists Jean Twenge, Roy Baumeister, and Christopher Nuss gave forty college students a fake personality test, randomly assigning them to three groups based on their supposed "results." The first group—the "future belonging" group—was told they'd have rewarding, caring relationships throughout their lives. The second group—the "future alone" group—was told that their friendships would fade, their marriages would end, and they'd likely spend most of their lives alone. The third group wasn't told anything about relationships; instead, they learned they'd be prone to physical accidents, such as car crashes.

The researchers then gave all three groups a timed IQ test. The "future alone" group bombed it, scoring significantly worse than the other two. In fact, the "future alone" group was the only group that seemed affected at all—even the accident-prone group scored as well as the "future belongers." The researchers concluded that it wasn't bad news in general that had produced a drop in test scores but rather the prospect of social exclusion. When confronted with thoughts of an imagined life alone, students' stress-response systems kicked in, draining their ability to think and reason with clarity.*

Down to our neurobiological core, we're terrified of not belonging, and for good reason. Over time, chronic exclusion invites depression, anxiety, and disease, making us sicker, sadder, and lonelier. Left unchecked, loneliness becomes a vicious cycle in which we push others away and avoid the very connections we crave. "You imagine that you're a misfit," writes Dr. Murthy. "You worry that you'll feel lonely even when you're with people. And most destructive of all, you question your self-worth, thinking that there might be something truly wrong with you that's causing this pain."

Even a *slight* rejection can start us down this path. In 1983, professor Kip Williams of Purdue University was relaxing in a park when a rogue Frisbee struck him in the back. He turned around and threw it to the two strangers behind him. To the professor's surprise, they threw it back to him again, and soon a spirited, spontaneous game of catch was underway among Williams and his new friends.

Unfortunately, it didn't last. What happened next would change not only the professor's own life but also our scientific understanding of what happens when we feel left out. "For no apparent reason, the two original players started throwing the Frisbee only to each other," Williams recalls. Insulted—no, *wounded*—Williams went back to playing with his dog, shocked by how bad he felt. He was "sad, embarrassed, and a bit angry," despite the fact that he'd never met his two ex-friends. He wondered what he'd done to deserve their scorn. The incident hurt Williams deeply, but it also planted a seed.

Later in his career, Williams and his colleagues developed Cyberball, a computer game in which players toss a ball back and forth between digital

---

* Needless to say, the experimenters apologized after the experiment, assuring participants that their "results" had been assigned at random and had no basis in fact.

avatars. In an experiment, they recruited more than a thousand participants from all over the world, telling them the five-minute game would prime their "mental visualization skills" for use in a later task. They also told players that the avatars in the game represented real people who were playing in separate rooms—people who didn't actually exist. (In reality, each participant played against a computer.) After a few friendly games, the computer would isolate the player to varying degrees. Some players would get the ball for half the remaining throws, some for a third, and some for a sixth. Some never got the ball again at all.

"The results astounded us," wrote Williams and his colleagues. "Although participants were playing a game with a disk or ball that did not actually exist and with fictitious others whom they did not know and whom they did not expect to meet, they actually cared about the extent to which they were included." The more players were ostracized, the lower their levels of belonging and self-esteem, and the less they considered their very existence to be meaningful. This held true even when participants learned that the other players weren't real. In other words, even when they *knew* that their exclusion was a ruse—one concocted by nothing more than a computer code—they still felt just as hurt.

In another study, Williams and his colleagues convinced participants that the other "players" were people they disagreed with (such as people with opposing politics) or people they downright hated (such as members of the Ku Klux Klan). It didn't matter. "Even when playing with people they openly despise, ostracized participants reported similarly low levels of belonging, self-esteem, control, and meaningful existence, and similarly lower mood levels as well." In another version of the game, called Cyberbomb, participants were blown up and eliminated altogether. And even *that* didn't hurt as badly as being rejected.*

---

* It's worth noting that the pain caused by exclusion can be quite real. Using Cyberball and functional magnetic resonance imaging, psychologist Naomi Eisenberger of the University of California found activation of the anterior cingulate cortex—the same part of the brain that registers physical pain.

It's long been known, of course, that people sometimes respond to rejection by lashing out. "The child who is not embraced by the village," a popular proverb warns, "will burn it down to feel its warmth." With this in mind, University of Kentucky psychologist C. Nathan DeWall and his colleagues designed a different Cyberball experiment: one in which participants who'd been ostracized could act aggressively toward innocent bystanders. Sure enough, the more participants felt ostracized, the more they showed signs of aggression.

But here's the good news: Aggressiveness *decreased* among people who felt included by at least one "player." Feeling accepted by even a single person, it turns out, can make us less lonely and hostile—even if that person only exists on a screen.

"We Need to Know That We're Worth Being Proud Of"

The trolley returns from Make-Believe, and Mister Rogers waits for us as usual. But here in his bright, comfortable living room, he doesn't look so happy.

On the contrary, he looks downright depressed.

"King Friday and Bob Dog were remembering times when people were playing [a] game and didn't want them to play," says Rogers. "That made the king and Bob Dog *really* sad."

Rogers pauses, letting his words linger in the white space. He casts his glance downward, and it's suddenly clear where King Friday's story had come from. The music stops; the *Neighborhood*'s set goes quiet. "I remember a time when I wasn't too good at playing basketball," says Rogers. "And nobody wanted me on their team."

If anything characterized Fred Rogers' childhood, it was the feeling of not fitting in. Though his material needs were more than met, Freddy still struggled. His peers had little use for the chubby, sickly, sensitive, rich kid. With no one to sit with during lunches at school, Freddy went home to play by himself. Once, a group of bullies chased him through Latrobe, calling him "Fat Freddy" and threatening to pummel him. Even at home, he sometimes felt like he didn't fit in. When his parents held their huge annual Christmas party, Freddy secluded himself in his room, hearing the music and laughter as it seeped up the stairs.

While our go-to guidance for children like Freddy is often to tell them to ignore other people's opinions, such advice is futile, as the Cyberball studies make clear. Worse, it can make kids think that their pain means something is wrong with them. Instead, writes Dr. Murthy, kids who feel left out need to be reminded "of the people who do value and accept them, whether they be in a different group of friends, a club or community group, or their favorite family members."

It's a lesson Rogers himself learned at an early age. As the target of bullies, "the advice I got from the grown-ups was, 'Just let on you don't care, then nobody will bother you,'" he recalled. Of course, it didn't work—Rogers *did* care, and pretending otherwise only made things worse. So he sought solace in the few people who seemed to accept him, particularly his mother and his maternal grandfather.

"Fred McFeely liked to tell him, 'I like you just the way you are,'" says Maxwell King. "Lots of people read that and think, 'Oh, he was just trying to make the boy feel good.' But that's not true—McFeely was trying to open up the world to him! He knew how shy and introverted Fred Rogers was. He wanted to give Rogers the confidence to explore the world and to learn about himself. He wanted to let Rogers know that he was appreciated—that he was *enough*."

Relationships like these helped Rogers weather the storms of his childhood. And as he grew older, he sought a sense of belonging in more and more places. After failing to find it at Dartmouth, he flew to Florida to visit Rollins College, which had a superior music program that had been recommended by a mentor. There, a group of students he'd never even met came to the airport to greet him—a gesture that must have seemed extraordinary to Rogers after so many years of rejection. "We were hanging out the windows of the car when he came out," recalls one of those students, Joanne Byrd. "We grabbed him, and took him right with us, and made him one of us."

Rogers had clearly found what he was looking for. He transferred to Rollins at once. And a few years later, Joanne Byrd became Joanne Rogers.

Rogers tried to re-create that feeling of belonging when he came to Studio A. The *Neighborhood*, he once told author Jeanne Marie Laskas, was less a television program than an "atmosphere"—one that "allows people to be comfortable enough to be who they are."

That atmosphere permeates every frame, from the opening message of acceptance (*I have always wanted to have a neighbor / just like you*) to the closing promise of continued connection tomorrow (*I'll be back when the day is new / and I'll have more ideas for you / And you'll have things you'll want to talk about / I will too*). Wherever he goes, Rogers introduces each new person to his television neighbor: the viewer. "At every point," notes the children's writer Roderick Townley, "the child sitting at home is included, acknowledged, [and] treated as a collaborator."

The *Neighborhood*'s atmosphere informs even the subtler aspects of the program. Rogers' steady eye contact with the camera mimics the face-to-face interaction that signals belonging and worth. His donning a sweater at the start of each episode recalls the soft, cloth-covered surrogate preferred by Harlow's rhesus monkeys. In fact, the boxes of vulnerable, sometimes heartbreaking correspondence in the Fred Rogers Archive suggest that some viewers saw him as exactly that: a surrogate caregiver who couldn't provide food but who could (and did) provide comfort for the children who needed it most.

"Nothing can replace the influence of unconditional love in the life of a child," Rogers said. "Children love to belong. They long to belong." The *Neighborhood* normalized this admission. Characters talk openly—if not always eagerly—about their need for human connection. We see this in King Friday's struggle to express his loneliness. It's difficult, he tells his subjects, but he knows that what's mentionable becomes more manageable. Again and again, the *Neighborhood*'s characters reap the rewards of admitting their longing to belong, gradually nudging viewers in the direction of doing the same.

"Mister Rogers wants to lead us into admitting that we all need to be loved, loved not for our accouterments or appendages but for ourselves alone," writes author William Guy. "Until we can make such an admission, we are fooling ourselves as we search for what we think will be our happiness."

Above all, the *Neighborhood*'s atmosphere combats the corrosive effects that loneliness and a lack of belonging can have on humans' self-worth. As Rogers put it in a speech:

> I'm proud of you! Does that sound familiar? It seems I say that a good deal in our Neighborhood. Well, whether we're a preschooler or young teen, a graduating college senior or a retired person, we human beings all want to know that we're acceptable, that our being alive somehow makes a difference in the lives of others. We need to know that we're worth being proud of.

Indeed, knowing that we matter to someone else—that we belong in the lives of others—may be the key to happy, healthy lives of our own. Study after study has revealed the importance of *mattering* at every age and every stage of life, from the very beginning to the very end.

In 2019, researchers from the University of Washington announced findings from a long-term study of some eight hundred adults whom they'd followed since elementary school. Throughout the early 1980s, the parents and teachers of one group received a series of lessons designed to help them build stronger bonds with their kids. The parents and teachers of the other group received no intervention at all. When researchers compared the two groups more than thirty years later, they couldn't believe what they found.

Those whose parents and teachers had been taught to build stronger relationships outperformed their peers on every measure of well-being:

physical health, mental health, relationships, income, civic engagement, and more. This held true across gender, race, and class. "The most important thing we've learned," said one of the researchers, summing up three decades of study, "is to provide opportunities for kids to have positive social involvement. Make sure your kids have the opportunity to engage with you as a parent. Play with them, hold them; don't just sit on your phone when you're with them. When kids feel bonded to you, they're less likely to violate your expectations. And you are likely to be setting them up to have better lives long into the future."

The more kids feel that they matter—that someone accepts them just the way they are—the better they tend to do. In Oakland, California, several public schools added an extra class to the school day. Taught by Black male educators and meant specifically for Black boys, these classes affirmed students' identities and boosted their sense of belonging by emphasizing Black history and culture and by providing personalized college and career counseling. "More than anything," reported the *New York Times* upon visiting a class, "it is the deep relationships between instructors and students . . . that hold the key to ending the soul-numbing disenfranchisement that so many young men experience at school."

Among the boys enrolled, researchers found, the dropout rate fell by nearly half. And although the initiative did not include Black girls, *their* dropout rate fell, too, suggesting that a sense of belonging had spilled beyond the classroom. The Oakland Unified School District has since launched similar initiatives for Black girls and other students who've been marginalized by the system. At the college level, programs designed to affirm students' identities and foster a sense of belonging have reduced gender gaps in STEM courses and achievement gaps between first- and continuing-generation college students.

Belonging can even help when we're physically ill or psychologically distressed. Being in the presence of people who accept us, scientists say, makes us less susceptible to pain. That's why having someone at our bedside can help us feel better when we're sick, even if all they're doing is sitting and keeping us company, notes Howard Ross. In speeches, Rogers himself often remembered visiting a friend, the psychoanalyst Helen Ross, at the end of her life. He sat at her bedside, he said, and held her hand in silence.

Likewise, knowing that someone is there for us can make our difficult days easier. As Rogers explained, we can sometimes diffuse a person's volatility "just by offering one kind word or sentence such as, 'It's really tough some days, isn't it?' It's amazing what can happen when an angry person feels understood and appreciated."

The Empathy Muscle

Despite his royal stature—the flowing robe, the high-up perch on the castle balcony, and the kingly roman numerals he affixes to his name—King Friday XIII has yet to feel like he matters. He's yet to feel like Make-Believe *sees* him, like his neighbors know there's a man beneath the crown. If anything, his regal regalia keeps a sense of belonging at bay. Who, after all, would be foolish enough to try to befriend a *king*?

Enter Randy S. Caribou: a six-foot reindeer with a self-proclaimed love for foolish things. He's starting a Make-Believe soccer team with Daniel Tiger, he says. At first, he'd called it the Reindeer-Tiger Team, but then Prince Tuesday and Ana Platypus had asked to join it, too. So he'd called it the Boy-Girl-Reindeer-Tiger Team. Then Lady Aberlin and Bob Dog joined, so *now* it's the Woman-Dog-Boy-Girl-Reindeer-Tiger Team, Randy explains. And now everyone's ready to play!

Everyone, that is, except for King Friday.

Before today, the sovereign might simply have outlawed soccer altogether. He might have lashed out at the Woman-Dog-Boy-Girl-Reindeer-Tiger Team, couching his anger at being left out in a long royal pronouncement. But something has shifted in Friday. After going around the mulberry bush a couple of times, he's felt the enormous weight of his loneliness finally begin to lift. The once-proud king has been humbled—and he likes it.

"Um, would it be possible to place a king on that team?" he timidly asks his subjects.

"You mean you would, King Friday? I was afraid to ask!" says Randy.

"That's the trouble!" Friday cries. "Everybody's afraid to ask. Kings are human, too!"

"Well, *I'm* asking you," Randy replies. "How about being on our *King-Woman-Dog-Boy-Girl-Reindeer-Tiger Team*?"

King Friday accepts, and Randy buys jerseys for the team: pink, sleeveless, laughably too-large jerseys to show the world that despite their differences, this team chooses togetherness.

In his book *Sapiens*, Yuval Noah Harari explores how human beings managed to break the rules of our wiring and form huge, diverse societies far larger than the tight-knit groups in which we'd evolved. The secret, he writes, was probably the appearance of fiction: stories and structures that don't exist in nature but which serve as a shared experience for people from different tribes. "Large numbers of strangers," Harari writes, "can cooperate successfully by believing in common myths," whether those myths are expressed by churches; by flags; or by pink, oversized jerseys. Myths provide ways of relating to other people across our lines of difference. They do this in part by setting the stage for empathy: the human ability to imagine other people's experiences and to attempt to understand their feelings, thoughts, and points of view.*

In recent years, it's been touted as the cure for almost everything. "There's a lot of talk in this country about the federal deficit," said then senator Barack Obama in a 2006 commencement speech. "But I think we should talk more about our empathy deficit—the ability to put ourselves

---

* There are actually two kinds of empathy: *cognitive* empathy, which refers to understanding another's point of view, and *affective* empathy, which refers to understanding people's feelings. However, most of us simply use "empathy" as an umbrella term for both.

in someone else's shoes; to see the world through those who are different from us—the child who's hungry, the laid-off steelworker, the immigrant woman cleaning your dorm room."

Others have called empathy the key to world peace and a possible solution to climate change. It's been said to make us better teachers, better doctors, better business professionals, and even better athletes. Not only does it drive us to build belonging with others, experts say, it also helps *us*. According to psychologist Michele Borba,

> The ability to empathize affects our kids' future health, wealth, authentic happiness, relationship satisfaction, and ability to bounce back from adversity. It promotes kindness, prosocial behaviors, and moral courage, and it is an effective antidote to bullying, aggression, prejudice, and racism. Empathy is also a positive predictor of children's reading and math test scores and critical thinking skills, prepares kids for the global world, and gives them a job market boost.

For all the hype about empathy, it's a relatively recent concept. The word itself was only coined in 1909, but since then, an explosion of research has helped uncover how empathy works in the brain. In *Wired to Connect*, author Britt Andreatta relates a fascinating study in which scientists watched participants' brains light up when shown a scene from a movie. Afterward, when asked to explain the scene to others, participants' brains lit up as if they were still watching the film. "Even more fascinating, listeners' brains lit up the same way," Andreatta writes. Even though the listeners were simply hearing another person's description, their brains reacted as if they were watching the film themselves. This suggests that to a certain extent, we can share an experience—or at least a *facsimile* of an experience—that we haven't encountered ourselves.

Empathy affects some of us more than others. Some people, for example, may experience physical pain when they see someone else get hurt. For a select few, empathy can even be debilitating as they struggle to differentiate between their own pain and that of other people. (The existence of these "extreme empaths" has been hotly debated by scientists.) On the whole, however, data suggests that Obama was right—that we really are facing an "empathy deficit."

Psychologist Sara Konrath and her colleagues at the University of Michigan found that between 1979 and 2009, empathy levels among college students fell by about 40 percent. Compared to their analog peers, digital-age college students were far less likely to agree with statements like *I sometimes try to understand my friends better by imagining how things look from their perspective*, or *I often have tender, concerned feelings for people less fortunate than I am*. The researchers found a similar decline in kindness and volunteerism.

Though their analysis stopped short of pinpointing specific causes, Konrath and her colleagues theorized that media saturation and pressure to achieve have overwhelmed today's students, making them feel as if there's simply no time for thinking about, listening to, or trying to understand other people. Today's young people aren't inherently less kind or empathetic than their predecessors, but they *are* more anxious and stressed out and worn down and scared. And it's difficult to exercise empathy when that's the way you feel.

Rogers himself knew this well. In fact, to keep himself grounded, he woke up every morning at 5:00 a.m. to give himself a couple of hours of unhurried quiet. He spent those early mornings actively exercising empathy: "He would read the Bible, pray for other people, and then he would think about the coming day," says Maxwell King. "He would spend that time envisioning who he was going to see and how he would be fully engaged and thoughtful and considerate and kind with whomever he encountered."

Rogers understood that empathy can be developed and strengthened like a muscle. "Empathic ability is a bit like musical ability—part nature and part nurture," explains Roman Krznaric, author of *Empathy: Why It Matters, and How to Get It*. "Some people just seem to be born with innate musical skills—they've got perfect pitch or can pick up almost any instrument and play it beautifully. But musicality is also learned. It is best if we start young, yet most people could still learn to play the guitar pretty well at 45, as long as they put in the effort to practice. And that is how it is with empathy."

One of the best ways to "practice" empathy, experts say, is through storytelling. Stories make abstract concepts visceral; they make invisible policies visible. They help us look past our assumptions and see the people behind them: people with pains and joys, motivations and fears. They help us see neighbors instead of "others." We watch the *Neighborhood*'s stories, writes psychologist Susan Linn, "because we have come to care about the essence of these characters. We, and our children, watch because we know them. We recognize ourselves in their complexity."

Indeed, storytelling works both ways: By learning the stories of others, we come to better understand our own. When we strive to see the perspectives of people beyond our immediate tribes, we expand our concerns and see the world and its injustices more clearly. Remember the *Saturday Light Brigade* from Chapter 1—the radio program where kids make podcasts and audio documentaries? The program's students interview people confronting homelessness, racism, the difficulties of being LGBTQ, and more. As part of their reporting, the young producers speak with experts, community leaders, and people with lived experience—a process that, for some kids, can completely upend their worldview. "By the time they put a finished product together, they're thinking about their subjects in ways they never had before," says Larry Berger, the program's founder. "They're full of so much empathy. The work changes them. And it changes their peers who hear it."

Of course, empathy does *not* mean we condone or tolerate everybody's beliefs. When we empathize with someone, we simply aim to discern where they're coming from so that we might understand them. It doesn't require us to agree with or even accept the things they say or do. In fact, empathy can be a powerful tool for changing someone's mind, because it makes human connection possible. And it's often a sense of connection that persuades a person to change.

In one small study, published in *Child Development*, researchers from the National Institute of Mental Health recruited sixteen mothers and their (roughly) two-year-old children. Over the course of several months, the mothers recorded incidents in which their children caused another child's distress, whether by biting, hitting, or snatching away a toy. The researchers found that the kids who were most likely to make amends when they'd hurt someone were those whose mothers were both intensely nurturing and intensely moral. These mothers were *horrified* when their children caused someone pain, and they let their children know it: "Look what you did! Don't you see you hurt Amy? Don't *ever* pull hair!"

This sort of reaction was far more effective than calmly dispensed reasoning. But—and this is essential—it only worked in the context of "empathic caregiving," in which mothers and children had close relationships that were otherwise warm and in which mothers did not attack their children's character.

Rogers himself said it best. "I think people don't change very much when all they have is a finger pointed at them," he once told a reporter. "I think the only way people change is in relation to somebody who loves them."

Who Is My Neighbor?

In 1970, psychologists John Darley and Daniel Batson shared the parable of the Good Samaritan with a few dozen seminary students in Princeton, New Jersey. In the Gospel of Luke, a lawyer asks Jesus, "Who is my neighbor?"

Jesus replies with a story:

A certain man was going down from Jerusalem to Jericho, and he fell among robbers, who both stripped him and beat him, and departed, leaving him half dead. By chance, a certain priest was going down that way. When he saw him, he passed by on the other side. In the same way a Levite also, when he came to the place, and saw him, passed by on the other side. But a certain Samaritan, as he travelled, came where he was. When he saw him, he was moved with compassion, came to him, and bound up his wounds, pouring on oil and wine. He set him on his own animal, and brought him to an inn, and took care of him. On the next day, when he departed, he took out two denarii, gave them to the host, and said to him, "Take care of him. Whatever you spend beyond that, I will repay you when I return." Now, which of these three do you think seemed to be a neighbor to him who fell among the robbers?

Darley and Batson asked the students to give a three- to five-minute sermon on the story, to be recorded in another building on campus. Some of the students were told that they could take their time getting there; others were told they were already late and should hurry as fast as they could. The route required them to pass through an alley, where Darley and Batson had placed an actor—a "victim" that each student would find slumped in a doorway, coughing and groaning.

The researchers watched to see which students helped and to what degree. The results would make the study famous. Among those who'd been told they could take their time, 63 percent offered the victim help. Among those who'd been told to hurry, however, only 10 percent bothered to stop. "A person in a hurry is likely to keep going," Darley and Batson concluded. "Ironically, he is likely to keep going even if he is hurrying to speak on the parable of the Good Samaritan, thus inadvertently confirming the point of the parable. Indeed, on several occasions, a seminary student going to give his talk on the parable of the Good Samaritan literally stepped over the victim as he hurried on his way!"

Did the Princeton seminarians lack empathy? Not necessarily. In post-experiment interviews, some said that they'd noticed the victim but hadn't realized he'd needed help until later, once they'd had time to reflect. In these cases, Darley and Batson theorized, the students' "empathic reactions" were likely delayed by their hurrying. Like today's overwhelmed college students, the pressure of their circumstances had prevented them from empathizing. Others, though, had clearly felt empathy in real time—they were visibly shaken as they passed the victim in the alley. But they still hadn't offered to help.

It's tempting to ascribe this to heartlessness or hypocrisy, and many people have. But in the young ministers' minds, they were *already* helping someone: the researchers themselves. They'd seen the victim and empathized with his plight. But by stopping to offer their help, they felt they'd be letting down the scientists who'd asked for it first. "Conflict, rather than callousness, can explain their failure to stop," Darley and Batson wrote.

Empathy, in other words, isn't necessarily enough. What good is empathy to the victim who's left on the street? Empathy, on its own, doesn't put a roof over the victim's head or take him to a hospital or put him up in an inn. Empathy can even be self-serving—when we pat ourselves on the back for feeling someone's pain, we risk mistaking that feeling for having done something about the problem.

Empathy can also reinforce our biases. We don't deploy it equally, and our reasons for empathizing with some people over others can be exceedingly petty. Let's say you're a soccer fan, and your favorite team is the King-Woman-Dog-Boy-Girl-Reindeer-Tiger Team—you just can't get enough of those pink, oversized jerseys. And let's say you're taking a stroll one day when you see a stranger trip, fall, and injure himself. In deciding whether to help, does it matter what the stranger is wearing?

Science suggests that it does. In fact, when researchers at Lancaster University in the United Kingdom studied this exact scenario (using an actor as the injured stranger), they found that soccer fans were far more likely to help someone who supports their favorite team. When thirteen fans of the British soccer club Manchester United saw an actor trip and fall, all but one stopped to help when the actor was wearing a Manchester jersey. Meanwhile, among the ten Manchester fans who witnessed a Liverpool fan get injured, seven ignored the incident entirely. And among the twelve fans who watched a plainclothes actor slip and fall, only four bothered to help.

Indeed, despite its reputation as a social panacea, empathy has limitations and pitfalls that we ought to be aware of. Yale psychologist Paul Bloom wrote a whole book about them—one with the rather surprising title of *Against Empathy*. "One reason why being against empathy is so shocking is that people often assume that empathy is an absolute good," he explains. "You can never be too rich or too thin . . . or too empathetic. Empathy is unusual in this regard." When it comes to our other feelings and capacities, Bloom argues, we tend to be more nuanced. He gives anger as an example—anger can be constructive, destructive, or both, depending on how it's used.

Still, even critics like Bloom concede that *some* empathy is required for human connection. The Samaritan can't help the victim at all if he doesn't recognize that the victim needs help in the first place. Likewise, "if I'm buying a present for my niece, you don't have to be a moral philosopher to appreciate that I should try to get her something that she wants, not something that I want," he writes. "To make a positive difference, you need some grasp of what's going on in others' minds."

That's why some empathy experts want to tweak our oldest, most universal moral directive: *Do unto others as you would have them do unto you.* The Golden Rule, they argue, is insufficient—"we might end up treating people in a way that would suit ourselves, but that could be wholly inappropriate from their perspective," writes Roman Krznaric. Instead, we ought to upgrade to what's been called the Platinum Rule, which takes other people's feelings, needs, and experiences into account. *Do unto others*, the Platinum Rule states, *as they would have you do unto them.*

Life Is for Service

As Rogers walked with his new friends and his future wife through the campus of Rollins College, he passed an unassuming plaque on a walkway near the quad. The plaque's inscription struck him as so simple—yet so profound—that it would shape the rest of his years. He copied it down on a tiny slip of paper, put it in his wallet, and carried it with him for decades. Eventually, he hung a photo of the plaque on the wall of his office in Pittsburgh. "LIFE IS FOR SERVICE," it read in capital letters—a reminder that, above all, we're put on this planet to help each other.

"People tend to think that Rogers' great passion in life was the education of young children, and that certainly was *one* of his great passions," says Maxwell King. "Another was television and television programming. But I think his overarching, dominant passion was to be a good person and to be good to other people. He felt that it was the number-one job he had in life."

Most of us would more or less agree. Nationally, parents say their highest hope for their children is to grow into loving, caring adults who prioritize family and generosity over everything else. Parents and teachers alike say caring for other people is far more important to them than children's intelligence or achievements. On surveys, at least, our priorities seem loud and clear.

But according to a 2014 report released by Harvard University's Graduate School of Education, our children hear something else entirely. About 80 percent of young people say their parents are more concerned about achievement than they are about being loving or caring. A similar proportion say the same is true of their teachers. When asked what would make their parents prouder—getting good grades or being a caring community member—kids were three times more likely to pick the former.

According to the researchers who conducted the survey, the messages adults convey about achievement and happiness are far more powerful— and far more frequent—than the ones we convey about caring. For kids, this can be confusing at best, and counterproductive at worst. Those under the most pressure to achieve tend to report the lowest levels of empathy, and those whose parents emphasize happiness aren't necessarily happier.

The good news is that kids themselves still value caring for others. Of the ten thousand young people surveyed, about two-thirds listed kindness among their top three values. Many described the strong moral codes they'd developed over time. As one young person wrote, "I feel that people should always put others before themselves and focus on contributing something to the world that will improve life for future generations."

Young people like this are onto something, scientists say. Not only does service to others benefit the world at large, it also benefits young people themselves, making them less lonely and more likely to find a sense of belonging. It reduces stress and boosts well-being. And it helps them find that all-important sense that they matter.

To become loving and caring people, kids first have to know that they're worthy of love and care themselves. That's why, when Rogers gave speeches, he often helped his audiences see exactly that. "From the time you were very little," he'd say, "you've had people who have smiled you into smiling, people who have talked you into talking, sung you into singing, loved you into loving."

Some of them may be here right now. Some may be far away. Some . . . may even be in heaven. But wherever they are, if they've loved you, and encouraged you, and wanted what was best in life for you, they're right inside your self. And I feel that you deserve quiet time, on this special occasion, to devote some thought to them. So, let's just take a minute, in honor of those [who] have cared about us all along the way. One silent minute.

Whomever you've been thinking about, imagine how grateful they must be that during your silent times, you remember how important they are to you. It's not the honors and the prizes, and the fancy outsides of life which ultimately nourish our souls. It's the knowing that we can be trusted. That we never have to fear the truth. That the bedrock of our lives, from which we make our choices, is very good stuff.

Tears were not uncommon by the minute's end. The exercise immersed participants in gratitude and belonging, reinforcing the notion that they, too, can be loving, caring people. And understanding that notion can be critical. "The greatest thing we can do," Rogers liked to say, "is let people know that they are loved and capable of loving."

The exercise is closely related to a form of meditation called *metta*, or loving-kindness meditation—a Buddhist practice that strengthens the sense of connection among loved ones, acquaintances, and even strangers. In one *metta* practice, participants call to mind someone who has loved them deeply. They let themselves feel that person's love; then they imagine themselves reflecting that love back to the world. According to Emma Seppälä of Stanford University, loving-kindness meditation can increase feelings of happiness while reducing self-focus and turning our attention toward others. It can prepare us, in other words, for service.

Valerie Kinloch remembers the people who loved her, who encouraged her, who wanted what was best in life for her. She knows that even today, they're right inside her self. Many years later and many miles from home, she can still list their names: Ms. Kirkland, Ms. Ferguson, Ms. Smalls, Ms. Green, Ms. Thompson. "It was the presence of these teachers—these Black women teachers—that provided me with an understanding of what can happen if I would only imagine it. If I would only *think* it. If I would only put myself in someone else's position, even as a kid in elementary school, and have empathy," she says. "They helped me embrace the idea that, 'You can always become. You can always strive to *be*.'"

Kinloch followed that idea from a childhood in Charleston, South Carolina, to a life of service that has spanned the country. As an educator; the author of several books about race, literacy, and service learning; and the dean of the School of Education at the University of Pittsburgh, Kinloch has spent her career building something better for young people—building a kind of learning that, like her own teachers did for her, shows kids that they matter just the way they are.

It's something that the education system too often fails to do, says Kinloch, especially for children who look like she does. "Kids walk into classrooms and learning spaces excited. They want to learn, they want to make, they want to redesign worlds. And when we, the adults, don't make space for that, we squash all of that creativity," she says. "We tell them, 'You *can't* do these things that you're dreaming about. Now, fit this mold and meet these standards.' How do we think about *possibilities* instead? How do we think about the ways that people dream and imagine better futures? Why don't we start by asking, 'What do you dream about that you never talk about? What would you do if only you could?'"

By starting there, says Kinloch, we can start to build spaces where everyone—kids and parents and families alike—can feel a sense of belonging. We can start to build spaces where everyone's a learner and everyone's a teacher, and where the learning that happens at home and in communities is just as valued as the learning that happens in school. We can build spaces that look, in other words, a lot more like the *Neighborhood*: where humanity and justice go hand in hand, and where we're valued for *who we are* rather than *what we do*.

To that end, Kinloch also cochairs Remake Learning, the network of schools, libraries, museums, and out-of-school programs in Pittsburgh comprised of the people and organizations we've met throughout this book (and many, many others). At its core, the network exists to nudge us closer to the *Neighborhood*, providing the space for desires and dreams on one hand, and tools for turning possibilities into realities on the other. Whether kids are recording interviews at the *Saturday Light Brigade* or spinning pottery at the Manchester Craftsmen's Guild or weaving community at the Global Minds Initiative, they all come to see that in order to learn, we need only stop and listen—to ourselves and to one another.

It's a lesson Kinloch learned from an early age. What her teachers helped her see, she says, is that the people around her were "a series of books that I hadn't been reading. Everything my teachers were trying to teach me was always right in front of me. I didn't have to open a book to read it—I could just sit and listen to the conversations happening on the front porches or at the kitchen table or even in the hallways at school. And when I realized that, that's when I fell deeply in love with learning."

It's also when she fell deeply into her *self*—the person she'd become as she read the people around her. One memory in particular remains especially vivid: "We were in Ms. Ferguson's classroom, and a kid stood up and said he was sick. And then all of a sudden, he just threw up all over the place," Kinloch recalls, laughing. "Of course, we were all screaming. 'It stinks! Ms. Ferguson, it stinks!'

"And very calmly, Ms. Ferguson said something like, 'We're going to get some supplies and we're going to clean it up. We'll make sure it doesn't soak into the carpet. Anyone who feels like they don't have the stomach for it can go to the other side of the room or in the hallway, but I need someone who's willing to help.'"

Kinloch's fourth-grade self stayed in the room to clean. "I remember it so clearly," she says. "Ms. Ferguson looked at me and said, 'You are going to be someone who cares for people and who does good in the world.' And even today, that's my work: The type of cleaning up that means being willing to show humanity to others—being willing to go there even when it's nasty and messy. It means not ignoring human suffering. It means working with other people to make the world better. If we want to clean up, we've got to be *out there*, whatever *out there* looks like for each of us. That's the work. That's service."

One Little Buckaroo

Fred Rogers was just out of college, taking his first steps on the path that would lead to the *Neighborhood*. He'd moved to New York City to learn the art and craft of television production by working behind the scenes at NBC Studios. Among the programs he helped produce was *The Gabby Hayes Show*: a short-lived, Western-themed program for children. Starring George "Gabby" Hayes as a folksy, bandanna-clad cowboy with a whistle in his speech, the program was as much an ad for its sponsor, Quaker Oats, as it was an original program. But one thing in particular caught Rogers' eye: *The Gabby Hayes Show* began and ended, just as the

Neighborhood would some fifteen years later, with its star speaking directly into the camera.

"Mr. Hayes," Rogers asked the make-believe cowboy, "what do you think about when you look in the camera and know that there are thousands of people looking at you?"

Hayes didn't hesitate. "Freddy," he said, "I think of one little buckaroo."

The comment stuck with Rogers for the rest of his career. In the *Neighborhood*, he later wrote, he tried to do the same thing, imagining one "television friend" as he talked to the camera. His aim, of course, was to do what Hayes had done and what countless others have tried to do since: connect with children through a screen.

In the spring of 2020, when COVID-19 closed schools around the world, the upheaval thrust smartphones, videoconferencing, and virtual instruction into the spotlight. The sudden and near-total shift to online learning sparked a wave of frustration from kids, families, and educators alike. Forging human connection is difficult enough under ideal circumstances, when kids and adults can gather in classrooms and communities. Take away that face-to-face interaction, and the difficulty grows by magnitudes—especially with younger kids, for whom interpersonal time is essential to learning and development.

The outbreak of COVID-19 was a case study in what can happen when human connections are severed. Parents found themselves largely on their own, coping with financial fallout, childcare concerns, and the health of their families. Educators, for the first time, had to rely almost entirely on digital tools—tools that many of their students couldn't afford or acquire. Kids themselves lost the very connections that helped them define and develop themselves as human beings: connections with friends, peers, and the people beyond their homes. It takes a village to raise a child, but what happens when the villagers all stay home?

"It's hard. There's no getting around it," says Valerie Kinloch. "It's even harder when we think about young kids, because for them, it's often about being able to smell and hear and touch and experience. But in the absence of being able to see one another face-to-face, I go back to building relationships. Because learning *always* starts with relationships. And I don't have to be in front of a person to learn how to be in relation with that person."

Instead, it helps to do what Gabby Hayes did and what Fred Rogers did: be there for that one little buckaroo on the other side of the screen.

It's a message that Rogers impressed upon his staff. "When I first met Fred for advice after completing my bachelor's degree in psychology," says Hedda Sharapan, "he suggested that I study child development at the graduate level if I wanted to do work in children's television. And what I heard in that was that the important question is not, 'What can *I give* to children?' The important question is, 'What are *they bringing* to us?' We, as adults, learn so much when we're curious about who children are. What a great opportunity for us to learn from what they're noticing and expressing—things we might have never considered ourselves."

This is especially important as kids carry the weight of the world, whether in the form of climate change, racism, a global pandemic, or all of the above and more. Whatever it is that kids are bringing, it's the job of adults to recognize it; to let kids express it if they want to; and to let kids know that their feelings are all right, whatever those feelings might be.

"When children want us to listen, they're not just saying, 'I want you to hear my words,'" says Kinloch. "They're saying, 'I want you to figure out my body movements. I want you to figure out what you think my eyes are saying. I want you to hear what I'm saying in ways where—if for only a minute—you suspend your beliefs about me. You suspend the judgments you're carrying and the point you want to make, and you just sit back and truly listen.'"

It's by doing this, experts say, that we begin to restore the connections we've lost. It's a slow, sometimes difficult process—one that requires every tool for learning that the *Neighborhood* left us. We have to be curious about kids. We have to let them be creative in the ways they reveal themselves to us. We have to listen to them deeply and talk to them lovingly, and we have to show up for them if we want them to show up for us. "Whether we're talking through a computer or face-to-face," says Kinloch, "if I don't have a connection with students, I'm not going anywhere."

Fortunately for us, connection doesn't require that we always have the answers. On the contrary, revealing our own vulnerability—our fears, our self-doubts, our uncertainties—models for kids that it's okay to *not* know and that it's good to ask for help. It models for kids that it's okay to admit that we need one another. "In times of stress," said Rogers, "the best thing we can do for each other is to listen with our ears and our hearts, and to be assured that our questions are just as important as our answers."

It's in those questions and in that listening that human connection can thrive—whether we're kids, adults, or make-believe kings.

⋯⋯⋯⋯⋯

"Welcome!" King Friday exclaims, donning the jersey that covers his robe. "Team members, I presume?"

"Correct as usual, King Friday!" his teammates shout as one.

From the castle balcony, Make-Believe's ruler waves to his subjects. No—he waves to his *friends*. He waves to those caring people and puppets who've shown him that he, King Friday XIII, matters—that he's part of something special. That even though he's been brash and volatile and insecure, and even though he might be those things again, he can still find grace in connection with others. He can still do what he's been put here to do: serve his beloved community.

The team's all here. They've even added a few new players. With Henrietta Pussycat and X the Owl on board, the Pussycat-Owl-King-Woman-Dog-Boy-Girl-Reindeer-Tiger Team is finally ready to play. Whether the game is soccer or hide-and-seek or dancing around the mulberry bush, it makes no difference to the jubilant king. It just feels nice to be part of a team.

"Every time we get together in our outfits," King Friday tells his pink-jerseyed friends, "we can decide what we'll play and we'll play it! And we'll win the game of having *fun*! Let's hear it for our team!"

⸻

Back in his living room, Mister Rogers waits for us like always. He looks much happier now that Friday has found a team, and he hopes that we can find one, too. "And no matter what game you play," he tells us, "you can be yourself. And that's all you ever have to be. You are *you*, and that's enough for anybody. And knowing that can give you such a good feeling."

Mister Rogers smiles—he's felt that feeling himself. He thinks, perhaps, about *his* team: about his parents and grandparents; about the car full of friends on a tarmac in Florida; about his wife, Joanne; and his mentor, Margaret, for whom he wrote this episode. Perhaps he thinks of all the people who have smiled him into smiling, talked him into talking, and sung him into singing.

Or perhaps he thinks, just for a moment, of Helen Ross, the friend he'd visited at the end of her life. It was Helen, after all, who had liked to remind him: "Don't forget the *fun*." It was Helen who had spent a lifetime studying the wonders of human development, and it was Helen who—during Rogers' final bedside visit—revealed what she had learned.

"I found Helen very frail," Rogers recalled. "Some of the time, I just held her hand and we said nothing. We didn't have to.

"After one of those silences, Helen said to me, 'Do you ever pray for people, Fred?'

"'Of course I do,' I simply said. 'Dear God, encircle us with thy love wherever we may be.'

"And Helen replied, 'That's what it is, isn't it? It's love. That's what it's all about.'"

WHAT MIGHT YOU DO?

- Have you ever felt like you didn't belong? Each of us has, at some point, felt isolated. We clearly weren't wanted on the team, or our peers decided to reject us. Talk to children about why it hurts when you feel like you don't belong and how they might seek ways to build bridges beyond their friends. Who else could be on their "team"? Who might be feeling excluded? *Encourage your child to ask the quiet kid across the street to play. Or ask your child to paint a picture for the neighbor who's stuck inside. How can kids say, in their own way, "I have always wanted to have a neighbor just like you?"*

- King Friday and Bob Dog learned that they were more alike than they might have assumed. While they'd been separated materially by King Friday's regal clothes and high perch, they found that they shared an experience—they'd both been left out. They connected with each other by coming to understand the other character's perspective. *Talk with your kids about their friends and neighbors. What unexpected experiences, feelings, and beliefs might they share? What might they gain by learning about other lives—and imagining themselves in other people's shoes?*

- Empathy—like doing a cartwheel or drawing a really good circle— is something that has to be practiced. Help your kids to identify small things they can do to put themselves in other people's positions. *On their birthdays, Gregg's kids receive lots of gifts. Each year, however, they're only allowed to keep three or four of them. The rest are set aside for a charitable organization called Beverly's Birthdays, which arranges birthday parties for kids experiencing homelessness. The conversations that ensue help children understand why some of their peers don't receive gifts, why some kids don't have homes, and why it's good to share with others. Is there something relatable you can do with your own kids to help them build their empathy muscles?*

- Allow yourself to be vulnerable with your children. Adults, says Valerie Kinloch, "have to be vulnerable and willing to show that we're human beings who have feelings and who don't have all the answers. When we can show that to kids, they will always show it to us." *Be honest when you don't know the answer to something, and invite your children along on your quest to discover the answer.*

- Be willing to give your children—and yourself—a break when things get overwhelming. *"Some days," said Rogers, "doing 'the best we can' may still fall short of what we would like to be able to do, but life isn't perfect on any front—and doing what we can with what we have is the most we should expect of ourselves or anyone else."*

The Beginning of Something Else

Long before this was a book—back when it was just an *idea* for a book—its premise was this: In a time of rapid social and technological change, the tools for learning that Fred Rogers taught would grow more and more essential.

We had no idea how much rapid change was in store.

It took more than two years to write *When You Wonder, You're Learning*, and in many ways, the world in which we started the manuscript looked wholly different from the one in which we finished it. A strange and deadly virus spread across the planet, killing far too many people and putting countless more out of work. Much of what had once been modern life—commuting and commerce and getting together for coffee—came to a grinding halt. At the same time, a reckoning came to America: The country's centuries-old legacy of racism took center stage in the national discourse, and millions of people risked brutality and illness and worse to march for justice.

Amid it all, for the first time in history, millions of kids started their school years behind computer screens. Parents and caregivers quickly added a new word to their jam-packed job descriptions: *educator*. Though parents and caregivers have long been the people whom we learn from the most, they haven't always been considered educators—at least in the traditional sense of the word. In "normal" times, kids *learned* from their parents, but *education* came from their teachers.

The pandemic shattered that dichotomy. Families got a firsthand glimpse at digital-age teaching, with all its difficulties and joys. And teachers peered into kitchens and living rooms and saw, more clearly than ever, what matters to families at home.

It's too soon to tell where all of this will take us, though by the time you read this book, perhaps we'll have some signals. For now, all that's clear is that change—even big change—can happen far more quickly than we might have once assumed. What was "normal" yesterday doesn't *have* to define tomorrow. And though the time in between may be weighted by grief, with change comes a sense of possibility—a door to something better, if we're willing to push it open. "Often, when you think you're at the end of something, you're at the beginning of something else," Fred Rogers said. And that's exactly where we find ourselves now.

It can be tempting, at such junctures, to want to hide in the *Neighborhood*. The two of us have felt it as strongly as anyone. It's just *nicer* in there—the days begin and end predictably; neighbors treat each other like human beings; and it's almost always sunny and warm. Who *wouldn't* want to cast aside reality and get lost in Make-Believe instead? Who wouldn't prefer the *Neighborhood*'s comfort over the pain outside our windows?

But here's the thing: The *Neighborhood* isn't a hiding place.

It never was.

It's easy to forget with the program so squarely in our rearview mirrors, but the *Neighborhood* never shielded us from the world or its horrors. During the program's first few minutes in February 1968, King Friday

XIII decided to build a border wall, declaring a war on outsiders and change. By the end of that year—which saw Martin Luther King Jr. murdered in Memphis, millions of people marching for justice, and a strange and deadly virus spreading across the planet—the program would cover sickness, assassination, burning buildings, and more. Even today, *Daniel Tiger's Neighborhood* bravely does the same, tackling difficult topics like racism and COVID-19.

So why do we find such comfort in the world of Mister Rogers? If the *Neighborhood* was more than beautiful days and pleasant songs and the sheer *niceness* for which we revere it, why does it feel like a refuge? Actress Mary Rawson, who played Cousin Mary Owl in the Neighborhood of Make-Believe, offers a theory. In the *Neighborhood*, "violence and war, hatred and intolerance are not painted out of the picture," she writes, "but neither are they allowed to destroy the canvas."

The real gift that Fred Rogers gave us was hope—hope that with the tools for learning that he worked so hard to teach us, we would find within ourselves the strength to confront hard problems. Hope that we'd each find the courage to love thy neighbor. Hope that caring adults would protect us—and that each of us would, in turn, become caring adults ourselves. Rogers gave us hope that despite everything, the canvas was worth defending.

If the people we met while writing this book are any indication, such hope was not misplaced. Every day in Pittsburgh and beyond, parents, educators, and young people themselves are doing what Rogers did— combining timeless ideas with new ways of learning to make the world more accepting, more compassionate, and more humane. At the *Saturday Light Brigade* and at Steeltown, they're using podcasts and films to celebrate their differences and to shine a light on their similarities. They're using Simple Interactions to turn mundane moments into loving affirmations. They're learning side by side at Remake Learning Days, growing closer together in the process. And at programs like GirlGov, they're giving kids a direct say in democracy—in what "something else" will look like.

It's a kind of work that's never really finished. Rogers, of course, knew this all along: When he aired his final episode in August 2001, he gave no indication that we'd reached the end. There's an arts festival in Make-Believe; Rogers tells us he's proud of us; and as he walks out the door, he waves goodbye and tells us he'll see us again.

It must have seemed like an odd final line from a man who insisted, at every turn, that his program speak honestly to children. Why, at the end of something, would he focus on the beginning of something else? Why would he tell us he'd "be back next time" if next time hadn't been planned?

Perhaps because "next time" is now and "next time" is tomorrow and "next time" is the day after that. Perhaps because the work of the *Neighborhood*—which is the work of learning that we're loved and capable of loving—is infinite. "Love," Rogers said, "isn't a state of perfect caring. It is an active noun like struggle. To love someone is to strive to accept that person exactly the way he or she is, right here and now."

If we want to raise creative, curious, caring human beings, then we have our work cut out for us.

May we offer that love—and carry on with that striving—for the rest of our days.

Acknowledgments

I hope you're proud of yourself for the times you've
said "yes," when all it meant was extra work for you and
was seemingly helpful only to someone else.

—Fred Rogers

The number of people who said "yes" during the course of this project
continues to astound us. So many neighbors gave freely of their time, expertise, and care, often benefiting no one but the two of us. To properly
express our gratitude would require an additional book. We'll spare you
that for now, but we want to extend a special thanks to Bill Isler, without
whom this book would simply not exist. Bill's guidance provided the very
foundation for *When You Wonder, You're Learning.* He trusted us from the
start and generously opened door after door.

Likewise, we extend our unending gratitude to Joanne Rogers. Having
the blessing of Queen Sara Saturday herself is what helped us write when
writing seemed impossible. Joanne, thank you for believing in us and in
this project. We hope it carries forward the legacy that you marshaled
with grace.

Thank you also to Hedda Sharapan of Fred Rogers Productions and
the Fred Rogers Center. Hedda knows as much about the *Neighborhood*

as anyone, and she embodies its lessons in a way that inspires us both. Hedda, thank you for your time, insights, and feedback. All of it made this a better, more useful book.

We're also grateful to Maxwell King, both for his excellent biography and the commentary he provided for each chapter. We drew upon his knowledge every step of the way, and we're fortunate that such a critical source also happens to be a great writer and a genuinely likable guy. We're in your debt, Max. Both of us.

We'd also like to thank all the people who sat with us in person and on the phone and on Zoom, answering our good questions and our bad ones with utmost thought. The work they do—and the care they bring to that work each day—filled us with hope, even in our difficult moments. Thank you to Jason Brown and the Carnegie Science Center; Melissa Butler, the reimagining project, and the Children's Innovation Project; Larry Berger, Chanessa Schuler, and the *Saturday Light Brigade*; Kristin Morgan, Simon Rafferty, and The Labs @ Carnegie Library of Pittsburgh; Bill Strickland and the Manchester Craftsmen's Guild; Jane Werner and the Children's Museum of Pittsburgh; Dana Winters and the Simple Interactions team at the Fred Rogers Center; Wendy Burtner, Ian Altenbaugh, and Steeltown; Terry Richards, Patti Rote, and the Girls of Steel; Mary Kay Babyak, Sarah Brooks, Aaron Altemus, and the Consortium for Public Education; Peyton Klein and the Global Minds Initiative; Dorie Taylor, Yu-Ling Cheng, and the Remake Learning Days Across America team; Heather Arnet and the Women and Girls Foundation; and Valerie Kinloch and the University of Pittsburgh School of Education. Each of these people make the *Neighborhood* real, as do many, many others whom we couldn't include. We've been inspired by them in our hometown, across the United States, and around the world. There are so many good, caring, and creative people supporting our kids.

We'd also like to thank Fred Rogers' kind and generous colleagues, who—after helping to bring us *Mister Rogers' Neighborhood*—went on to do incredible, important work in other roles. In particular, we'd like to thank Roberta Schomburg of the Fred Rogers Center at Saint Vincent College, as well as such former directors and fellows as Rita Catalano, Rick Fernandes, Junlei Li, and Alice Wilder. Likewise, we're beyond grateful to Aisha White at the Positive Racial Identity Development in Early Education (P.R.I.D.E.) program at the University of Pittsburgh.

Special thanks also to Paul Siefken and Chris Arnold at Fred Rogers Productions and to the Right Reverend Douglas Nowicki and Emily Uhrin at the Fred Rogers Center.

Lots of people helped us navigate the mysterious world of books and publishing, and they did it with patience and good humor. Thank you to Bob Miller and Sarah Murphy at Flatiron Books for their selfless feedback on our initial ideas and for connecting us to our favorite literary agent: Jessica Papin at Dystel, Goderich & Bourret. Jessica, you are second to none, and we can hardly begin to thank you.

And then, of course, there's our editor, Dan Ambrosio, and the entire team at Hachette Books. Thank you all for your confidence in us and for helping us turn an idea into something real.

We'd also like to thank the people and institutions on which we've relied for expertise, support, and mentorship. Thank you to the Grable Foundation and its unflagging dedication to improving the lives of children and youth. Thank you in particular to the foundation's trustees—Chip Burke, Patsy Burke, Jan Nicholson, Barbara Nicholson McFadyen, Susan Brownlee, Bill Isler, and Rob Ivry—and to our second-floor colleagues: Kristen Burns, D'Ann Swanson, Tracey Reed Armant, Teresa Serrao, Jennifer Morris, Regina Archie, Wendy Belic, Dana Lamenza, Merrilynn Young, James Isler, Bart Rocco, and Bille Rondinelli.

Thank you, also, to the Remake Learning Council, to Remake Learning at large, and to the network's leaders past and present: Jim Denova, Valerie Kinloch, Sunanna Chand, Mary Murrin, Anne Sekula, Gerry Balbier, Ani Martinez, Temple Lovelace, Tyler Samstag, LaTrenda Leonard Sherrill, Rosanne Javorsky, Don Martin, Megan Collett, Lynne Schrum, Jess Trybus, and so very many others.

We're grateful to the many organizations that have made this work possible over the years, including the Sprout Fund (Cathy Lewis Long and Matt Hannigan), Root+All (Ryan Coon and Arielle Evans), Grantmakers of Western Pennsylvania (Barbara Taylor), the Motherhood (Cooper Munroe), DesignQuack (Deb Cavrak), and Melissa Rayworth.

Finally, two places in particular—one virtual, the other brick-and-mortar—were instrumental in bringing this book to fruition. The first is the *Mister Rogers' Neighborhood* Archive (neighborhoodarchive.com), an online resource meticulously maintained by Tim Lybarger. The number of times we've turned to Tim's site is probably in the thousands. Thank you, Tim, for such an incredible labor of love.

The second place is the Carnegie Library of Pittsburgh, where the bulk of this book was researched and written. Public libraries are pillars of our democracy; please support them however you can.

On a personal note, Gregg is forever thankful for the love and support of three people who fill his every day with joy, growth, and gratitude: Yu-Ling, Catheryn, and Caroline. It is his own family—Tom, Karen, and Scott—who long ago set the foundations and expectations for loving and kindness. His Taiwanese family—Weng-Sheng, Lee-May, and Robert—show repeatedly that generosity crosses cultures and oceans. And he's been lucky to surround himself with a lifetime of incredibly decent and amazingly inspiring friends, teachers, and colleagues. You know who you are—thank you.

Ryan would like to thank his parents and grandparents for building the loving neighborhood in which he grew up and which surrounds him still. Thanks also to his sister, Kathryn, and his siblings-in-law: Pat, Ed, Celia, Tom, and Joe. Then there are the people who've made him a better writer and a better human: his professors at Chatham and Pitt; his brilliant writer friends (who could forget Corey Florindi or Brittany Hailer?); and his former students in south Louisiana, who gave their teacher more patience and kindheartedness than he deserved. He'd also like to thank John Bixby, Shane Connelly, Bob Fischer, Will Gamble, Jordan Rydzewski, and Peter Topa—laughs can be few and far between in the middle of draft number six, but you kept them coming from start to finish. Thank you for the gift of belonging. Finally, and most of all, Ryan would like to thank Jackie Roth, whose presence allows him to write the word *love* and to know, deep down, exactly what it means.

About the Authors

Gregg Behr is a father, children's advocate, and director for the Grable Foundation whose work has drawn comparisons to his hero, Fred Rogers. For more than a decade, he has helped lead Remake Learning—a network of educators, scientists, artists, and makers he founded in 2007—to international renown. Formed in Rogers' real-life neighborhood of Pittsburgh, Remake Learning has turned heads everywhere from Forbes to the World Economic Forum for its efforts to ignite children's curiosity, encourage creativity, and foster justice and belonging in schools, libraries, museums, and more. A graduate of the University of Notre Dame and also Duke University, Gregg holds honorary degrees from Carlow University and Saint Vincent College. He's an advisor to the Brookings Institution and the Fred Rogers Center, and has been cited by Barack Obama, Richard Branson, and the Disruptor Foundation as an innovator and thought leader. Twitter: @greggbehr

Ryan Rydzewski is a writer whose science and education reporting has garnered several awards and fellowships. A graduate of the University of Pittsburgh, he taught elementary school in south Louisiana before earning an MFA in nonfiction writing from Chatham University. As a freelancer, his magazine stories have focused on everything from schools to space travel to *Mister Rogers' Neighborhood*, and his poems and other pieces have appeared in several journals. A native of Erie, Pennsylvania, Ryan lives in Pittsburgh with his wife, Jaqueline. Visit his website at ryanrydzewski. com. Twitter: @ryanrydzewski

Further Reading

To learn more about Remake Learning and its work,
visit remakelearning.org and remakelearningdays.org.

To learn more about the future of learning in Pittsburgh and beyond, visit
grable.org/publications.

Follow *When You Wonder, You're Learning* online:

Instagram: @When_You_Wonder
Twitter: @When_You_Wonder
Facebook: facebook.com/WhenYouWonder/
Website: WhenYouWonder.org

Send us your questions, ideas, and more at WhenYouWonderBook@gmail.com.

Sources

Introduction

2   **"Can you imagine what it's like":** Gillies, Judith S. "Back to Mr. Rogers' Neighborhood." *Washington Post*, December 28, 2003. https://www.washingtonpost.com/archive/lifestyle/tv/2003/12/28/back-to-mr-rogers-neighborhood/9b88d474-0a49-4580-a492-b302f4e7d4c7/.

2   **Studies of children who regularly watched:** Wilson, Barbara J. "Media and Children's Aggression, Fear, and Altruism." *CYC-Online*, no. 112 (May 2008). https://www.cyc-net.org/cyc-online/cyconline-june2008-wilson.html.

3   **Clearly, there's still a cultural craving:** "PBS KIDS Renews 'Daniel Tiger's Neighborhood' for a Fourth Season." PBS KIDS, October 11, 2017. https://www.fredrogers.org/2017/10/11/pbs-kids-renews-daniel-tigers-neighborhood-fourth-season/.

4   **They'd also find that their sixteenth-century:** Heywood, Colin. *A History of Childhood: Children and Childhood in the West from Medieval to Modern Times.* Cambridge, UK: Polity, 2001.

4   **What they've found is that kids:** Orme, Nicholas. *Medieval Children.* New Haven, CT: Yale University Press, 2003. Pg. 10.

5   **A child-rearing tract:** Cressy, David. *Literacy and the Social Order: Reading and Writing in Tudor and Stuart England.* Cambridge, UK: Cambridge University Press, 2009. Pg. 4.

6   **In fact, for a brief period in 2002:** Garvin, David A. "How Google Sold Its Engineers on Management." *Harvard Business Review*, December 2013. https://hbr.org/2013/12/how-google-sold-its-engineers-on-management.

6 **"If they become stuck, they'll ask":** Bryant, Adam. "Google's Quest to Build a Better Boss." *New York Times*, March 12, 2011. https://www.nytimes.com/2011/03/13/business/13hire.html.

9 **"More importantly, they'll use the facts":** Wagner, Melissa, Tim Lybarger, and Jenna McGuiggan. *Mister Rogers' Neighborhood: A Visual History*. New York, NY: Clarkson Potter, 2019. Pg. 241.

9 **They've been shown to be up to *ten times*:** *From a Nation at Risk to a Nation at Hope*. Aspen Institute's National Commission on Social, Emotional, and Academic Development, January 15, 2019. http://nationathope.org/wp-content/uploads/2018_aspen_final-report_full_webversion.pdf.

9 **What really matters is whether:** Rogers, Fred. *The World According to Mister Rogers: Important Things to Remember*. New York, NY: Hyperion, 2003.

Chapter 1: When You Wonder, You're Learning

12 **"Cancel. All. Curiosity.":** "Mister Rogers Talks About Curiosity." Episode. *Mister Rogers' Neighborhood* #1751, February 21, 2000.

13 **Actors posing as critics wandered:** Burns, Lucy. "Degenerate Art: Why Hitler Hated Modernism." BBC World Service, November 6, 2013. https://www.bbc.com/news/magazine-24819441.

13 **"What societies really, ideally, want":** Baldwin, James. "A Talk to Teachers." *Saturday Review*, December 21, 1963.

14 **According to one theory, the discovery:** Wrangham, Richard. *Catching Fire: How Cooking Made Us Human*. New York, NY: Basic Books, 2009.

14 **Before they learn to speak:** Leslie, Ian. *Curious: The Desire to Know and Why Your Future Depends On It*. New York, NY: Basic Books, 2015. Pg. xxi.

14 **Not only is it "the linchpin":** Engel, Susan. *The Hungry Mind: The Origins of Curiosity in Childhood*. Cambridge, MA: Harvard University Press, 2015. Pg. 3.

15 **"In a few people, intellectual curiosity":** Popova, Maria. "How We Think: John Dewey on the Art of Reflection and Fruitful Curiosity in an Age of Instant Opinions and Information Overload." Brain Pickings, March 27, 2017. https://www.brainpickings.org/2014/08/18/how-we-think-john-dewey/.

15 **It's been estimated that today's young:** Young, Jeffrey R. "How Many Times Will People Change Jobs? The Myth of the Endlessly-Job-Hopping

Millennial." EdSurge, July 20, 2017. https://www.edsurge.com/news/2017-07-20-how-many-times-will-people-change-jobs-the-myth-of-the-endlessly-job-hopping-millennial.

15 **Consider the priorities of any:** Clifford, Catherine. "5 Traits Tim Cook Looks for in an Apple Employee." CNBC, October 3, 2016. https://www.cnbc.com/2016/10/03/5-traits-tim-cook-looks-for-in-an-apple-employee.html.

15 **Addressing a crowd of college graduates:** Aiello, McKenna. "9 Most Inspiring Quotes from Oprah Winfrey's USC Commencement Speech." E! Online, May 11, 2018. https://www.eonline.com/news/934704/9-most-inspiring-quotes-from-oprah-winfrey-s-usc-commencement-speech.

15 **And Ta-Nehisi Coates:** Dyson, Michael Eric. "Ta-Nehisi Coates on Education, Religion and Obama." *Washington Post*, October 13, 2017. https://www.washingtonpost.com/outlook/ta-nehisi-coates-on-education-religion-and-obama/2017/10/13/adc054c6-ae84-11e7-be94-fabb0f1e9ffb_story.html.

17 **"[My grandfather] helped me":** "Mister Rogers Talks About Making and Creating." Episode. *Mister Rogers' Neighborhood* #1559, February 6, 1986.

17 **"Inciting children's curiosity":** Engel, *The Hungry Mind*, Pg. 17.

17 **The research team watched their brains:** Kang, Min Jeong, Ming Hsu, Ian M. Krajbich, George Loewenstein, Samuel M. McClure, Joseph Tao-yi Wang, and Colin F. Camerer. "The Wick in the Candle of Learning: Epistemic Curiosity Activates Reward Circuitry and Enhances Memory." *Psychological Science* 20, no. 8 (August 2009). https://doi.org/10.1111/j.1467-9280.2009.02402.x.

18 **"The researchers also found that":** Livio, Mario. *Why?: What Makes Us Curious*. New York, NY: Simon & Schuster Paperbacks, 2017. Pg. 96.

18 **"Curiosity may put the brain":** Cell Press. "How Curiosity Changes the Brain to Enhance Learning." ScienceDaily. www.sciencedaily.com/releases/2014/10/141002123631.htm.

20 **Chouinard concluded that curiosity:** Chouinard, Michelle M., P. L. Harris, and Michael P. Maratsos. "Children's Questions: A Mechanism for Cognitive Development." *Monographs of the Society for Research in Child Development* 72, no. 1 (2007): 1–129. http://www.jstor.org/stable/30163594.

20   **"That means 11-year-olds":** Engel, Susan. "The Case for Curiosity." *Educational Leadership.* ACSD, February 2013. http://www.ascd.org/publications/educational-leadership/feb13/vol70/num05/The-Case-for-Curiosity.aspx.

21   **There's a reason childproofing:** Dao, Amy, and Juliet McMullin. "Unintentional Injury, Supervision, and Discourses on Childproofing Devices." *Medical Anthropology* 38, no. 1 (January 2019): 15–29. https://doi.org/10.1080/01459740.2018.1482548.

22   **"The teacher stopped her midsentence":** Engel, "The Case for Curiosity."

22   **Moreover, those answers have:** Begus, Katarina, and Victoria Southgate. "Infant Pointing Serves an Interrogative Function." *Developmental Science* 15, no. 5 (September 2012): 611–617. https://doi.org/10.1111/j.1467-7687.2012.01160.x.

23   **"Even when you don't know the answer":** *The Sky Above Mister Rogers' Neighborhood: Teacher's Guide.* Pittsburgh, PA: Family Communications, n.d. https://www.peoriariverfrontmuseum.org/system/resources/BAhbBlsHOgZmSSIuMjAxMi8xMi8wMi8xMV8xOF8wMF8zNDhfVGVhY2hlcl9HdWlkZS5wZGYGOgZFVA/Teacher%20Guide.pdf.

23   **A child psychologist, educator, and professor:** Flecker, Sally Ann. "When Fred Met Margaret." Pitt Med. University of Pittsburgh, 2014. https://www.pittmed.health.pitt.edu/story/when-fred-met-margaret.

24   **His teachers at the seminary:** King, Maxwell. *The Good Neighbor: The Life and Work of Fred Rogers.* New York, NY: Abrams Press, 2018.

24   **As Rogers' mentor, McFarland left:** Flecker, "When Fred Met Margaret."

24   **They'd caught his curiosity:** Rogers, Fred. "At Play in the Neighborhood." In *Shakespeare Plays the Classroom,* edited by Stuart E. Omans and Maurice J. O'Sullivan. Sarasota, FL: Pineapple Press, 2003.

25   **"I love to have guests and presenters":** Lietz, Jeana. "Journey to the Neighborhood: An Analysis of Fred Rogers and His Lessons for Educational Leaders," 2014. https://ecommons.luc.edu/luc_diss/1097/.

25   **As founder of the reimagining project:** reimagining project. https://www.reimaginingproject.com/.

27   **The children who'd completed the project:** Engel, Susan. "Over-Testing Kids Is Not the Answer: Here's How We Really Spark Curiosity." *Salon,*

March 14, 2015. https://www.salon.com/2015/03/14/over_testing_kids
_is_not_the_answer_heres_how_we_really_spark_creativity/.

27   **"But so does the promise"**: Leslie, *Curious*, Pg. 14.

27   **Then, discovering that it refers:** Metzger, Nadine. "Battling Demons
with Medical Authority: Werewolves, Physicians and Rationalization."
History of Psychiatry 24, no. 3 (September 2013). https://doi.org/10.1177
/0957154x13482835.

28   **"He did the same thing the next day":** Junod, Tom. "Can You Say . . .
Hero?" *Esquire*, November 1998. https://www.esquire.com/entertainment
/tv/a27134/can-you-say-hero-esq1198/.

30   **Others, however, clung to their mothers:** Ainsworth, Mary D. Salter,
and Silvia M. Bell. "Attachment, Exploration, and Separation: Illustrated
by the Behavior of One-Year-Olds in a Strange Situation." *Child Development* 41, no. 1 (March 1970). https://doi.org/10.2307/1127388.

30   **"Curiosity is underwritten by love":** Leslie, *Curious*, Pg. 43.

30   **But when researchers injected them:** Pellow, Sharon, Philippe Cho-
pin, Sandra E. File, and Mike Briley. "Validation of Open: Closed Arm
Entries in an Elevated Plus-Maze as a Measure of Anxiety in the Rat."
Journal of Neuroscience Methods 14, no. 3 (August 1985). https://doi
.org/10.1016/0165-0270(85)90031-7.

30   **"I give an expression of care":** "Mr. Rogers—Testimony Before the U.S.
Senate on Funding for PBS." American Rhetoric, May 1, 1969. https://
www.americanrhetoric.com/speeches/fredrogerssenatetestimonypbs.htm.

31   **"You could relax and be ready":** Lietz, "Journey to the Neighborhood,"
Pg. 127. This quote has been slightly amended by Sharapan for inclusion
here.

31   **A simple show of warmth:** Terada, Youki. "Welcoming Students with a
Smile." Edutopia. George Lucas Educational Foundation, September 11,
2018. https://www.edutopia.org/article/welcoming-students-smile.

32   **What drew kids to the *Neighborhood*:** Lietz, "Journey to the Neighborhood," Pg. 9.

32   **Each episode taps two proven:** Engel, Susan. "Children's Need to Know:
Curiosity in Schools." *Harvard Educational Review* 81, no. 4 (December
2011). https://doi.org/10.17763/haer.81.4.h054131316473115.

32   **"The artistry of the program":** Grant recommendation. Fred Rogers
Archives.

33   **According to one nationally representative:** Elpus, Kenneth. "Arts Education and Positive Youth Development: Cognitive, Behavioral, and Social Outcomes of Adolescents Who Study the Arts." National Endowment for the Arts, n.d. https://www.arts.gov/sites/default/files/Research-Art -Works-Maryland.pdf.

33   **Young people who've studied:** Ibid.

33   **That means publishers have almost:** Wakefield, John F. "A Brief History of Textbooks: Where Have We Been All These Years?" Paper presented at the Meeting of the Text and Academic Authors, June 1998. https://eric .ed.gov/?id=ED419246.

33   **However, a number of studies:** Engel, "Children's Need to Know: Curiosity in Schools."

34   **Researchers have found that even:** Donahue, Elisabeth. "Font Focus: Making Ideas Harder to Read May Make Them Easier to Retain." Princeton University, October 28, 2010. https://www.princeton.edu/news/2010/10/28 /font-focus-making-ideas-harder-read-may-make-them-easier-retain.

34   **Studies have shown that kids:** Barnes, Jennifer L., and Paul Bloom. "Children's Preference for Social Stories." *Developmental Psychology* 50, no. 2 (2014). https://doi.org/10.1037/a0033613.

34   **They also crave stories:** Gray, Peter. "One More Really Big Reason to Read Stories to Children." Psychology Today, October 11, 2014. https:// www.psychologytoday.com/us/blog/freedom-learn/201410/one-more -really-big-reason-read-stories-children.

34   **"Precisely because [fiction]":** Ibid.

36   **The Reverend Paula Lawrence-Wehmiller:** Lawrence-Wehmiller, Paula. "Mister Rogers: Keeper of the Dream." In *Mister Rogers' Neighborhood: Children, Television, and Fred Rogers*, edited by Mark Collins and Margaret Mary Kimmel. Pittsburgh, PA: University of Pittsburgh Press, 1996.

36   **"He creates a sanctuary":** Ibid.

37   **He became a community activist:** DeFour, Matthew. "Madison Civic Activist Jeff Erlanger Dies." *Wisconsin State Journal*, June 12, 2007. https://www.newspapers.com/clip/47651874/jeff-erlanger-1970-2000/.

Chapter 2: Mud Pies and Block Buildings

42   **"Spoons, and the king":** "Mister Rogers Talks About Make-Believe." Episode. *Mister Rogers' Neighborhood* #1501, June 28, 1982.

42   **A full 98 percent scored:** Brady, Jocelyn, and Evan P. Schneider. "Stop Trying to Be Creative." PeopleScience, January 25, 2019. https://people science.maritz.com/Articles/2019/stop-trying-to-be-creative.

43   **"Block buildings have infinite variety":** Rogers, Fred. *You Are Special: Words of Wisdom for All Ages from a Beloved Neighbor.* New York, NY: Penguin Books, 1995.

43   **Their creativity has turned:** Yoshiaki, Nihei, and Higuchi Hiroyoshi. "When and Where Did Crows Learn to Use Automobiles as Nutcrackers?" *Tohoku psychologica folia* 60 (July 1, 2002): 93–97. http://hdl.handle .net/10097/54761.

43   **Barack Obama once called:** "Remarks by the President at the Import–Export Bank's Annual Conference, March 11, 2010." Office of the U.S. Intellectual Property Enforcement Coordinator. National Archives and Records Administration, March 11, 2010. https://obamawhitehouse .archives.gov/omb/intellectualproperty/quotes.

43   **in 2019, LinkedIn:** Petrone, Paul. "Why Creativity Is the Most Important Skill in the World." LinkedIn, December 31, 2018. https:// www.linkedin.com/business/learning/blog/top-skills-and-courses /why-creativity-is-the-most-important-skill-in-the-world.

44   **By Land's measure:** Smith, Oliver. "Mapped: Which Countries Have the Most Redheads?" *Telegraph*, January 12, 2017. https://www.telegraph .co.uk/travel/maps-and-graphics/country-with-the-most-redheads -gingers/.

44   **"What we have concluded":** Naiman, Linda. "Can Creativity Be Taught? Here's What the Research Says." Creativity at Work, June 6, 2014. https://www.creativityatwork.com/2012/03/23/can-creativity-be -taught/.

44   **"It merely becomes incidental":** Vygotsky, Lev Semenovich. "Imagination and Creativity in Childhood." *Journal of Russian and East European Psychology* 42, no. 1 (2004). https://www.marxists.org/archive/vygotsky /works/1927/imagination.pdf.

44   **But as kids enter adolescence:** Sharma, Sushil, Mariam Arain, Puja Mathur, Afsha Rais, Wynand Nel, Ranbir Sandhu, Maliha Haque, and Lina Johal. "Maturation of the Adolescent Brain." *Neuropsychiatric Disease and Treatment*, April 3, 2013. https://doi.org/10.2147/ndt.s39 776.

44   **This is where judgment:** Coutlee, Christopher G., and Scott A. Huettel. "The Functional Neuroanatomy of Decision Making: Prefrontal Control of Thought and Action." *Brain Research* 1428 (January 5, 2012). https://doi.org/10.1016/j.brainres.2011.05.053; Klinge, Kylah Goodfellow. "Mapping Creativity in the Brain." *Atlantic*, March 21, 2016. https://www.theatlantic.com/science/archive/2016/03/the-driving -principles-behind-creativity/474621/.

45   **"We also see this curtailment":** Vygotsky, "Imagination and Creativity in Childhood."

45   **There's a reason some comedy:** "Cheaper Tickets If You'll Sit in the Front Row..." Chortle, June 18, 2014. https://www.chortle.co.uk /news/2014/06/18/20414/cheaper_tickets_if_youll_sit_in_the_front _row . . .

45   **"Children, like laboratory rats":** Rogers, Fred. "Encouraging Creativity." Lecture at Thiel College, November 13, 1969.

46   **Subsequent cohorts scored better:** Bronson, Po, and Ashley Merryman. "The Creativity Crisis." *Newsweek*, July 10, 2010. https://www.newsweek .com/creativity-crisis-74665.

46   **The trend was so striking:** Kim, Kyung Hee. "The Creativity Crisis: The Decrease in Creative Thinking Scores on the Torrance Tests of Creative Thinking." *Creativity Research Journal* 23, no. 4 (November 9, 2011). https://doi.org/10.1080/10400419.2011.627805.

46   **Though her research stops short:** Ibid.

47   **"How will society meet the challenges":** Golinkoff, Roberta M., and Kathy Hirsh-Pasek. *Becoming Brilliant: What Science Tells Us About Raising Successful Children.* Washington, D.C.: American Psychological Association, 2016. Pg. 188.

47   **You will have created something:** Vonnegut, Kurt. *A Man Without a Country.* New York, NY: Random House, 2007.

52   **"The product, he notes":** Guy, William. "The Theology of *Mister Rogers' Neighborhood.*" In *Mister Rogers' Neighborhood: Children, Television, and Fred Rogers*, edited by Mark Collins and Margaret Mary Kimmel. Pittsburgh, PA: University of Pittsburgh Press, 1996.

52   **It's gotten so intense:** Epstein, David. "You Don't Want a Child Prodigy." *New York Times*, May 24, 2019. https://www.nytimes.com/2019/05/24 /opinion/sunday/kids-sports-music-choices.html.

53 **"The next day I went back":** Rogers, Fred. *The World According to Mister Rogers: Important Things to Remember.* New York, NY: Hyperion, 2003.

54 **"It's where you have imagination":** Skipper, Clay. "How (and Why) to Build Some Boredom Back into Your Life." *GQ*, November 8, 2018. https://www.gq.com/story/how-and-why-you-should-be-bored.

54 **A century ago, sociologists were:** Morozov, Evgeny. "Only Disconnect." *New Yorker*, October 21, 2013. https://www.newyorker.com/magazine/2013/10/28/only-disconnect-2.

54 **No wonder more than 70 percent:** Smith, Jacquelyn. "72% of People Get Their Best Ideas in the Shower—Here's Why." *Business Insider*, January 14, 2016. https://www.businessinsider.com/why-people-get-their-best-ideas-in-the-shower-2016-1.

54 **Albert Einstein was known:** Livni, Ephrat. "Albert Einstein's Best Ideas Came When He Was Aimless. Yours Can Too." Quartz, June 8, 2018. https://qz.com/1299282/albert-einsteins-best-ideas-came-while-he-was-relaxing-aimlessly-yours-can-too/.

54 **Maya Angelou considered:** Plimpton, George. "Maya Angelou, the Art of Fiction No. 119." *Paris Review*, 1990. https://www.theparisreview.org/interviews/2279/the-art-of-fiction-no-119-maya-angelou.

55 **Nakamatsu submerges himself:** Lidz, Franz. "Dr. NakaMats, the Man with 3300 Patents to His Name." Smithsonian.com. Smithsonian Institution, December 2012. https://www.smithsonianmag.com/science-nature/dr-nakamats-the-man-with-3300-patents-to-his-name-134571403/.

55 **Nakamatsu's more-questionable claims:** Jozuka, Emiko. "Japan's 87-Year-Old Patent King Is Trying to Invent Treatment for His Own Cancer." VICE, January 11, 2016. https://www.vice.com/en_us/article/bmvz48/japans-87-year-old-patent-king-is-trying-to-invent-treatment-for-his-own-cancer.

55 **"It can be right there":** Golinkoff and Hirsh-Pasek, *Becoming Brilliant*, Pg. 196.

55 **Its insistence on doing something:** Vygotsky, "Imagination and Creativity in Childhood."

57 **The color blue, for example:** University of British Columbia. "Effect of Colors: Blue Boosts Creativity, While Red Enhances Attention to Detail." ScienceDaily. www.sciencedaily.com/releases/2009/02/090205142143.htm.

57 **Though the task was the same:** McCoy, Janetta Mitchell, and Gary W. Evans. "The Potential Role of the Physical Environment in Fostering Creativity." *Creativity Research Journal* 14, no. 3–4 (October 2002). https:// doi.org/10.1207/s15326934crj1434_11.

59 **He had few resources:** Strickland, Bill, and Vince Rause. *Make the Impossible Possible: One Man's Crusade to Inspire Others to Dream Bigger and Achieve the Extraordinary.* New York, NY: Broadway Books, 2009. Pg. 7.

61 **"And *now* look at the things":** "Mister Rogers Talks About Art." Episode. *Mister Rogers' Neighborhood* #1644, November 28, 1991.

61 **In their book *The House of Make-Believe*:** Singer, Dorothy G., and Jerome L. Singer. *The House of Make-Believe: Children's Play and the Developing Imagination.* Cambridge, MA: Harvard University Press, 1990. Pg. 4.

62 **"Play is fundamentally important":** Yogman, Michael, Andrew Garner, Jeffrey Hutchinson, Kathy Hirsh-Pasek, and Roberta Michnick Golinkoff. "The Power of Play: A Pediatric Role in Enhancing Development in Young Children." *Pediatrics* 142, no. 3 (September 2018). https://doi .org/10.1542/peds.2018-2058.

63 **"I'm sure you'll find a way":** "Mister Rogers Talks About Make-Believe." Episode. *Mister Rogers' Neighborhood* #1502, June 29, 1982.

64 **"You see a child play":** "Erik Erikson, 91, Psychoanalyst Who Reshaped Views of Human Growth, Dies." *New York Times*, May 13, 1994. http:// movies2.nytimes.com/books/99/08/22/specials/erikson-obit.html.

64 **"But for children, play":** Moore, Heidi. "Why Play Is the Work of Childhood." Fred Rogers Center for Early Learning & Children's Media. Saint Vincent College, September 23, 2014. https://www.fredrogerscenter .org/2014/09/why-play-is-the-work-of-childhood/.

66 **They found that the kids without:** Pepler, Debra J., and Hildy S. Ross. "The Effects of Play on Convergent and Divergent Problem Solving." *Child Development* 52, no. 4 (December 1981). https://doi.org/10.2307/1129 507.

67 **"In constant reference to the traditional":** Rogers, "Encouraging Creativity."

68 **Adults who do something creative:** Suttie, Jill. "Doing Something Creative Can Boost Your Well-Being." Greater Good. Greater Good Science

Center at UC Berkeley, March 21, 2017. https://greatergood.berkeley.edu/article/item/doing_something_creative_can_boost_your_well_being.

68   **In fact, parents' emphasis:** Singer and Singer, *The House of Make-Believe*, Pgs. 161–162.

68   **"Art museums, school art exhibits":** Golinkoff and Hirsh-Pasek, *Becoming Brilliant*, Pg. 215.

69   **"[As] though, on a rainy day":** Bianculli, David. "The Myth, the Man, the Legend." In *Mister Rogers' Neighborhood: Children, Television, and Fred Rogers*, edited by Mark Collins and Margaret Mary Kimmel. Pittsburgh, PA: University of Pittsburgh Press, 1996.

Chapter 3: It All Works Out If You Talk and You Listen

72   **And then he leans in:** "Mister Rogers Talks About No and Yes." Episode. *Mister Rogers' Neighborhood* #1544, February 7, 1985.

72   **He'd been too wrapped up:** MacManus, Christopher. "Watch Now: Texting Man Ambushed by Bear." CNET, April 11, 2012. https://www.cnet.com/news/watch-now-texting-man-ambushed-by-bear/.

72   **Not that it had any effect:** "Distracted Walking Injuries on the Rise; 52 Percent Occur at Home." National Safety Council, June 17, 2015. https://www.prnewswire.com/news-releases/distracted-walking-injuries-on-the-rise-52-percent-occur-at-home-300100870.html; Short, John Rennie. *The Unequal City: Urban Resurgence, Displacement, and the Making of Inequality in Global Cities.* New York, NY: Routledge, 2018.

72   **We text while driving:** "Texting and Driving Accident Statistics—Distracted Driving." edgarsnyder.com, n.d. https://www.edgarsnyder.com/car-accident/cause-of-accident/cell-phone/cell-phone-statistics.html.

72   **By the time you finish:** Morreale, Megan. "Daily SMS Mobile Usage Statistics." SMSEagle, March 6, 2017. https://www.smseagle.eu/2017/03/06/daily-sms-mobile-statistics/.

73   **On average, Americans look:** Spangler, Todd. "Are Americans Addicted to Smartphones? U.S. Consumers Check Their Phones 52 Times Daily, Study Finds." *Variety*, November 14, 2018. https://variety.com/2018/digital/news/smartphone-addiction-study-check-phones-52-times-daily-1203028454/.

73   **The average adult spends:** He, Amy. "US Adults Are Spending More Time on Mobile Than They Do Watching TV." eMarketer, June 4,

2019. https://www.emarketer.com/content/average-us-time-spent-with
-mobile-in-2019-has-increased.

73   **teenagers log more:** Rideout, Victoria, and Michael B. Robb. *The Common Sense Census: Media Use by Tweens and Teens.* Common Sense Media, 2019. https://www.commonsensemedia.org/sites/default/files/uploads /research/2019-census-8-to-18-full-report-updated.pdf.

73   **Some companies:** Jeffries, Adrianne. "You'll Tweet When You're Dead: LivesOn Says Digital 'Twin' Can Mimic Your Online Persona." Verge, February 21, 2013. https://www.theverge.com/2013/2/21/4010016/liveson -uses-artificial-intelligence-to-tweet-for-you-after-death.

73   **Every notification, every text:** Haynes, Trevor. "Dopamine, Smartphones & You: A Battle for Your Time." Science in the News. Harvard University, May 1, 2018. http://sitn.hms.harvard.edu/flash/2018/dopamine -smartphones-battle-time/.

73   **nearly half of American adults:** Lardieri, Alexa. "Many Americans Report Feeling Lonely, Younger Generations More So, Study Finds." *U.S. News & World Report*, May 1, 2018. https://www.usnews.com /news/health-care-news/articles/2018-05-01/study-many-americans -report-feeling-lonely-younger-generations-more-so.

73   **The average person:** Renner, Ben. "The Average American Hasn't Made a New Friend in 5 Years. Here's Why." Study Finds, October 9, 2019. https://www.studyfinds.org/survey-average-american-hasnt-made -new-friend-in-5-years/.

74   **And in Japan, one survey:** "An Epidemic of Loneliness." Week, January 6, 2019. https://theweek.com/articles/815518/epidemic-loneliness.

74   **One study equated its health:** Lardieri, "Many Americans Report Feeling Lonely."

74   **A survey in Britain:** Ewens, Hannah. "What Young People Fear the Most." VICE, September 21, 2016. https://www.vice.com/en_uk/article /nnyk37/what-vice-readers-fear-the-most-hannah-ewens-love-loneliness.

74   **In 2018, Britain appointed:** Bourn, Chris. "The Loneliness Epidemic Is So Bad, World Leaders Have Been Forced to Intervene." MEL, July 17, 2019. https://melmagazine.com/en-us/story/the-loneliness-epidemic-is-so -bad-world-leaders-have-been-forced-to-intervene.

74   **But with smartphone-detox camps:** Jeong, Sophie. "The Teens So Addicted to Phones They're Going into Detox." CNN, October 21, 2019.

https://edition.cnn.com/2019/10/20/asia/smartphone-addiction-camp
-intl-hnk-scli/index.html.

74   **"To lead a happy"**: Metusalem, Ross, Daniel M. Belenky, and Kristen DiCerbo. *Skills for Today: What We Know about Teaching and Assessing Communication*. London, UK: Pearson, 2017.

74   **In Silicon Valley**: Anders, George. "That 'Useless' Liberal Arts Degree Has Become Tech's Hottest Ticket." Forbes, July 29, 2015. https://www .forbes.com/sites/georgeanders/2015/07/29/liberal-arts-degree-tech/.

75   **"Deep listening and loving speech"**: Nhat Hạnh, Thich. *The Art of Communicating*. New York, NY: HarperOne, 2014. Pg. 41.

76   **Answered well, the moment**: Carver, Raymond. *A New Path to the Waterfall*. New York, NY: Atlantic Monthly Press, 1989.

77   **"Conversing with children"**: Ginott, Haim G., Alice Ginott, and H. Wallace Goddard. *Between Parent and Child: Revised and Updated: The Bestselling Classic That Revolutionized Parent-Child Communication*. New York, NY: Random House, 2003. Pg. 5.

77   **According to Ginott**: Ibid., Pg. xiii.

78   **"The people we trust"**: Kris, Deborah Farmer. "What's Mentionable Is Manageable: Why Parents Should Help Children Name Their Fears." *Washington Post*, September 20, 2018. https://www.washingtonpost.com /news/parenting/wp/2018/09/20/whats-mentionable-is-manageable-why -parents-should-help-kids-name-their-fears/.

79   **Sometimes it's a professional**: Kamal, Rabah. "What Are the Current Costs and Outcomes Related to Mental Health and Substance Use Disorders?" Peterson-KFF Health System Tracker, July 31, 2017. https://www.healthsystemtracker.org/chart-collection/current-costs -outcomes-related-mental-health-substance-abuse-disorders/; Davidson, Jordan. "Americans Spend Over $200 Billion Treating Mental Health Conditions." Mighty, May 31, 2016. https://themighty.com/2016/05 /mental-health-conditions-are-costing-the-u-s-a-ton-of-money/.

79   **"At times of strong emotion"**: Ginott, Ginott, and Wallace, *Between Parent and Child*, Pg. 28.

79   **His friends and staff remember**: Sharapan, Hedda. "The Power of Listening." *What We Can Continue to Learn from Fred Rogers*. Fred Rogers Center for Early Learning & Children's Media, October 2016. http://www .fredrogerscenter.org/wp-content/uploads/2016/10/October-2016.pdf.

80 **"Whether that person is speaking":** Ibid.

80 **"A judgment may form":** Nhat Hạnh, *The Art of Communicating*, Pg. 42.

81 **"Being supportive often means":** Rogers, Fred. Keynote address presented at the NAEYC Annual Conference, 1983. https://radar.auctr.edu /islandora/object/auc.092:0041.

81 **"The more I think about it":** "Mister Rogers Talks About No and Yes." Episode. *Mister Rogers' Neighborhood* #1544, February 7, 1985.

82 **"Now we just listen":** Nhat Hạnh, *The Art of Communicating*, Pg. 44.

82 **"But let someone really listen":** Faber, Adele, and Elaine Mazlish. *How to Talk So Kids Will Listen & Listen So Kids Will Talk.* New York, NY: Scribner, 1980. Pg. 8.

83 **"That is true love":** Nhat Hạnh, *The Art of Communicating*, Pg. 77.

84 **Though Rogers largely avoided:** Galinsky, Ellen. "Mister Rogers Speaks to Parents." In *Mister Rogers Neighborhood: Children, Television, and Fred Rogers*, edited by Mark Collins and Margaret Mary Kimmel. Pittsburgh, PA: University of Pittsburgh Press, 1996.

87 **In classrooms, Simple Interactions:** Wanless, Shannon, and Dana Winters. "A Welcome Space for Taking Risks: Psychological Safety Creates a Positive Climate for Learning." *Learning Forward* 39, no. 4 (August 2018). https://learningforward.org/journal/august-2018-vol-39-no-4/a -welcome-space-for-taking-risks/.

88 **Thich Nhat Hanh writes that:** Nhat Hạnh, *The Art of Communicating*, Pgs. 73–75.

89 **"That kind of message can":** Rogers, Fred. "At Play in the Neighborhood." In *Shakespeare Plays the Classroom*, edited by Stuart E. Omans and Maurice J. O'Sullivan. Sarasota, FL: Pineapple Press, 2003.

89 **In 1951, during his final year:** Deb, Sopan. "'Mister Rogers' Neighborhood' at 50: 5 Memorable Moments." *New York Times*, March 5, 2018. https://www.nytimes.com/2018/03/05/arts/television/mister-rogers -neighborhood-at-50.html.

89 **By the time Rogers first saw:** "National Television Penetration Trends." Nielsen Company, n.d. https://www.tvb.org/Portals/0/media/file/TV _Households.pdf.

89 **Families all over town:** Waugh, Steve, and Peter Clements. *AQA The Making of a Superpower: USA, 1865–1975.* Cambridge, UK: Cambridge University Press, 2015.

89   **"And if there's anything":** Hollingsworth, Amy. *The Simple Faith of Mister Rogers: Spiritual Insights from the World's Most Beloved Neighbor.* Brentwood, TN: Integrity Publishers, 2005.

90   **After a brief detour to Canada:** Junod, Tom. "Can You Say . . . Hero?" *Esquire,* November 1998. https://www.esquire.com/entertainment/tv /a27134/can-you-say-hero-esq1198/; additional information provided by Hedda Sharapan.

90   **"A lot happens there":** "About Fred Rogers." Mister Rogers' Neighborhood. https://www.misterrogers.org/about-fred-rogers/.

90   **"a cardinal sin":** King, Maxwell. *The Good Neighbor: The Life and Work of Fred Rogers.* New York, NY: Abrams Press, 2018. Pg. 179.

91   **"Unfortunately, even parents":** Ginott, Ginott, and Wallace, *Between Parent and Child,* Pg. 1.

91   **"I bet you'd forget your head":** Ibid., Pg. 2.

92   **"We can express our angry":** Ibid., Pg. 49.

Chapter 4: Appreciation Is a Holy Thing

100   **And when the digging:** "Mister Rogers Talks About Work." Episodes. *Mister Rogers' Neighborhood* #1526–1529, April 4–7, 1984.

101   **Although they'd never met Warneken:** Tomasello, Michael. *Why We Cooperate.* Cambridge, MA: MIT Press, 2009.

101   **But it didn't work:** Ibid.

101   **Warneken and Tomasello concluded:** Tomasello, Michael, Alicia P. Melis, Claudio Tennie, Emily Wyman, and Esther Herrmann. "Two Key Steps in the Evolution of Human Cooperation." *Current Anthropology* 53, no. 6 (December 2012). https://doi.org/10.1086/668207.

102   **"You could say it's as if":** Surowiecki, James. *The Wisdom of Crowds.* New York, NY: Anchor Books, 2004. Pg. 162.

102   **Today, nearly nine out of ten:** Andreatta, Britt. *Wired to Connect: The Brain Science of Teams and a New Model for Creating Collaboration and Inclusion.* Santa Barbara, CA: 7th Mind Publishing, 2018. Pg. 6; Andreatta, Britt. "Better Together: The Neuroscience of Teams." May 4, 2017. https://www.td.org/insights/better-together-the-neuroscience-of -teams.

102   **and in survey after large-scale survey:** Campbell, Marissa. "Top 5 Skills Employers Look For." Nth Degree, n.d. https://newmanu.edu/top-5-skills

-employers-look-for; "Qualifications and Attributes Critical to Employers." Youth.gov, n.d. https://youth.gov/youth-topics/youth-employment /qualifications-and-attributes-employers-believe-are-critical.

102 **Some companies have even hired:** Hansen, Morten T., and Scott Tapp. "Who Should Be Your Chief Collaboration Officer?" *Harvard Business Review*, October 11, 2010. https://hbr.org/2010/10 /who-should-be-your-chief-colla.

102 **To become a fellow:** Cross, Rob, Reb Rebele, and Adam Grant. "Collaborative Overload." *Harvard Business Review*, 2016. https://hbr.org/2016/01 /collaborative-overload.

102 **Predictably, people who work:** Ibid.

102 **Learning scientists have long known:** Kuhl, Patricia K. "Brain Mechanisms in Early Language Acquisition." *Neuron* 67, no. 5 (September 9, 2010). https://doi.org/10.1016/j.neuron.2010.08.038; Banks, Duncan. "What Is Brain Plasticity and Why Is It So Important?" Conversation, April 4, 2016. https://theconversation.com/what-is-brain-plasticity-and -why-is-it-so-important-55967.

103 **Even better, the students:** Cohen, Elizabeth G., and Rachel A. Lotan. *Designing Groupwork: Strategies for the Heterogeneous Classroom.* 3rd ed. New York, NY: Teachers College Press, 2014.

103 **In 2015, the Programme:** "PISA 2015 Results (Volume V)." *OECD Programme for International Student Assessment*, 2017. https://doi.org/10 .1787/9789264285521-en.

103 **Worldwide, just 8 percent:** Ibid.

103 **Girls scored significantly higher:** Ibid.

104 **"So, too, are we less able":** *What We Do Together: The State of Associational Life in America.* Joint Economic Committee, May 2017. https://www.lee .senate.gov/public/_cache/files/b5f224ce-98f7-40f6-a814-8602696714d8 /what-we-do-together.pdf.

104 **Less than a third of Americans:** Persily, Nathaniel, and Jon Cohen. "Americans Are Losing Faith in Democracy—and in Each Other." *Washington Post*, October 14, 2016. https://www.washingtonpost .com/opinions/americans-are-losing-faith-in-democracy—and-in-each -other/2016/10/14/b35234ea-90c6-11e6-9c52-0b10449e33c4_story.html.

104 **"When groups engage in cooperative":** Cohen and Lotan, *Designing Groupwork.*

105 **"And all those people care":** "Mister Rogers Talks About Work." Episode. *Mister Rogers' Neighborhood* #1530, April 8, 1984.

106 **"Most confounding of all":** Duhigg, Charles. "What Google Learned from Its Quest to Build the Perfect Team." *New York Times*, February 25, 2016. https://www.nytimes.com/2016/02/28/magazine/what-google -learned-from-its-quest-to-build-the-perfect-team.html.

107 **At the same time, fewer than:** Salmon, Nadine. "Speak Up for Safety." RN.com, 2012. https://www.rn.com/nursing-news/speak-up-for-safety/.

107 **Perhaps it's no surprise:** "Study Suggests Medical Errors Now Third Leading Cause of Death in the U.S." Johns Hopkins Medicine, May 3, 2016. https://www.hopkinsmedicine.org/news/media/releases/study_suggests _medical_errors_now_third_leading_cause_of_death_in_the_us.

107 **But on teams that have established:** Edmondson, Amy. "Psychological Safety and Learning Behavior in Work Teams." *Administrative Science Quarterly* 44, no. 2 (1999). https://doi.org/10.2307/2666999.

108 **By contrast, teams that felt:** "Re:Work—How Google Thinks About Team Effectiveness." Google, October 25, 2017. https://rework.with google.com/blog/how-google-thinks-team-effectiveness/.

108 **Googlers on psychologically safe:** "Re:Work." Google, n.d. https:// rework.withgoogle.com/print/guides/5721312655835136/.

108 **On average, kids who had *not*:** "PISA 2015 Results (Volume V)," *OECD*.

108 **Those who felt respected:** Ibid.

108 **The more students felt safe:** Ibid.

109 **And Dylan replied:** Fine, Jason, and Jann Wenner. *Harrison*. New York, NY: Simon & Schuster, 2002.

109 **"We'll bury 'em in the mix":** Traveling Wilburys, n.d. http://www .travelingwilburys.com/music.

110 **"If we can help our children":** "Mister Rogers' Neighborhood: The Music." Fred Rogers Productions, n.d. https://www.misterrogers.org /the-music/.

111 **"If my child could find":** Friedrich Cofer, Lynette. "Make-Believe, Truth, and Freedom: Television in the Public Interest." In *Mister Rogers Neighborhood: Children, Television, and Fred Rogers*, edited by Mark Collins and Margaret Mary Kimmel. Pittsburgh, PA: University of Pittsburgh Press, 2019.

112 **"But in every case, what is common":** Ibid.

112   **Just as Friedrich Cofer discovered:** Wilson, Barbara J. "Media and Children's Aggression, Fear, and Altruism." *CYC-Online*, no. 112 (May 2008). https://www.cyc-net.org/cyc-online/cyconline-june2008-wilson.html.

115   **"Quite literally, just when we":** Delizonna, Laura. "High-Performing Teams Need Psychological Safety. Here's How to Create It." *Harvard Business Review*, August 24, 2017. https://hbr.org/2017/08/high-performing-teams-need-psychological-safety-heres-how-to-create-it.

116   *This person wishes to be loved:* Dass, Ram, and Mirabai Bush. "Just-Like-Me Compassion Meditation by Ram Dass, Mirabai Bush: Spiritual Practice: Spirituality & Practice." Spirituality and Practice, n.d. https://www.spiritualityandpractice.com/practices/practices/view/27782/just-like-me-compassion-meditation.

118   **As Surowiecki notes:** Surowiecki, *Wisdom of Crowds*, Pg. 31.

119   **A double community pool!:** "Mister Rogers Talks About Work."

120   **"Each person is in some way":** Friedrich Cofer, "Make-Believe, Truth, and Freedom," Pg. 160.

120   **Already, the generation born:** Krogstad, Jens Manuel. "Reflecting a Demographic Shift, 109 U.S. Counties Have Become Majority Nonwhite Since 2000." Pew Research Center, August 21, 2019. https://www.pewresearch.org/fact-tank/2019/08/21/u-s-counties-majority-nonwhite/.

120   **In 2017, some forty-four million:** Cilluffo, Anthony, and D'Vera Cohn. "6 Demographic Trends Shaping the U.S. and the World in 2019." Pew Research Center, April 11, 2019. https://www.pewresearch.org/fact-tank/2019/04/11/6-demographic-trends-shaping-the-u-s-and-the-world-in-2019/.

120   **Though the statistics have improved:** Hunt, Darnell, Ana-Christina Ramon, and Michael Tran. *Hollywood Diversity Report.* UCLA College Social Sciences, 2019. https://socialsciences.ucla.edu/wp-content/uploads/2019/02/UCLA-Hollywood-Diversity-Report-2019-2-21-2019.pdf.

121   **One analysis found that among:** Wong, Jessica. "Kids' TV Lacks Gender Balance and Diversity, New Study Suggests." CBC News, May 4, 2019. https://www.cbc.ca/news/entertainment/childrens-tv-study-diversity-1.5118385.

121   **In 1983, about a year:** Dobrow, Julie, Calvin Gidney, and Jennifer Burton. "Why It's So Important for Kids to See Diverse TV and Movie Characters." Conversation, March 7, 2018. https://theconversation.com

/why-its-so-important-for-kids-to-see-diverse-tv-and-movie-characters
-92576.

121   **you might start to wonder:** "Study Finds TV Can Decrease Self-Esteem
in Children, Except White Boys." Indiana University, May 30, 2012.
https://newsinfo.iu.edu/news-archive/22445.html.

122   **about six hours' worth:** Rideout, Victoria, and Michael B. Robb. *The
Common Sense Census: Media Use by Tweens and Teens.* Common Sense
Media, 2019. https://www.commonsensemedia.org/sites/default/files
/uploads/research/2019-census-8-to-18-full-report-updated.pdf.

122   **Not only did *Black Panther*:** Tartaglione, Nancy. "'Pacific Rim:
Uprising' Tops $150M in Global Bow; 'Black Panther' Now #1
Solo Superhero Movie WW—International Box Office." Deadline,
March 25, 2018. https://deadline.com/2018/03/pacific-rim-uprising
-china-black-panther-tomb-raider-coco-peter-rabbit-international
-box-office-weekend-results-1202353014/; Easter, Makeda. "'Black Panther' Breaks Another Record, Becoming the Most Tweeted-About Film
of All Time." *Los Angeles Times*, March 21, 2018. https://www.latimes
.com/entertainment/movies/la-et-mn-black-panther-twitter-20180321
-htmlstory.html; Couch, Aaron. "Oscars: 'Black Panther' Gets Historic Best
Picture Nomination." Hollywood Reporter, January 22, 2019. https://www
.hollywoodreporter.com/heat-vision/black-panther-best-picture-oscars
-nomination-is-historic-1177708.

122   **According to research compiled:** "About P.R.I.D.E." Positive Racial
Identity Development in Early Education. University of Pittsburgh, n.d.
https://www.racepride.pitt.edu/about-pride/; *Positive Racial Identity Development in Early Education: Understanding PRIDE in Pittsburgh.* University
of Pittsburgh School of Education Race and Early Childhood Collaborative, 2016. http://www.racepride.pitt.edu/wp-content/uploads/2018/06
/PRIDE_Scan.pdf.

122   **And perhaps not surprisingly:** Rivas-Drake, Deborah, Eleanor K. Sea-
ton, Carol Markstrom, Stephen Quintana, Moin Syed, Richard M. Lee,
Seth J. Schwartz, Adriana J. Umaña-Taylor, Sabine French, and Tiffany
Yip. "Ethnic and Racial Identity in Adolescence: Implications for Psycho-
social, Academic, and Health Outcomes." *Child Development* 85, no. 1
(2014). https://doi.org/10.1111/cdev.12200.

123   **"If our brains are presented":** Andreatta, *Wired to Connect*, Pg. 66.

124 **This happens regardless of parents':** Wanless, Shannon B., and Patricia A. Crawford. "Reading Your Way to a Culturally Responsive Classroom." *Young Children* 71, no. 2 (May 2016). https://www.naeyc.org/resources /pubs/yc/may2016/culturally-responsive-classroom.

126 **Together with this kind:** Wilson, Barbara J. "Media and Children's Aggression, Fear, and Altruism." *CYC-Online*, no. 112 (May 2008). https:// www.cyc-net.org/cyc-online/cyconline-june2008-wilson.html

Chapter 5: It's You Who Have to Try It and It's
You Who Have to Fall (Sometimes)

134 **Mister Rogers has failed:** "Mister Rogers Talks About Learning." Episode. *Mister Rogers' Neighborhood* #1651, August 24, 1992.

134 **Remaining in print for forty-plus:** Scharnhorst, Gary, and Jack Bales. *The Lost Life of Horatio Alger, Jr.* Bloomington, IN: Indiana University Press, 1985.

136 **we wouldn't have WD-40:** "Our History." WD-40 Company, n.d. https://www.wd40company.com/our-company/our-history/.

136 **Dyson vacuum cleaners:** Loftus, Jack. "Praising Failure: James Dyson Talks Vacuum's 5,127 Prototypes." Gizmodo, April 10, 2011. https://gizmodo .com/praising-failure-james-dyson-talks-vacuums-5-127-proto-5790556.

136 **The fruit was eaten:** Bryson, Bill. *The Body: A Guide for Occupants.* New York, NY: Doubleday, 2019. Pg. 42.

136 **Horatio Alger, of all people:** Scharnhorst and Bales, *The Lost Life of Horatio Alger, Jr.*

136 **Albert Einstein never flunked math:** Roos, Dave. "10 False History 'Facts' Everyone Knows." HowStuffWorks, May 6, 2014. https://history .howstuffworks.com/history-vs-myth/10-false-history-facts8.htm.

136 **Michael Jordan was never cut:** Grossman, Samantha. "A Myth Debunked: Was Michael Jordan Really Cut from His High-School Team?" *Time*, January 16, 2012. https://newsfeed.time.com/2012/01/16/a-myth -debunked-was-michael-jordan-really-cut-from-his-high-school-team/.

136 **In fact, of all the icons:** Ward, Maria. "5 Things You Didn't Know About Oprah Winfrey." *Vogue*, January 29, 2017. https://www.vogue.com/article /oprah-winfrey-5-things-you-didnt-know.

136 **Winston Churchill never said:** O'Keefe, M. M. "How Popular History Distorts Churchill's 'Never Give Up' Speech." Medium, February 2, 2019.

https://medium.com/@MM_OKeefe/how-popular-history-does-you-a-disservice-distorting-churchills-never-give-up-speech-5d429ef97346.

136 **Vince Lombardi quit:** O'Keefe, M. M. "Lombardi: A Winner Who Quit." Medium, January 28, 2019. https://medium.com/the-ascent/https-theascent-pub-vince-lombardi-disproved-winners-never-quit-1cc264f9aa99.

137 **Instead, in its original form:** O'Toole, Garson. "Purpose and Persistence Are Required for Success: Unrewarded Genius Is Almost a Proverb." Quote Investigator, January 12, 2016. https://quoteinvestigator.com/2016/01/12/persist/.

137 **Nor is it particularly easy:** Credé, Marcus. "What Shall We Do About Grit? A Critical Review of What We Know and What We Don't Know." *Educational Researcher* 47, no. 9 (September 18, 2018). https://doi.org/10.3102/0013189x18801322.

137 **In fact, "eventual elites":** Epstein, David. *Range: Why Generalists Triumph in a Specialized World.* New York, NY: Riverhead Books, 2019. Pg. 7.

138 **"We need to help children":** Rogers, Fred. *Many Ways to Say I Love You: Wisdom for Parents and Children from Mister Rogers.* New York, NY: Hachette Books, 2006.

138 **"The type of work they do":** West, Darrell M. "The Need for Lifetime Learning During an Era of Economic Disruption." Brookings Institution, May 21, 2018. https://www.brookings.edu/blog/brown-center-chalkboard/2018/05/21/the-need-for-lifetime-learning-during-an-era-of-economic-disruption/.

138 **As Epstein puts it:** Epstein, *Range,* Pg. 157.

139 **The goal is absolutely secondary:** Emphasis added. "Hunter S. Thompson's Letter on Finding Your Purpose and Living a Meaningful Life." Farnam Street, May 2014. https://fs.blog/2014/05/hunter-s-thompson-to-hume-logan/.

140 **The three of them link:** "Mister Rogers Talks About Learning." Episode. *Mister Rogers' Neighborhood* #1653, August 26, 1992.

141 **"And do you know what":** "Mister Rogers Talks About Learning." Episode. *Mister Rogers' Neighborhood* #1652, August 25, 1992.

141 **A vicious cycle commences:** Boaler, Jo. *Limitless Mind: Learn, Lead, and Live Without Barriers.* New York, NY: HarperOne, 2019.

141 **Tactics like these might aim:** Ibid., Pg. 36.

142 **Their bodies prepare to run:** Knurek, Sean. "Understanding Cortisol, the Stress Hormone." Healthy Relationships. Michigan State University Extension, November 27, 2018. https://www.canr.msu.edu/news /understanding_cortisol_the_stress_hormone.

142 **It can help us rise:** Ibid.

143 **The constant presence of stress:** "Chronic Stress Puts Your Health at Risk." Mayo Clinic, March 19, 2019. https://www.mayoclinic.org/healthy -lifestyle/stress-management/in-depth/stress/art-20046037.

143 **Nearly a quarter reported three:** "About the CDC-Kaiser ACE Study." Centers for Disease Control and Prevention, April 13, 2020. https://www .cdc.gov/violenceprevention/acestudy/about.html.

143 **People with six or more ACEs were:** Tough, Paul. *How Children Succeed: Grit, Curiosity, and the Hidden Power of Character.* Boston, MA: Houghton Mifflin Harcourt, 2012. Pgs. 10–11.

143 **One found that people with six or more:** Brown, David W., Robert F. Anda, Henning Tiemeier, Vincent J. Felitti, Valerie J. Edwards, Janet B. Croft, and Wayne H. Giles. "Adverse Childhood Experiences and the Risk of Premature Mortality." *American Journal of Preventive Medicine* 37, no. 5 (November 1, 2009). https://doi.org/10.1016/j.amepre.2009.06.021.

143 **Another found that while ACEs:** Merrick, Melissa T., Derek C. Ford, Katie A. Ports, and Angie S. Guinn. "Prevalence of Adverse Childhood Experiences from the 2011–2014 Behavioral Risk Factor Surveillance System in 23 States." *JAMA Pediatrics* 172, no. 11 (November 2018). https:// doi.org/10.1001/jamapediatrics.2018.2537.

144 **Even years after their time:** Tough, *How Children Succeed*, Pgs. 10–11; Teplin, Linda A., Karen M. Abram, Jason J. Washburn, Leah J. Welty, Jennifer A. Hershfield, and Mina K. Dulcan. "The Northwestern Juvenile Project: Overview." Office of Justice Programs. U.S. Department of Justice, February 2013. https://ojjdp.ojp.gov/sites/g/files/xyckuh176/files/pubs /234522.pdf.

144 **That creates more stress:** Tough, Paul. "How Kids Learn Resilience." *Atlantic*, June 2016. https://www.theatlantic.com/magazine/archive /2016/06/how-kids-really-succeed/480744/.

144 **Experts call toxic stress:** Hickman, Jim. "Toxic Stress: The Other Health Crisis Politicians Should Be Talking About." STAT, June 21, 2019. https:// www.statnews.com/2019/06/21/toxic-stress-health-crisis-politicians/.

145 **"Instead of suspending and expelling":** Gaines, Patrice. "California's First Surgeon General: Screen Every Student for Childhood Trauma." NBC News, October 11, 2019. https://www.nbcnews.com/news/nbcblk /california-s-first-surgeon-general-screen-every-student-childhood-trauma -n1064286.

145 **Preventing and healing ACEs:** "Preventing Adverse Childhood Experiences." Centers for Disease Control and Prevention, April 3, 2020. https:// www.cdc.gov/violenceprevention/childabuseandneglect/aces/fastfact .html.

145 **An extra 1.5 million students:** Chatterjee, Rhitu. "CDC: Childhood Trauma Is a Public Health Issue and We Can Do More To Prevent It." NPR, November 5, 2019. https://www.npr.org/sections /health-shots/2019/11/05/776550377/cdc-childhood-trauma-is-a-public -health-issue-and-we-can-do-more-prevent-it.

145 **and communities would collectively save:** "Preventing Adverse Childhood Experiences." Centers for Disease Control and Prevention, April 3, 2020. https://www.cdc.gov/violenceprevention/childabuseandneglect /aces/fastfact.html.

145 **"By ensuring that all children":** Merrick, Ford, Ports, and Guinn, "Prevalence of Adverse Childhood Experiences."

145 **"When a pup received":** Tough, *How Children Succeed*, Pg. 30.

145 **Among the study's small sample:** Chatterjee, "CDC: Childhood Trauma."

146 **The higher their positive childhood:** Bethell, Christina, Jennifer Jones, Narangerel Gombojav, Jeff Linkenbach, and Robert Sege. "Positive Childhood Experiences and Adult Mental and Relational Health in a Statewide Sample." *JAMA Pediatrics* 173, no. 11 (September 9, 2019). https://doi .org/10.1001/jamapediatrics.2019.3007.

148 **According to data collected:** "How Remake Learning Days Build Family Engagement, Create Demand for More STEAM Learning Opportunities, and Contribute to a More Equitable STEAM Learning Ecology." Global Family Research Project. Remake Learning, 2019. https://remakelearning days.org/wp-content/uploads/2020/04/RLDAA_LearningMemo3.pdf.

151 **As a classmate remembers:** King, Maxwell. *The Good Neighbor: The Life and Work of Fred Rogers*. New York, NY: Abrams Press, 2018. Pg. 45.

151 **"[I] was scared to death":** Ibid., Pg. 46.

151   He'd found a door: Ibid., Pg. 45.

151   "Despite the fact that the two": Useem, Jerry. "Is Grit Overrated?" *Atlantic*, May 2016. https://www.theatlantic.com/magazine/archive/2016/05/is-grit-overrated/476397/.

152   One survey of academics: Leslie, Sarah-Jane, Andrei Cimpian, Meredith Meyer, and Edward Freeland. "Expectations of Brilliance Underlie Gender Distributions Across Academic Disciplines." *Science* 347, no. 6219 (January 16, 2015). https://doi.org/10.1126/science.1261375.

152   Parents are more likely to Google: Stephens-Davidowitz, Seth. "Google, Tell Me. Is My Son a Genius?" *New York Times*, January 18, 2014. https://www.nytimes.com/2014/01/19/opinion/sunday/google-tell-me-is-my-son-a-genius.html.

152   Teachers, too, are more likely: Voyer, Daniel, and Susan D. Voyer. "Gender Differences in Scholastic Achievement: A Meta-Analysis." *Psychological Bulletin* 140, no. 4 (July 2014). https://doi.org/10.1037/a0036620.

152   Likewise, when six- and seven-year-olds: Cimpian, Andrei, and Sarah-Jane Leslie. "Why Young Girls Don't Think They Are Smart Enough." *New York Times*, January 26, 2017. https://www.nytimes.com/2017/01/26/well/family/why-young-girls-dont-think-they-are-smart-enough.html.

152   "Once people get this terrible idea": Boaler, *Limitless Mind*, Pg. 20.

152   In Britain, for example: Dixon, Annabelle. "Editorial." *FORUM* 44, no. 1 (2002). http://www.wwwords.co.uk/pdf/freetoview.asp?j=forum&vol=44&issue=1&year=2002&article=Forum_44-1_Core Content.

153   "Once we tell young students": Boaler, *Limitless Mind*, Pg. 24.

154   "The third group (elite college)": Andreatta, Britt. *Wired to Connect: The Brain Science of Teams and a New Model for Creating Collaboration and Inclusion*. Santa Barbara, CA: 7th Mind Publishing, 2018. Pg. 69.

154   Sure enough, the group: Steele, Claude M. "Thin Ice: Stereotype Threat and Black College Students." *Atlantic*, August 1999. https://www.theatlantic.com/magazine/archive/1999/08/thin-ice-stereotype-threat-and-black-college-students/304663/.

154   When they fail, it's a reflection: Dweck, Carol S. *Mindset: The New Psychology of Success*. New York, NY: Ballantine Books, 2016.

154   People with fixed mindsets: Ibid., Pg. 61.

155   **"And then it can become fancier":** "Mister Rogers Talks About Learning." Episode. *Mister Rogers' Neighborhood* #1651, August 24, 1992.

155   **And it means, as the educational researcher:** Bloom, Benjamin. "New Views of the Learner: Implications for Instruction and Curriculum." ASCD Annual Conference. Address, 1978. http://www.ascd.org/ASCD/pdf/journals/ed_lead/el_197804_bloom.pdf.

155   **"Although people may differ":** Dweck, *Mindset*, Pg. 7.

156   **"The worse they felt":** Ibid., Pg. 38.

156   **"We all need to accept some":** Ibid., Pg. 50.

156   **Well, when researchers described:** Cimpian and Leslie, "Why Young Girls Don't."

157   **All thanks to an online program:** Yeager, David S., Paul Hanselman, Gregory M. Walton, Jared S. Murray, Robert Crosnoe, Chandra Muller, Elizabeth Tipton, et al. "A National Experiment Reveals Where a Growth Mindset Improves Achievement." *Nature* 573, no. 7774 (August 7, 2019). https://doi.org/10.1038/s41586-019-1466-y.

157   **There is, however, a catch:** Yeager, David S. "Creating Schools That Support Growth Mindset Is What's Next." Holdsworth Center, November 20, 2019. https://holdsworthcenter.org/blog/creating-schools-that-support-growth-mindset-is-next/.

157   **In fact, when this happened:** Steele, "Thin Ice."

158   **"How we deal with the big":** Rogers, Fred. *You Are Special: Words of Wisdom for All Ages from a Beloved Neighbor.* New York, NY: Penguin Books, 1995.

159   **Instead, writes Dweck:** Dweck, *Mindset*, Pg. 16.

160   **But on tests of recall:** Boser, Ulrich. "Boser: Students Want Learning to Be Easy. But for Learning to Be Valuable, the Brain Has to Struggle." 74, April 13, 2020. https://www.the74million.org/article/boser-students-want-learning-to-be-easy-but-for-learning-to-be-valuable-the-brain-has-to-struggle/; Chew, Stephen L. "Improving Classroom Performance by Challenging Student Misconceptions About Learning." Association for Psychological Science, April 1, 2010. https://www.psychologicalscience.org/observer/improving-classroom-performance-by-challenging-student-misconceptions-about-learning.

160   **"Tolerating big mistakes can create":** Epstein, *Range*, Pg. 86.

160   **"Let the children know":** Sharapan, Hedda. *What We Can Continue to Learn from Fred Rogers.* Fred Rogers Center for Early Learning & Children's Media, February 2020. https://www.fredrogerscenter.org/wp-content/uploads/2020/02/February-2020.pdf.

162   **"If you're a musician":** Shanley, Mike. "Eric Kloss: About Time." Jazz-Times, April 25, 2019. https://jazztimes.com/archives/eric-kloss-about-time/.

163   **The machine, he says:** "Mister Rogers Talks About Learning." Episode. *Mister Rogers' Neighborhood* #1654, August 27, 1992.

164   **To suggest otherwise:** Love, Bettina L. *We Want to Do More Than Survive: Abolitionist Teaching and the Pursuit of Educational Freedom.* Boston, MA: Beacon Press, 2019. Pg. 86.

164   **"Until those arrangements have":** Kohn, Alfie. "The 'Mindset' Mindset." August 16, 2015. https://www.alfiekohn.org/article/mindset/.

Chapter 6: Such a Good Feeling

172   **And then, his voice beginning:** "Mister Rogers Talks About Fun & Games." Episode. *Mister Rogers' Neighborhood* #1603, February 22, 1989.

173   **In Italy, quarantined residents:** Carella, Leonardo. "Italians in Lockdown All Over Italy Are Keeping Each Other Company by Singing, Dancing and Playing Music from the Balconies. A Thread to Celebrate the Resilience of Ordinary People." Twitter, March 13, 2020. https://twitter.com/leonardocarella/status/1238511612270690305.

173   **And in Pittsburgh, neighbors:** "Residents Put on Concert for Their Community." ABC News, March 26, 2020. https://www.youtube.com/watch?v=CahmcLHJgTc.

173   **"Quite simply," writes Dr. Vivek:** Murthy, Vivek H. *Together: The Healing Power of Human Connection in a Sometimes Lonely World.* New York, NY: Harper Wave, 2020. Pg. 11.

174   **"The high mortality," Spitz wrote:** Spitz, Renée A. "The Role of Ecological Factors in Emotional Development in Infancy." *Child Development* 20, no. 3 (September 1949). https://doi.org/10.2307/1125870; "History Module: The Devastating Effects of Isolation on Social Behaviour." Brain from Top to Bottom. McGill University, n.d. https://thebrain.mcgill.ca/flash/capsules/histoire_bleu06.html.

174   **The infants chose:** "History Module," Brain from Top to Bottom; Mc-
        Leod, Saul. "Attachment Theory." Simply Psychology, February 5, 2017.
        https://www.simplypsychology.org/attachment.html.

174   **Early humans who could bond:** Harari, Yuval Noah. *Sapiens: A Brief
        History of Humankind.* New York, NY: HarperCollins, 2015. Pg. 10.

175   **You've been doing this since:** Ross, Howard J., and JonRobert Tarta-
        glione. *Our Search for Belonging: How Our Need to Connect Is Tearing Us
        Apart.* Oakland, CA: Berrett-Koehler, 2018. Pg. 109.

175   **Even before the COVID-19 pandemic:** Gordon, Serena. "Coronavirus
        Pandemic May Lead to 75,000 'Deaths of Despair' from Suicide, Drug
        and Alcohol Abuse, Study Says." CBS News, May 8, 2020. https://www
        .cbsnews.com/news/coronavirus-deaths-suicides-drugs-alcohol-pandemic
        -75000/.

175   **"It is in our DNA to want":** Ross, *Our Search for Belonging,* Pg. xiii.

176   **"It's much more important":** Harari, *Sapiens,* Pg. 22.

176   **"The gossip theory might sound":** Ibid., Pg. 24.

176   **University of Toronto professor:** Craig, Lindsey. "Racial Bias May
        Begin in Babies at Six Months, U of T Research Reveals." Univer-
        sity of Toronto News, April 11, 2017. https://www.utoronto.ca/news
        /racial-bias-may-begin-babies-six-months-u-t-research-reveals.

177   **Babies, it seems, like:** Hamlin, J. Kiley, Neha Mahajan, Zoe Liberman,
        and Karen Wynn. "Not Like Me = Bad: Infants Prefer Those Who Harm
        Dissimilar Others." *Psychological Science* 24, no. 4 (April 2013). https://
        doi.org/10.1177/0956797612457785.

177   **The point is that we're wired:** Turner, Cory, and Anya Kamenetz.
        "Kindness vs. Cruelty: Helping Kids Hear the Better Angels of Their Na-
        ture." NPR, July 5, 2019. https://www.npr.org/2019/07/05/731346268
        /kindness-vs-cruelty-helping-kids-hear-the-better-angels-of-their
        -nature.

177   **When children reach adolescence:** Albert, Dustin, Jason Chein, and
        Laurence Steinberg. "The Teenage Brain: Peer Influences on Adolescent
        Decision Making." *Current Directions in Psychological Science* 22, no. 2
        (April 2013). https://doi.org/10.1177/0963721412471347.

177   **"As a result, those differences":** Lorde, Audre. "Age, Race, Class,
        and Sex: Women Redefining Difference." Presented at the Copeland

Colloquium, Amherst College, April 1980. https://www.colorado.edu
/odece/sites/default/files/attached-files/rba09-sb4converted_8.pdf.

179   **"To combat this silencing effect":** Murthy, *Together*, Pg. 11.

179   **Students from schools with high rates:** Ross, *Our Search for Belonging*,
Pg. 29.

179   **"That is something to watch":** Capps, Kriston. "A New Study Links
Gentrification and Kids' Anxiety." Bloomberg CityLab, September 4, 2019. https://www.citylab.com/equity/2019/09/gentrification
-effects-children-depression-economic-data/597292/.

179   **The third group wasn't told:** Baumeister, Roy F., Jean M. Twenge,
and Christopher K. Nuss. "Effects of Social Exclusion on Cognitive
Processes: Anticipated Aloneness Reduces Intelligent Thought." *Journal of Personality and Social Psychology* 83, no. 4 (2002). https://doi
.org/10.1037/0022-3514.83.4.817.

180   **"And most destructive of all":** Murthy, *Together*, Pg. 27.

180   **"For no apparent reason":** Williams, Kipling D., and Blair Jarvis. "Cyberball: A Program for Use in Research on Interpersonal Ostracism and
Acceptance." *Behavior Research Methods* 38, no. 1 (2006). https://doi
.org/10.3758/bf03192765.

181   **In another version of the game:** Ibid.

182   **Feeling accepted by even a single:** Dewall, C. Nathan, Jean M. Twenge,
Brad Bushman, Charles Im, and Kipling Williams. "A Little Acceptance
Goes a Long Way: Applying Social Impact Theory to the Rejection–
Aggression Link." *Social Psychological and Personality Science* 1, no. 2
(2010). https://doi.org/10.1177/1948550610361387.

183   **When his parents held their huge:** King, Maxwell. *The Good Neighbor:
The Life and Work of Fred Rogers.* New York, NY: Abrams Press, 2018.
Pg. 4.

183   **Instead, writes Dr. Murthy:** Murthy, *Together*, Pg. 253.

183   **"of the people who do value":** Ibid.

183   **As the target of bullies:** King, *The Good Neighbor*, Pg. 31.

184   **"We grabbed him":** Ibid., Pg. 52.

184   **The *Neighborhood*, he once told:** Laskas, Jeanne Marie. "The Mister
Rogers No One Saw." *New York Times*, November 19, 2019. https://www
.nytimes.com/2019/11/19/magazine/mr-rogers.html.

184 **"At every point," notes:** Townley, Roderick. "Fred's Shoes: The Meaning of Transitions in *Mister Rogers' Neighborhood.*" In *Mister Rogers Neighborhood: Children, Television, and Fred Rogers*, edited by Mark Collins and Margaret Mary Kimmel. Pittsburgh, PA: University of Pittsburgh Press, 1996.

184 **"They long to belong":** King, *The Good Neighbor*, Pg. 18.

185 **"Until we can make such":** Guy, William. "The Theology of Mister Rogers' Neighborhood." In *Mister Rogers' Neighborhood: Children, Television, and Fred Rogers*, edited by Mark Collins and Margaret Mary Kimmel. Pittsburgh, PA: University of Pittsburgh Press, 1996.

185 **We need to know that we're worth:** Rogers, Fred. "Commencement Address." Goucher College, May 14, 1993. Fred Rogers Archives.

186 **"And you are likely to be setting":** Eckart, Kim. "Decades After a Grade-School Program to Promote Social Development, Adults Report Healthier, More Successful Lives." UW News. University of Washington, July 25, 2019. https://www.washington.edu/news/2019/07/25/decades-after-a-grade-school-program-to-promote-social-development-adults-report-healthier-more-successful-lives/.

186 **Taught by Black male educators:** Dee, Thomas, and Emily Penner. "My Brother's Keeper? The Impact of Targeted Educational Supports." Stanford University Center for Education Policy Analysis, October 2019. https://cepa.stanford.edu/sites/default/files/wp19-07-v201910.pdf.

186 **And although the initiative:** Barnum, Matt. "Oakland High Schools Offered an Extra Class to Support Black Boys. A New Study Shows It Substantially Cut Their Dropout Rate." Chalkbeat, October 21, 2019. https://www.chalkbeat.org/2019/10/21/21109062/oakland-high-schools-offered-an-extra-class-to-support-black-boys-a-new-study-shows-it-substantially.

186 **At the college level:** "Belonging." Mindset Scholars Network, n.d. https://mindsetscholarsnetwork.org/learning-mindsets/belonging/.

186 **That's why having someone:** Ross, *Our Search for Belonging*, Pg. 114.

187 **"It's amazing what can happen":** Rogers, Fred. "At Play in the Neighborhood." In *Shakespeare Plays the Classroom*, edited by Stuart E. Omans and Maurice J. O'Sullivan. Sarasota, FL: Pineapple Press, 2003.

188 **"Large numbers of strangers":** Harari, *Sapiens*, Pg. 27.

188 **"But I think we should talk":** "Obama to Graduates: Cultivate Empathy." Northwestern University News, June 19, 2006. https://www.north western.edu/newscenter/stories/2006/06/barack.html.

189 **It's been said to make us better:** Cox, Stefani. "Empathy Is the Key to World Peace." Big Think, December 24, 2015. https://bigthink.com /stefani-cox/empathy-could-be-key-to-world-peace; Drewes, Felix. "Empathy—A Solution to Global Climate Change Threats." Research-Gate, May 4, 2013. https://www.researchgate.net/publication/262172477 _Empathy_-_A_Solution_to_Global_Climate_Change_Threats; Morin, Amanda. "Teaching with Empathy: Why It's Important." Understood, n.d. https://www.understood.org/en/school-learning/for-educators /empathy/teaching-with-empathy-why-its-important; Hirsch, Elliot M. "The Role of Empathy in Medicine: A Medical Student's Perspective." *AMA Journal of Ethics* 9, no. 6 (2007). https://doi.org/10.1001/virtual mentor.2007.9.6.medu1-0706; "Why Empathy Is the Most Important Business Skill." Laserfiche, n.d. https://www.laserfiche.com/ecmblog /why-empathy-is-the-most-important-business-skill/; "Empathy Is a Winning Strategy." Ashoka, September 14, 2011. https://www.ashoka.org/en /story/empathy-winning-strategy.

189 **Empathy is also a positive predictor:** Borba, Michele. *UnSelfie: Why Empathetic Kids Succeed in Our All-About-Me World.* New York, NY: Touchstone, 2016. Pg. xiv.

189 **The word itself was only coined:** Krznaric, Roman. *Empathy: Why It Matters, and How to Get It.* New York, NY: Perigee, 2014. Pg. 9.

189 **Even though the listeners were simply:** Andreatta, Britt. *Wired to Connect: The Brain Science of Teams and a New Model for Creating Collaboration and Inclusion.* Santa Barbara, CA: 7th Mind Publishing, 2018. Pg. 32.

189 **Some people, for example, may:** Thomson, Helen. "We Feel Your Pain: Extreme Empaths." New Scientist, March 10, 2010. https://www .newscientist.com/article/mg20527511-700-we-feel-your-pain-extreme -empaths/.

189 **For a select few, empathy:** Ewens, Hannah. "Super Empaths Are Real, Says Study." VICE, November 8, 2018. https://www.vice.com/en_us /article/xwj84k/super-empaths-are-real-says-study.

190   **The researchers found a similar:** "Empathy: College Students Don't Have as Much as They Used To." University of Michigan News, May 27, 2010. https://news.umich.edu/empathy-college-students-don-t -have-as-much-as-they-used-to/.

190   **"Empathic ability is a bit like":** Krznaric, *Empathy*, Pg. 10.

191   **"And that is how it is":** Ibid., Pg. 27.

191   **"We recognize ourselves":** Linn, Susan. "With an Open Hand: Puppetry on *Mister Rogers' Neighborhood.*" In *Mister Rogers' Neighborhood: Children, Television, and Fred Rogers,* edited by Mark Collins and Margaret Mary Kimmel. Pittsburgh, PA: University of Pittsburgh Press, 1996.

192   **But—and this is essential:** Zahn-Waxler, Carolyn, Marian Radke-Yarrow, and Robert A. King. "Child Rearing and Children's Prosocial Initiations toward Victims of Distress." *Child Development* 50, no. 2 (1979). https://doi.org/10.2307/1129406; Turner and Kamenetz, "Kindness vs. Cruelty."

192   **"I think the only way people":** Laskas, Jeanne Marie. "What Is Essential Is Invisible to the Eye." In *Mister Rogers' Neighborhood: Children, Television, and Fred Rogers,* edited by Mark Collins and Margaret Mary Kimmel. Pittsburgh, PA: University of Pittsburgh Press, 1996.

193   **Now which of these three:** Luke 10:30.

194   **"Conflict, rather than callousness":** Darley, John M., and C. Daniel Batson. "'From Jerusalem to Jericho': A Study of Situational and Dispositional Variables in Helping Behavior." *Journal of Personality and Social Psychology* 27, no. 1 (1973): 100–108. https://doi.org/10.1037/h0034449.

194   **Meanwhile, among the ten:** Ross, *Our Search for Belonging,* Pg. 138; Prosser, Amy, Mark Levine, David Evans, and Stephen Reicher. "Identity and Emergency Intervention: How Social Group Membership and Inclusiveness of Group Boundaries Shape Helping Behavior." *Personality and Social Psychology Bulletin* 31, no. 4 (2005), https://journals.sagepub.com /doi/10.1177/0146167204271651.

195   **"To make a positive difference":** Bloom, Paul. *Against Empathy: The Case for Rational Compassion.* New York, NY: Ecco, 2016. Pg. 36.

195   **The Golden Rule, they argue:** Krznaric, *Empathy,* Pg. 58.

196   **Eventually, he hung a photo:** Davis, Bobby. "Farewell to Our Favorite Neighbor: In Honor of Fred Rogers '51, March 20, 1928–February 27, 2003." Rollins Alumni Record. Rollins College, 2003. https://lib.rollins

.edu/olin/oldsite/archives/golden/Rogers.htm; Owen, Rob. "There Goes the Neighborhood: Mister Rogers Will Make Last Episodes of Show in December." *Pittsburgh Post-Gazette*, November 12, 2000. https://old .post-gazette.com/tv/20001112rogers2.asp.

196 **Nationally, parents say their highest:** *Culture of American Families: A National Survey.* University of Virginia Institute for Advanced Studies in Culture, 2012. https://s3.amazonaws.com/iasc-prod/uploads/pdf /4a18126c1a07680e4fbe.pdf.

196 **As one young person wrote:** "The Children We Mean to Raise: The Real Messages Adults Are Sending About Values." Making Caring Common. Harvard University, July 2014. https://mcc.gse.harvard.edu/report s/children-mean-raise.

197 **That the bedrock of our lives:** "Revisiting Fred Rogers' 2002 Commencement Address." Dartmouth News, March 28, 2018. https:// news.dartmouth.edu/news/2018/03/revisiting-fred-rogers-2002 -commencement-address.

198 **They let themselves feel:** "Loving-Kindness Meditation." Greater Good in Action. Greater Good Science Center at UC Berkeley, n.d. https://ggia .berkeley.edu/practice/loving_kindness_meditation.

198 **It can prepare us:** Seppälä, Emma. "A Gift of Loving Kindness Meditation," May 28, 2014. https://emmaseppala.com/gift-loving-kindness -meditation/.

201 **"Freddy," he said:** Danielson, Louisa. "The Gentle Tongue: How Language Affected the World of *Mister Rogers' Neighborhood.*" *Interdisciplinary Journal of Popular Culture and Pedagogy* 2, no. 1 (2015). http:// journaldialogue.org/issues/the-gentle-tongue-how-language-affected-the -world-of-mister-rogers-neighborhood/.

204 **"Let's hear it for our team!":** "Mister Rogers Talks About Fun & Games." Episode. *Mister Rogers' Neighborhood* #1605, February 24, 1989.

204 **"'That's what it's all about'":** Rogers, Fred. "South Padre Island Speech." Speech, November 27, 1978. Fred Rogers Archives.

Epilogue

209 **By the end of that year:** "1968 Pandemic (H3N2 Virus)." Centers for Disease Control and Prevention, January 2, 2019. https://www.cdc.gov /flu/pandemic-resources/1968-pandemic.html.